SOFTWARE ASSESSMENT

SOFTWARE ASSESSMENT
Reliability, Safety, Testability

Michael A. Friedman
Hughes Information Systems

Jeffrey M. Voas
Reliable Software Technologies Corporation

A WILEY-INTERSCIENCE PUBLICATION

JOHN WILEY & SONS, INC.

New York • Chichester • Brisbane • Toronto • Singapore

This publication is designed to provide accurate and
authoritative information in regard to the subject
matter covered. It is sold with the understanding that
the publisher is not engaged in rendering legal, accounting,
or other professional services. If legal advice or other
expert assistance is required, the services of a competent
professional person should be sought.

Library of Congress Cataloging-in-Publication Data:

Friedman, Michael A.
    Software assessment : reliability, safety, testability / Michael
A. Friedman, Jeffrey M. Voas.
        p.   cm.
    Includes index.
    ISBN 0-471-01009-X (acid-free paper)
    1. Computer software—Quality control.   I. Voas, Jeffrey M.
  II. Title.
    QA76.76.Q35F75   1995
    005.1—dc20   94-49676

Printed in the United States of America

10 9 8 7 6 5 4 3 2 1

To my wife Christine and my parents.
—M.A.F.
To my parents Larry Keith Voas and Sarah Jane Voas.
—J.M.V.

PREFACE

The quality of executing software reveals itself in two broad aspects: software reliability and software safety. Software reliability is a measure of the extent to which the software meets its specified requirements. Whenever the software behavior does not meet those requirements, a software failure is said to have occurred. Software reliability concerns itself with the frequency of such failures—predicting, measuring, modeling, and demonstrating the software's failure rate. Software reliability has to do with the "good" things you want the software to do.

Software safety is concerned with unintended software behavior that results in loss. Software in medical devices, aircraft, industrial plants, trains, cars, weapon systems, and nuclear power plants—to name a few—can cause serious harm to life, limb, and property in the event of a software failure or incorrect software requirements. The loss could be financial or something intangible, like goodwill of customers or the general public. Software safety has to do with the "bad" things you don't want the software to do.

Verification of both reliability and safety has traditionally been assessed via testing. Exhaustive testing is intractable, so projects usually try for coverage; test all statements at least once, or all branches, or all conditions. But a program can have so many states that the coverage testing really does not accomplish much. It produces a "warm fuzzy" feeling that fosters overconfidence.

The solution is to employ intelligent testing. This is done by employing the cutting-edge concept of software testability. Software testability analysis predicts the likelihood that if there are faults in the software, they will be revealed through testing. The analysis is used to optimize the testing process to determinine how much testing is enough, determine where to concentrate scarce resources, and determine the value of any particular testing approach.

Testability is based upon a theoretical model of the relationship between software faults and software failures. This theory was pioneered by one of the authors of this book (JMV) in the early 1990s and is widely considered to be the next generation in software verification. He himself has published over 50 papers on software testability. Much of his research has been sponsored by NASA and other agencies that need to achieve ultrahigh levels of reliability and safety. Already many software developers are utilizing the principles of software testability. Testability tools are beginning to appear in the commercial marketplace. These tools can pinpoint the areas (specific modules, lines of code) in a computer program that have high testability and those that have low testability. We know that testing is going to do well on the high-testability areas. The areas of low testability can be subjected to nontesting means of verification, such as inspections, walkthroughs, or formal analysis.

This book teaches the theoretical underpinnings of software testability, software reliability and software safety, and discusses the practical assessment of these important software qualities. The reader will come away with a thorough understanding of the nature of these qualities and practical means of assessing those qualities. While the emphasis is on assessment of these qualities, the achievement of these qualities is also discussed at certain points. For example, Chapter 4 addresses design for testability.

This book reflects experience gained on major software projects the authors have worked on.

This book is geared toward practitioners such as software engineers, reliability engineers, and safety engineers and is usable as a textbook for an upper-division or graduate-level course on software assessment. It is assumed that the reader is familiar with basic software concepts and probability and statistics.

Chapter 1 talks about the nature of testing, dispelling myths and describing a simple urn model of software testing. Chapters 2 and 3 introduce the PIE model of software testability, which allows testability analysis to be automated. Chapter 4 addresses design for testability— that is, how the software engineer should design and code a program to maximize testability. Chapters 5 and 6 deal with the assessment of software safety. Chapters 7–10 comprehensively cover the assessment of software reliability. Chapter 11 is devoted to the generation of test cases to support both testing and testability analysis.

Each chapter is followed by questions that can be used for self-assessment or class assignments.

Acknowledgments

We would like to acknowledge colleagues who, through their inspiration, influence, and commentary, helped shape the methodologies described in this book. To name a few: Larry James, Tom Pliska, Nancy Leveson, Peggy Tran, Pete Goddard, Tony Zenga, Vishwa Hässan, Steve Cha, Leo Marcus, Dolores Wallace, Mark Bouler, Tim Shimeall, Keith Miller, Larry Morell, Dick Hamlet, Wayne Bryant, John McManus, and Jeff Payne.

MICHAEL A. FRIEDMAN

Fountain Valley, California

JEFFREY M. VOAS

Arlington, Virginia

CONTENTS

Introduction

Software, a complex intellectual product, inevitably emerges from development with undesirable defects called *faults,* popularly referred to as "bugs." Faults are measured by the number of faults in a program or by fault density (average number of faults per, say, 1000 lines of program code). Faults are introduced from several possible causes: The developer may misunderstand the problem to be solved or the customer's expectations. The developer might inadequately translate those expectations into technical requirements. The program design may be lacking. The coding into a programming language can be flawed, perhaps because the developer misunderstood some aspect of the programming language or other rules of the computing environment.

When the computer encounters a fault during execution, a software *failure* can result. A failure is the departure of the external results of program operation (i.e., output) from requirements. The program may enter an inoperable state by prematurely terminating (a "crash") or by appearing to freeze up (a "hang"). Oftentimes a failure is simply an event in which an incorrect result is output; there is a discrepancy between an output value and that dictated by requirements. The program may continue running, and the next result the program produces may be perfectly correct.

The higher the frequency of failures, the worse the reliability of the software is judged to be. The average number of failures per unit time is called the *failure rate.* For example, you might observe a particular piece of software to fail on average three times per 10,000 hours. The software failure rate in this case would be $3/10,000 = 0.0003$ failures per hour. We've lumped all failures together, but failures might differ in the severity of their consequences. We could categorize failures as major, minor, and so forth, and calculate a different failure rate for each. If one of those three failures was major and two were minor, the major failure rate would be 0.0001 and the minor failure rate would be 0.0002.

After a failure has occurred, a programmer tracks down the fault that caused the failure by a process called "debugging." Many software development environments include debuggers, which are utility programs that let you step through the program and observe its inner workings. Sometimes in the course of tracking down one fault the programmer discovers one or more related faults. Faults can also be found by manually walking through the code or by performing some type of analysis. Some "software failures" cannot be traced to software faults and are ultimately found to be the result of hardware failures or operator mistakes.

At least for the time being, computer programming is a labor-intensive task. Programming started out as an art form but in more recent years has matured into a discipline called *software engineering*. While programming is still very much a creative activity, methodologies, tools, and management procedures have emerged that result in improved productivity and quality. But advances in software engineering have not kept pace with the rapid advancements in hardware performance and capacity. Each year, the trend has been for software projects undertaken to become bigger and more complex. Complexity arises from humans' limited capability in understanding both the way a system behaves and the way it is put together. Unlike hardware, the size and intricacy of software are not constrained by physical laws such as power, weight, and number of parts. Nor does software have inherent form or function limitations such as strength, density, or malleability. Even the constraint of "common sense" is lacking. Software is perceived as flexible, and often little thought is given to the consequences of modifying requirements in the middle of development. Software involves manipulation of intangible, abstract symbols and is sensitive to tiny errors such as punctuation, the kind of errors called "typos" in documents. A silly mistake like an extra hyphen or the substitution of a comma for a period can have catastrophic consequences. Each and every step that the computer must follow must be painstakingly spelled out fully and correctly.

Another problem, although some may argue that it is not, is that, at the current level of maturity of the field of software engineering, there is currently a lack of professional standards determining who is a qualified software engineer. There are no minimum education or experience requirements.

Computers are increasingly being employed in monitoring and controlling systems where unintended software behavior can hurt people, damage property, or cause other loss. Our society is becoming more and more dependent on the proper functioning of software-intensive systems. When software is deployed in cardiac pacemakers, patient monitoring equipment, fly-by-wire aircraft, aircraft collision avoidance systems, train control systems, air traffic control, and other vital applications, safety is a serious concern. Software has caused and contributed to many accidents.

Achieving software reliability and safety is difficult, but it is disheartening that *assessing* software reliability and safety may be even harder in practice than achieving those qualities. Testing and verification and validation (V&V) frequently account for 50% of software development costs. Numerous testing techniques are available with little or no theoretical basis.

Programs generally have a combinatorial explosion of input states and paths, making exhaustive testing and analysis intractable. For example, a program that reads in two integers has over four billion input states. A 100-line program might produce 32 million paths. Because exhaustive testing is out of the question, statistical testing has been proposed. But ultrahigh reliability systems—failure rate of 10^{-7} per hour or less—pose special problems because apart from the difficulty of achieving such high reliability, there are practical limits on how we can statistically ascertain that that level of reliability has actually been achieved.

The solution to many of the limitations of testing is to employ the concept of *software testability* to guide the verification of the software. Software testability is a measure of the degree to which a piece of software tends to "wear its faults on its sleeve"—that is, the degree to which it tends to reveal its faults during testing. Testability is an important software quality in itself, but is also a powerful concept for efficiently assessing reliability and safety. If we can establish, to a high degree of confidence, that any faults that exist will be "obvious" to testing, then we can establish the absence of faults more quickly. By designing for high testability by isolating and removing software characteristics that discourage software from revealing faults during testing, and selecting tests that have a greater ability to reveal the existence of faults, it is possible to construct a methodology that uses fewer tests and gains higher confidence in the reliability and safety of the software. By measuring the testability of different parts of the code, testability provides guidance on which parts can be verified by testing and which parts should best be verified by nontest means such as desk checking, analysis, and modeling.

Note that software assessment is not development process assessment. Many practitioners have fallen into the trap of thinking that if the process used to develop the code is correct, then the code itself is correct. This is absurd. Just because you use a computer-aided software engineering (CASE) tool does not suggest that you have properly input your schematic into it. And if you have made an error in getting your schematic into the tool, that will likely show up as incorrect software. We are not suggesting that a good development process should not be sought, because a good process will almost certainly produce better software. Instead, this book emphasizes assessing how good the software is once you have applied the best processes available. From time to time throughout the book, we will comment on various phases in the development of the software that might improve your process.

CHAPTER 1

The Balls and Urn View of Software Testing

SOFTWARE QUALITY: ASSESSING VERSUS ACHIEVING

Software quality is perhaps the biggest issue of the 1990s in software circles. We hear speakers at conferences talking about structured design methodologies, metrics, reusability, new language standards, ISO-9000, object-oriented systems, portable common tool environment (PCTE), maintainability, seemingly endless types of software testing techniques and tools, independent verification and validation (IV&V), software experience factories, Software Engineering Institute (SEI) process maturity models, cleanroom methodologies, formal methods, computer-aided software engineering (CASE) tools, and the list of software quality characteristics and quality enhancement techniques never ends. What they are all trying to do, and often not articulating very well, is to teach the software engineering community methods for improving both their software end-product and the process they use to produce software. The goals of the speakers and conference program committees are worthy, but the confusion all of these ideas and methodologies carry with them can be quite overwhelming to your typical attendee. For example, it is often unclear as to whether a method for attaining one software characteristic is detrimental and will cause you to lose another characteristic that you want.

Furthermore, it is unscientific to merely assert that applying some "grab bag" of software quality improvement techniques makes the software "more" reliable than if the techniques had not been used. If you know that a specific technique makes the software more reliable, then put a number on the degree to which the reliability was actually improved. What we need in software engineering are ways to *quantify* how much benefit a particular technique provides before that technique is applied. If this information were available, then software engineers could convincingly argue that even though they have only assessed a reliability of X, they know that the reliability is $X + Y$ because some technique Z provides Y more reliability. But measuring the process may be harder than measuring the product, and much research is still needed before we can confidently do this. This process-measuring approach can be described as showing that the processes used to develop the software were right instead of showing that the software itself is right.

The software engineering life cycle, whether you consider it to be more of a spiral model (Boehm, 1988) or waterfall model (Royce, 1970), is simply a process, where many development decisions are made at various points during the process. These decisions (1) directly impact future decisions during the process and (2) eventually affect the software product itself. At the early phases in the life cycle, the emphasis is on *achieving* quality in the end-product; later in the life cycle, we shift attention toward *assessing* how much quality we have actually been able to achieve. This is not to say that assessing and achieving reliability cannot be performed simultaneously. For example, if an assessment of quality comes up deficient, then we will want to achieve higher levels of quality by performing more work, such as specialized debugging and testing.

Testing plays a role in both achieving and assessing quality. As we test–debug–fix, we achieve higher levels of quality; when we system test before product release, we assess how good our system is. Often a particular testing technique is geared toward either achieving or assessing software, but not both. A common problem in practice is that an organization will try to use a quality achievement testing technique for an assessment technique, which is possible but difficult. An example is when a unit testing technique such as branch coverage is used as a measure of reliability, which is of course not directly possible. Although 100% branch coverage will make us feel better about the reliability than will 50% branch coverage, the true reliability of the code will be the same.

It is interesting to note, and possibly hard to believe, that it may be more difficult to assess quality in software than it is to achieve quality, for a variety of reasons that will become more obvious in later sections and chapters. This has driven us to try to assess the quality of the software development process rather than the software. You might think that it would be harder to produce a correct air traffic control system than to assess whether it is correct. The opposite appears to be true. Thus software quality assessment may be the hardest problem in the software life cycle, and assessment is the focus of this book.

TWO SOFTWARE ANALYSIS PERSPECTIVES: SEMANTIC VERSUS SYNTACTIC

The 19th-century philosopher of science Auguste Comte declared that astronomy would always be limited to the study of celestial bodies and their movements, since the composition of the stars could never be determined (Comte, 1848). Comte had reached this decision because of his belief that man would never be able to reach the stars; he never envisioned that there might be alternative ways of assessing the composition of the heavens. Soon after Comte's death in 1857, Bunsen and Kirchhoff developed spectroscopy to the precise degree that the elements of the stars could indeed be measured by the color of the light that they give off; that work continues today through the Hubble telescope.

Computer science is struggling with what can and cannot be measured in software, and software metrics research is at the center of this debate. The issues raised today by software researchers are not so unlike those raised by Comte's; for example, Butler and Finelli (1991) argue that we will never be able to test software to the levels necessary to assess that software has *ultrareliability* because of the enormous number of test cases needed. Although true given today's methods for testing, some-day an alternative technique may be invented that will allow us to poll (test) the input space that provides ultrahigh levels of reliability.

The artifacts that are studied in software are not physical but logical. They do not give off light, but they do have measurable properties and effects. No matter what the current state of software metrics theory and practice, we must not prematurely dismiss the possibility of future developments that will prove revolutionary in our use of software measurement.

In established scientific disciplines, the mutually supportive roles of empirical and theoretical methods are assumed. However, in computer science there is debate as to what should constitute legitimate science in the field. At best, contention can help us be creative and can help us judge all our research with a healthy skepticism; at worst, this contention can make us blind to the contributions others make in our field. Skepticism is healthy in science; cynicism is not!

Software assessment is generally performed in one of two manners: *black-box* or *white-box*. Black-box software assessment quantifies the quality of the software strictly as a function of the external behavior of the code—for instance, a mean-time-to-failure estimate based on the code, specification, frequency that the code is executed, and input distribution. In contrast, white-box (Probert, 1982) assessment techniques consider the structure of the code when making an assessment. An example here is the simple source lines of code metric. There is also a "gray-box" type of an assessment, such as failures observed per 1000 lines of code or faults detected per some number of lines of code. In this chapter, we mainly focus attention on those techniques that are white-box and that are based on the code itself.

White-box software analysis methods can largely be viewed in one of two ways: *structurally* and *semantically*. When you take the structural view of software, you limit your knowledge about the software to the operators and operands that comprise it. When the semantic perspective is adopted, you instead attach meaning to the operands and operators; that is, you consider what transpires when an input value is fed to the software and an output value is produced. Historically, software metrics have taken the structural perspective, and have been used to predict other characteristics (that are not directly measurable) of a program by only analyzing the source code. As an example, the first software metric was simply a count of the number of lines of code, which was used at that time to suggest how hard it would be to test and debug the code. Later, Halstead's (1977) volume metric counted operators and operands. His volume measure is $V = N \log_2 \eta$, where N is the total number of operator and operand occurrences, and η is total number of distinct operators and operands. This too was considered as a measure of how difficult it would be for testing and debugging. Today we are seeing a shift from static metrics to metrics that consider the semantics behind what the code computes. The differences between the semantic and syntactic view of software is analogous to the difference between looking at a car at the dealer's show-room floor and actually test-driving the car. Test-driving a car to ascertain the behavior of the car under different conditions in the "automobile" domain is exactly what semantic metrics are doing in the software domain.

The rationale for adopting the semantic perspective is that *computation*, in its purest sense, is simply the transformation of an input value, i, to an output value, o; i and o may be multidimensional. These transformations are what really define the software; they are what we pay for when we purchase software, and they are far more important to us than the underlying syntax. For example, if the program works efficiently and correctly, who really cares if the programmer used a **while** loop or a **for** loop?

We view a program P as an implementation of a function g that maps a domain of potential inputs to a range of potential outputs. Another function f with the same domain and perhaps different range represents the desired (or expected) behavior of g. Essentially f is just the specification of P. An *oracle* is a recursive predicate on input/output pairs that determines whether f has been implemented for an input: oracle $w(x, y)$ is TRUE iff $f(x) = y$. Then the oracle is used with $g(x)$ for y. In other words, an oracle is a procedure that tells you whether or not a program's output was correct on a particular run. As an example, suppose that your program computes the square root of a positive number. The oracle might square the output value and compare the result with the input. If they agree (to within a specified tolerance), then the oracle pronounces the test case to have been successful; if they do not agree, then the oracle says the test failed. During testing, it is necessary to say whether an output value of a program is correct or incorrect with respect to a particular input value, x, with the latter implying that $g(x) \neq f(x)$ and the former implying that $g(x) = f(x)$.

During a transformation from i to o, many intermediate program states are possible based on the incoming state; a successor program state is a function of a predecessor state and the code that performs the transformation. The meaning of the function that is computed by a program P, denoted by $[P]$, is dependent on the structural features of the code and the inputs that are fed into the program. For example, suppose that a program begins with several read statements followed by a conditional statement; and suppose that at the conditional branch statement, the program takes the true branch if one of the integer input values is odd and takes the false branch if it is even. Further suppose that the computation in the true branch is trivial but that the computation coded in the false branch is very syntactically complex and detailed. If you only looked at the code, you would see the complex section in the false branch and you might conclude that, in general, the code is complicated. However, if this program never reads in an even value for that integer, then the program is actually quite trivial, because the complex region is "dynamically" dead.

You cannot know this without knowledge concerning how the program behaves with respect to the inputs that it will receive. Hence the semantic perspective provides detailed and precise information on the code's behavior that is unavailable from its structural counterpart. However, the reader should be forewarned that assessing the semantic perspective is not without additional costs; you do not get that additional information for free. In the following chapters, we emphasize the semantic, white-box perspective of software, because it provides an enhanced ability to predict where in a program *faults* ("bugs") are more likely to hide and estimate the degree of testing that will be necessary to uncover those faults (which, by the way, are the two main reasons for performing software testability analysis).

A program P is a function over an input domain I to an output range O, where there are many (and for our purposes an effectively infinite number of) intermediate program states S that may be created. (We will frequently refer to the domain of a program as the *input space*, and to the output range as the *output space*.) I is the space of all "legal" inputs on which P should function. A program state S_i is simply a snapshot into the state of an executing program on some element of I. On a single execution, there can be many different program states. A *program state* contains the values of all programmer-defined variables, the current value of the program counter, the current scope, and information such as the contents of cache memory, main memory, and the program registers. In short, the program state is all of the information needed to restart an execution if we temporarily halted execution. We can further prune down the amount of information in a program state to what is termed a *data state*, which is simply all of the information that the programmer at the source level has access to; this includes programmer defined variables, the program counter, and the scope of the program. A data state does not include information pertaining to the contents of registers, main memory, or cache memory, since that is information that is controlled by the operating system, assembler, compilers, and so on, and not the application programmer.

Program states have a dynamic and fluid nature; they are in constant transition during execution. Data states are also subject to change, however, not only because of changes caused by the code, but because you have the option to include any information available in the data state. Why? Because a data state is an intangible entity that can be modified and redefined to fit the needs of the model or technique for which it is being defined. For instance, you might want to include the input value that started the execution as a member of every data state in the program. Another option would be to include a listing of all previous statements that have been executed up to the point where some data state occurs. If the program is a parallel/distributed system, then information concerning either "global" system time or the time on a particular local task might also be included. In short, the data state can include any data that your application needs to perform some dynamic analysis. The reason for separating the data state from the program state is that the goal of software testability is to predict *where* "programmer-induced" faults might be hiding. We are only concerned with where in the source code programmer-created bugs can hide, not where computer system problems may be originating from. This distinction must be clearly understood: We are solely concerned with the software's testability as it relates to the code produced by the programmer, and not problems that can arise from incorrect compilers, faulty hardware, or other system facilities.

A computation for each element of I eventually produces an element of O if the computation terminates. A sequence of zero or more data states are produced during an execution. We refer to this sequence of states as a *state chain*. For every unique member of I, there may or may not be a unique state chain, depending on whether the input value that began the computation is included as information in a data state. If it is, then there will be a unique state chain for each input value.

We define D to be the operational profile, the probability mass function over I; that is, D represents the likelihood of any member of I being selected during testing (or during actual use if the operational distribution is known). Often, the operational definition of D is unknown, and hence a uniform distribution over I may be assumed. D is the mechanism that is generally used for system quality assessment, and frequently it will be used to benchmark whether the software is ready for release. There is an interesting relationship between D and the code. Different D values will cause internal data states to be created with different frequencies. Different I values will almost certainly cause different data states to be created as well as different state chains. Data states are a direct product of I and the code. We conjecture that data states and state chains contain useful information concerning the quality of the code and the quality of D. For example, suppose we have the code

```
read(x);
x:=x mod 2;
{look at the data states created here}
```

and I is over all even integers for x with equilikely D. If we were to look at the data states after the modulus operation, we would see all zeros. This would immediately tell that D does not represent all integers, but only even integers. To testers, we might recommend modifying I ever so slightly as to use at least one odd integer. If for no other reason, this will increase the reusability of the code, because the next user may have an I containing odd integers.

We need to formally define several terms that are relevant to our study of software testability—in particular, error, fault, and failure. An *error* is a mental mistake that is made by the programmer or designer, and a *fault* is the manifestation of that error in the code (IEEE Std. 610.12-1990). We define a *software failure* to be the occurrence of an output value that is not correct with respect to the input value that P received with respect to the specification or oracle. For now, we consider I to only contain legal inputs, which means that the only type of software failure we are interested in is a failure caused by programmer faults, and not problems associated with the hardware environment or faulty inputs values that are fed to the program during testing. It should also be noted that O is not defined with respect to a correct version of P, but with respect to the current version of P, which may or may not be correct. If P or I changes, O may also change.

SOFTWARE TESTING

Software testing is a verification process for software quality assessment and software quality improvement. Software testing assesses the correctness for both the syntactic and semantic views of software. For example, a compiler tests the syntax, and dynamic testing checks the semantics. The results of testing can be used to assess quality because testing checks the correctness of the output of a program. Testing can be used to improve quality (i.e., to make the program more reliable) as a vital part of the "test–debug–fix" cycle—the process of testing until failure occurs, applying debugging, and then modifying the code. This process is performed repeatedly until the frequency with which failure occurs drops to an acceptable threshold.

Software testing is a validation and verification (V&V) technique that occurs late in the software life cycle. Boehm (1981) nicely differentiates between validation and verification in the following manner: *Validation* is the process of ensuring that the software is doing the right thing, and *verification* is the process of ensuring that the software is doing its purpose correctly. For instance, validation would ensure that we have produced a compiler instead of an operating system, and verification would check to see that our compiler is producing the correct assembler code.

Software testing has several advantages over other verification forms: It relies on less formal analysis than does a technique such as proof of correctness, it replicates operational behavior, and it has a statistical basis. However, software testing has drawbacks: Any predictions based on software testing depend on an assumed input distribution. If the assumed input distribution is inaccurate or if the input distribution changes over time, any predictions based on software testing can be invalidated. When testing reveals a failure, it provides little help in locating the fault. Testing can also require enormous amounts of execution time; in fact, it may take longer to test a program than it did to develop the code. And finally, testing requires an oracle. Because automated oracles are rarely available, human oracles who require time and sometimes get the wrong results (which misleads testers) are required.

Software assessment can be broken into two broad classes: *static* and *dynamic*. Software testing is a class of dynamic assessment techniques. Testing involves actual executions of the program. Test cases are generated, and the resulting outputs are compared to correct outputs that are known *a priori*. *A priori* knowledge as to what the correct outputs are is problematic. In this book, we are mainly interested in assessing software with dynamic executions; if the reader is interested in exploring static analysis methods, we recommend obtaining *Software Testing Techniques*, 2nd edition (Beizer, 1990).

Like all software assessment techniques, dynamic testing can be further divided into two classes: *white-box* and *black-box*. In white-box testing (Probert, 1982), the code is considered when determining what test cases are used. For instance, if the first statement is **if (read(a) = 500)**, then we might want to try testing the program with a test case of 500. Black-box testing is the opposite of white-box testing—that is, it does not consider the code when test cases are selected.

Software testing is the most widely applied class of techniques that are used to show that a program is computing the correct function. Even so, software testing is plagued by many criticisms: (1) Automated oracles are rarely available, (2) human oracles can frequently be wrong and are limited in the amount of testing that they can perform, (3) specifications can be incorrect (even though they stand as the referee when deciding whether an output is correct), (4) operational input distributions can be completely unknown, and (5) the number of members of I may be so large that any amount of system-level testing is analogous to a drop of water in the ocean.

In software testing and analysis, most of the problems are unfortunately either undecidable or intractable. An *undecidable* problem is one for which no algorithmic solution is possible. An *intractable* problem is one whose best solution requires inordinate resources. Whether an arbitrary program will terminate is undecidable, and testing on every possible input value is generally intractable; Huang (1975) shows that to exhaustively test a program that inputs two 32-bit integers would take nearly 50 billion years to test at a rate of 1 test case per millisecond.

Software testing is generally performed for one of two reasons: (1) to estimate reliability or (2) discover the existence of faults in order that they might be corrected. When a program does not fail during nonexhaustive testing, we cannot automatically assume that there are no defects and that the program is 100% reliable. In fact, for reliability estimation, it would be far easier if the code did fail some $x\%$ of the time, so that we could roughly assess a reliability of $1 - x\%$. And for defect detection, a program that does not fail is not receiving any quality improvements (fixes). It is ironic that we have a better idea of what to do with a program that is failing than with a program that is not failing.

Typically, when it is determined that a program is defective, debugging will begin, code corrections will be made, and testing will be resumed. As the test–debug–fix cycle repeats itself, it is expected that both the period of time between failures (MTTF) and the reliability will increase. After tests are performed, the number of failures and times at which the failures occurred will be used as parameters in various reliability models to predict whether (and when) future failures will occur. In this capacity, testing *estimates* current failure behavior that is then used to *predict* future failure behavior.

Software testing occurs late in the software development life cycle. It begins after design and coding are completed, usually beginning with module (or unit) testing and ending with system (or integration) testing. Because testing occurs late, it is sometimes argued that testing occurs too late in the overall development process to greatly improve software quality. This is true for certain types of defects, specifically design and specification errors. Whenever testing reveals that a design or specification error has occurred, the costs to fix the problem in the code are much greater than if the problem had been caught earlier. There is a general trend to apply testing techniques at precode phases of the life cycle—that is, test throughout the entire development process.

Testing of physical objects has been performed for years. However, software testing is an anomaly in the test-and-evaluation (T&E) arena, and well-informed persons recognize the distinctions between testing software systems and testing physical systems. The most obvious difference is that physical systems suffer from environmental damage and material imperfections; software, however, only suffers from mental imperfections. It is far easier to find a crack in a piece of glass than it is to find logic errors in algorithms. Also, few persons may truly understand a program's logic; and if their interpretation is incorrect, locating the manifestation of the mental error could be virtually impossible.

Software testing is generally done at one of two levels in the code: integration (or system), and unit (or module). *Unit testing* tests the modules in isolation from the rest of the system, while integration testing tests the complete system with all of its modules. In general, *integration testing* is performed to detect system and interface errors that are not easily detected at the unit level. Unit testing is generally done as part of development, and thus it is geared more toward achieving quality. Integration testing is geared more toward assessing quality; however, if problems are found at this stage, defect detection and removal will be applied to improve quality. The chronology of how different software testing techniques came into existence is interesting. In general, it was a piggyback type of evolution, where a new technique was a modification or a slight twist on a previous technique. *Functional testing* was the traditional testing technique; it was used before there were any serious attempts to develop better methods. Informally, functional testing meant that the programmer should think about the different functions that the system is supposed to perform and develop test cases for them. Today, this is commonly referred to as *requirements testing* and is a form of integration testing. Intuitively, this seems better than simple random selection over the entire input domain because random testing may fail to consider some of the functions that the software is suppose to compute.

Serious attempts were later made to make testing more systematic and less *ad hoc*. This was done because empirical studies showed that functional testing that was thought to be "thorough" was only covering 50% or so of the code. This started with the development of various *single statement* unit testing coverage measures such as *statement* and *branch*. Statement coverage ensures that every statement in the code is covered at least once, and branch coverage ensures that each branch has a true and false outcome at least once (Myers, 1979). Coverage was viewed as the next best alternative to *path testing*, in which all possible sequences of control flow through program are exercised. Path testing is generally infeasible, due to the enormous number of paths that can be created when the code contains an indefinite loop. Another problem with path testing is that some of the paths are termed infeasible, meaning that there is no way that the code can be traversed. For example, consider the loop condition: **while ((*a* > 5) and (*a* < 5)) do**. Because this condition cannot be satisfied, the code in the loop can never be executed, making the paths that contain the statements in the body of the loop infeasible. And finally, path testing is unable to detect *missing paths*, which is an important class of errors that testing needs to be able to detect.

More stringent single-statement unit testing coverages such as *condition, decision/condition*, and *multiple condition coverage* ensued. Condition coverage ensures that each condition in a decision has a true and false outcome, decision/condition requires that each branch have a true and false outcome, each condition in a branch have a true and false outcome, and each point of entry to the code be invoked at least once; and multiple condition coverage requires that all possible combinations of condition outcomes in a decision occur and that all points of entry be invoked at least once (Myers, 1979).

Unit testing coverage advocates then moved toward covering *groups* of statements with coverage techniques such as data flow (Rapps and Weyuker, 1985) and linear code sequence and jump (LCSAJ) (Woodward et al., 1980). (LCSAJ units are program units that may be concatenated to form program paths; basically a LCSAJ is a body of code through which the flow of control may proceed sequentially and which is terminated by a jump in the control flow.) "Statement grouping" criteria are generally more difficult to satisfy than the single statement coverages. These more advanced techniques were developed to provide a "feeling" that the code has been more thoroughly exercised. Note we say feeling, and not higher reliability, since there is no formal means for mapping testing coverage to reliability assessment; it is unfortunately just a "warm fuzzy" when someone says that they have performed coverage criteria x and hence the software is more reliable than had they not performed that coverage. This goes back to the problem of showing that the process is good versus showing that the code is good and the inability to assess a reliability estimate based solely on this information.

Subsumption has been widely used as a way of analytically comparing coverage testing techniques. Subsumption is a very important capability given the many different coverage schemes; we need some way to rank schemes according to coverage. We follow Weiss (1989) and Frankl and Weyuker (1988) for our definition of subsumption. A criterion C_1 *subsumes* another criterion C_2 iff for every program, and test set T that satisfies C_1 also satisfies C_2. Frankl and Weyuker actually used the term *includes*. The term *subsumption* was defined by Clarke et al. (1985): A criterion C_1 subsumes a criterion C_2 iff every set of execution paths P that satisfies C_1 also satisfies C_2. The term *subsumption* is currently the more widely used of the two terms, and the definitions are equivalent.

Note from our previous definitions of various single statement coverages that multiple condition coverage subsumes decision/condition, which subsumes condition, which subsumes branch, which subsumes statement. All of these single-statement coverages are subsumed by complete path testing. Similarly, one can show that different data flow criteria (a group of statements) subsume single-statement coverage criteria, but data flow coverage, although more stringent, is still subsumed by path testing. And path testing is subsumed by exhaustive testing, provided that any infeasible paths are deleted from the set of possible paths. Amazingly, even with all of these techniques available, the industry standard for unit testing coverage achieved is only 85% branch coverage. This means that most organizations test only 85% of their branches before integrating a unit into the system for integration testing.

Testing schemes such as branch and data flow are termed *partition testing* methods. This is because these techniques partition the program domain into equivalence classes termed *subdomains*. For example, if there is only one branch in a program, we could think of all the test cases that exercise the true branch as being in one subdomain, and those that exercise the false branch as being in the other. Although the subsumes hierarchy provides a way of ranking the strength of various criteria, there is a general lack of a theoretical framework for explaining why one partition testing method is better than simple random test case selection. Research has been published on this subject: Hamlet and Taylor (1990) described the effectiveness of a testing method as the probability that its use would cause at least one program failure; they gave examples that indicated that partition testing was not superior to random testing under a variety of circumstances. They also described special circumstances under which partition testing would be superior, namely, knowing the optimal way to partition the input space for the particular faults that are in the code. Similar findings that support Hamlet's observations were published by Weyuker and Jeng

(1991). Also, Duran and Ntafos (1984) provided simulation results that suggest that random testing may be often more cost-effective than partition testing schemes. In their paper, results from actual random testing experiments are provided, which dispel the myth that random testing is a worst-case type of software testing.

Later, fault-based testing techniques came along. *Fault-based testing* shows that a particular class of faults are not resident in a program. The problem is that they are restricted by the fault classes that they employ. Because the set of all fault classes possible is infinite, fault-based techniques are restricted in their power to only the fault classes considered. These techniques can show that certain fault classes are not in a program; methods here include symbolic error flow testing (Morell, 1990), algebraic testing (Howden, 1978), domain testing (White and Cohen, 1980), and mutation testing (DeMillo et al., 1978). Another method, *perturbation testing*, attempts to determine a sufficient set of paths to test for various faults. In perturbation testing, faults are modeled as vector spaces, and characterization theorems describe when sufficient paths have been tested to discover both computation and domain errors (a domain error puts you on the wrong subpath). Additional paths will not need testing if they cannot reduce the dimensionality of the fault space (Zeil, 1983; Zeil, 1988). However, these techniques cannot show a complete absence of faults for most programs.

Although we could belabor the problems of software testing and dismiss it as a chaotic process altogether, we will instead address the problem associated with an inability to test a program on every input and will also show the benefit that software testability can have on decreasing the impact of this problem. This criticism is a concern because there are so many legal input values that even if we test with many different input values, we still will have not scratched the surface with respect to all of the other input values that we could have been selected. Beizer (1990) describes this situation as shifting from a "deduction" to a "seduction," meaning that the best that we can do is to demonstrate that the code works on a reasonable set of test cases and assume that it will work correctly for the rest. *Exhaustive* software testing selects and tests with every possible (and legal) test case; only when the size of I is small is this feasible. Exhaustive testing is rarely feasible.

The ideal situation for testers is what we term the "tester's utopia": the situation where any fault in a program is detected on the first test performed. This would guarantee that faults cannot hide during testing. Furthermore, on the first test that resulted in success, we would have evidence that the code is correct, with no further testing needed. That's why we call this a utopia—a big unreachable dream.

Because we cannot attain this wish, we should consider what the typical successful test provides in terms of quality assessment. It provides no information other than the program worked successfully once, and it suggests that the next test may also work correctly. So what does a long string of successful tests suggest? It more strongly suggests that the next test will also be successful than does a single successful test. But the problem is that a limited number of successful tests does not guarantee future successful tests.

This problem can be described as a classical hypothesis test. Let the null hypothesis H_0 be that the proportion of input values to the program that fail is 0. Let the alter-

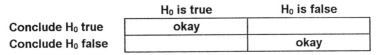

Figure 1-1. Hypothesis test situations.

native hypothesis H_a be that the proportion of input values that will result in failure is greater than 0. The hypothesis test is to test the program T times; if no failures occur, we conclude that H_0 is true; if one or more failures occurs, we conclude that H_0 is false.

In this situation, there are four situations that can occur, as shown in Figure 1-1. If we concur with what the truth is, then we are okay; however, there are two incorrect conclusions that we could arrive at: (1) The program is incorrect when it is correct, and (2) the program is correct but we conclude that it is incorrect. This second scenario is not possible, since we will not have observed a failure during our T tests, and hence we could not conclude that the program is incorrect. We must avoid the first incorrect conclusion, because that mistake could lead to a catastrophic failure. Only when testing is exhaustive can we be guaranteed that we have not made this mistake.

When software is exhaustively tested and each test case results in a correct output, the software is *correct*. Exhaustive testing is one empirical method for assessing correctness. Proofs-of-correctness, when feasible, also show that a program is correct; however, they suffer from a reliance on a correct specification and confidence that the proof itself was done correctly. Proofs are not empirical, but rather formal. Today, proofs-of-correctness are generally not performed, and instead a less rigorous technique termed *formal verification* is applied. The same problems with proofs-of-correctness occur with formal verifications; however, a successful formal verification does not assert correctness, it merely suggests correctness. Formal verification cannot be applied to large systems at the system level, and it is usually applied to smaller and more critical portions of a large system.

In summary, software testing can alert us to the existence of many types of problems, regardless of where in the software life cycle the problems were first introduced. Testing, however, is not a silver bullet: It relies heavily on either an oracle or correctness assertions; and if they are incorrect or ambiguous, testing's value is questionable at best and detrimental at worst. In the final analysis, testing is only as good as we are.

CORRECT OUTPUTS FROM INCORRECT CODE

An interesting issue arises during software development and particularly during testing; it is the issue of correct code versus correct outputs. What is it that we truly want? We want correct outputs from correct code, but we are willing to concede that correct outputs from incorrect code is not all bad. During dynamic testing, it is virtually impossible to determine which situation is true when correct outputs are produced. Certainly a correct output, no matter how derived, is good when the software is in use. And a correct output is a partial indication that the code is correct. However, if we limit this question to critical failures, then any incorrectness in the code may eventually cause a critical failure, in that case, correct outputs from incorrect code during testing are unacceptable (but during use they are acceptable). Whether we are willing to accept correct outputs from incorrect programs is more dependent on whether the code is operational or being tested. Code under test does not cause catastrophic problems, but operational code does. This issue will be raised again in Chapter 2 when we address the issue of software fault tolerance.

SOFTWARE TESTABILITY

The *IEEE Standard Glossary of Software Engineering Terminology* (IEEE, 1990) defines testability as:

> (1) the degree to which a system or component facilitates the establishment of test criteria and the performance of tests to determine whether those criteria have been met, and (2) the degree to which a requirement is stated in terms that permit establishment of test criteria and performance of tests to determine whether those criteria have been met.

Software testability is a software metric that refers to the ease with which some formal or informal testing criteria can be satisfied. For instance, if branch coverage is the testing criteria that is desired, and it is easy to find a set of inputs that satisfies that criteria, then the code would be considered to be of "high" testability. As another example, McCabe's cyclomatic complexity metric is frequently described as a measure of software testability, but is really a complexity measure of the digraph that represents the control flow of a program. The measure is determined by counting decision points (McConnell, 1993): We start with 1 for the straight path through the module. Every time we see one of the following keywords, we add 1: **if, while, repeat, for, and, or**. We add 1 for each case in a case statement. If the case statement lacks a default case, we add 1 more. If a McCabe's score is less than 10, the code may also be considered to be of high testability.

The formal or informal testing criteria considered for assessing testability can generally be classified as a structural coverage threshold or as an absolute absence of all faults. Voas defines the *testability* of a program P to be a prediction of the probability that if a fault exists in P, the fault will be detected by "whatever" testing scheme or test distribution is applied. In this definition, we are interested in whether the testing scheme or test distribution is capable of catching *all* existing faults. This can be in conflict with the other definitions for testability, and it often is (Voas et al., 1993). This definition of testability helps answer the question we just asked: *Are the correct outputs coming from correct code or incorrect code?*" In *Software Testing Techniques,* Beizer (1990) writes:

> We don't have testability metrics yet—but we have complexity metrics and we know that more complexity means more bugs and more testing to find those bugs.

It is this pervasive attitude in the software engineering community that has caused practitioners to automatically assume that software complexity measures are software testability measures. If you were to ask the typical software quality assurance person if they assess testability on their projects, they'd probably say: "Oh yes, we do cyclomatic complexity analysis." It is true that cyclomatic complexity estimates how difficult it will be to test all program paths, and hence provides an assessment of how difficult it will be to satisfy that particular coverage criteria. However, if your interest is not in only exercising the code but rather in detecting all of the faults, McCabe's measure will be less useful. In summary, complexity measures and coverage criteria are only two classes of measures that fit into the class of testability metrics.

TESTING AND TESTABILITY: TWO CLASSES OF SOFTWARE VALIDATION

Software validation generally refers to the process of showing that software is computing an expected function. According to the IEEE Standard Glossary of Software Engineering Terminology, *validation* is the

> process of evaluating a system or component during or at the end of the development process to determine whether it satisfies specified requirements.

The glossary defines software *verification* to be the

> process of evaluating a system or component to determine whether the products of a given development phase satisfy the conditions imposed at the start of that phase.

Software testing is used for both processes and is able to judge the quality of the code produced. Software testability, on the other hand, is not able to judge the quality of the code, because software testability has no information concerning whether the code is producing correct or incorrect results. It is only able to predict the likelihood of incorrect results occurring if a fault or faults exist in the code. For instance, a high McCabe score would predict reachability problems, while a high Voas score would indicate little likelihood of faults hiding for any reason, including reachability. This is a subtle yet fundamental difference between testability and testing.

Software testability is a validation technique, but in a different definition of the term "validation" that the IEEE Standard Glossary allows for. Software testability is assessing behavioral characteristics that are not related to whether the code is producing correct output. These behavioral characteristics are related to whether the program is capable of revealing problems within itself during testing. Software testing is designed to assess whether the function computed, which is a behavioral characteristic of the code, is correct. Thus testability and testing should be considered as performing validation, given a broader definition for "validation" than the IEEE standard provides for.

There is another interesting comparison that can be made between testing and testability; it is how these two techniques view the code. Testing is an assessment of the relationship between inputs and outputs, and hence has a black-box perspective to it (we are not talking here about white-box versus black-box testing, but rather in vaguer terms). In contrast, software testability is a metric that analyzes the code itself, and thus is classified as white-box. So not only are these two techniques validating different behavioral information, but they are analyzing these behaviors differently.

THE BALLS AND URN MODEL OF SOFTWARE TESTING

In our previous discussion, we presented two different perspectives on how to view software: (1) semantic and (2) structural. We have also presented several different definitions for software testability assessments. We now present a simple model that will be used throughout the next three chapters: We term it the *balls and urn model.* It nicely demonstrates the problem of trying to test software until we are confident that the software is not hiding faults. This model will help the reader better understand why nonexhaustively testing a program and not observing a failure is *not* a demonstration of correctness.

In the balls and urn model, there are two components: (1) an urn that represents the software and (2) balls that represent the legal input values that the program can receive (see Figure 1-2). In short, the balls represent what we previously denoted by *I*. In the balls and urn illustrations to follow, it may appear that an urn contains only a few balls that could be exhaustively sampled; that is not true. For the types of software that we are interested in, the number of balls in the urn will be overwhelming, and exhaustive sampling will be infeasible. As you will see later, only when exhaustive testing is infeasible is software testability an issue. If you can exhaustively test, then do so!

During testing, inputs can be selected in either a random or nonrandom manner. For instance, you could choose to select input values sequentially: 1, 2, 3, . . ., *n*. Or

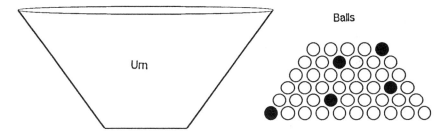

Figure 1-2. Two different colors of balls.

you could use a pseudorandom number generator to produce randomly generated integers for you: 94773, 2000332245, 3253322, ... *Random software testing* is the process of randomly selecting test cases with certain selection constraints and then testing a program on these test cases. The beauty of random testing is its probabilistic nature, which allows us to automate testing and to apply many different statistical models to the results.

Random testing serves a very important role in nonexhaustive software testing. Because we are unable to test all potential inputs and we can never know for certain what inputs the program will receive in operation, we probabilistically try to approximate this via random selection. This uncertainty creates a degree of randomness in the results.

We now add an assumption to our model about how the balls are distributed in the urn; since there is an associated probability of selecting any member of *I* during testing according to the testing scheme *D*, we will weight the likelihood of selecting a ball from the urn according to its probability in *D*. There will be at least one ball in the urn for each element of *I*. For instance, in Figure 1-3, we show that an input value of "1" is five times as likely to be selected as an input value of "2," and thus we put five balls in the urn representing "1" and one ball in the urn representing "2." Notice also that a value of "3" is four times as likely to be chosen as a value of "2," and so there are 4 balls representing "3" in the urn. Sampling from the urn is equivalent to sampling according to *D*.

In the balls and urn model, the reader should visualize a huge urn containing an enormous number of balls. The number need not be infinite, but large enough that for practical purposes we could never sample each ball in the urn in a reasonable amount of time. We assume that sampling is *with replacement*, even though sampling with replacement does not reveal as much information as sampling without replacement. Because the number of balls in the urn is so large, we can only hope to sample a small portion, and thus the effect on the results between drawing with or without replacement is minor. We do this mainly because the mathematics of sampling with replacement is simpler.

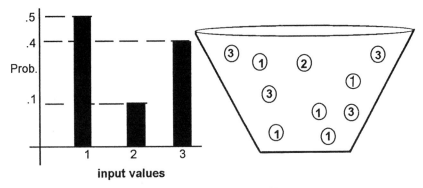

Figure 1-3. Relative frequencies of input values.

Each ball in the urn represents one input value to a program undergoing testing. (This input value may represent an *n*-dimensional input.) The balls represent the input domain of the program. Because some inputs in a program are more likely to be selected than others, we account for this in the urn. Initially, every ball in the urn is colored white (or clear) and has the input value it represents attached to it.

Now suppose that someone determines whether the program will produce the correct output for each ball. And further suppose that the person was able to find any ball in the urn representing an input value for which the program will fail. After they located these balls (if there were any), they paint them black. The black balls are put back into the urn and mixed together well with the uncolored white balls. This urn now represents the failure points in *I* with respect to *D*.

Now you are told to sample balls. You are ignorant as to whether there are any black balls in the urn. You must blindly determine whether any black balls exist. Of course, you can never be certain because you are limited in the number you can select, but if you do select many balls and observe none, you can at least gain a confidence that there are none. If there are many black balls in the urn with respect to the total number of balls, you should discover this fact quickly, because of the high probability of sampling at least one black ball when there are many black balls. If there are few black balls, then the probability that you will select one is small.

It should be clear how this model is analogous to random black-box software testing: The person who colors the balls represents the oracle, whether a ball is colored or not is determined by the program and specification, and ball sampling is just test case selection. Because the program and specification determine the color of a ball, every modification (or correction) to the program potentially changes the contents of the urn. It is also important to remember that we assume that every ball in the urn has an equally likely chance of being selected; thus after a ball is sampled and replaced, we assume that the urn is again homogeneously mixed. In this analogy, the urn should not necessarily be viewed as a static entity but rather a dynamically changing entity. Only once the program, *D*, and *I* become stable and are not being modified does the view of a static unchanging urn apply.

Before testing begins, it is not known whether there are any faults in the program, and we continue to choose test cases until we either observe a failure (a black ball is found) or observe no failures (no black balls) and eventually quit. Just because we quit testing after observing no failures does not mean that there are no inputs on which the program will fail. Remember that we are talking about nonexhaustive testing, because we assumed that the urn had so many balls that we could never sample all of them. All we gain after repeated sampling and finding no black balls is a *confidence* that there are none, *not a proof.*

This lack of proof is the downfall of dynamic software testing. It is simply Dijkstra's now famous adage that software testing can only show the existence of software faults, not their absence. Only one type of dynamic testing can prove that there are no existing faults, *exhaustive testing*, where every potential input to the program is executed and each output is evaluated for correctness. Thus nonexhaustive testing, which virtually all software programs receive, suffers from Dijkstra's insight. If we could exhaustively test and we knew *a priori* what each output should be for each input, we could program via look-up tables. We can easily argue that this is unrealistic, by asking the reader to recall how many times they have known *a priori* every input–output pair in the specification.

Random software testing is a probabilistic approximation technique for intelligently trying to determine the number of black balls in the urn. The more random sampling performed, the better the resulting approximation. If we could sample every ball at least once, we would no longer have an approximation, but instead, the exact answer.

In Chapter 2, we explore an approximation technique that gives insight into how many black balls are in the urn; this technique is not software testing in any form. It is a means of cheating—that is, looking down into the urn. It is not blind ball sampling, but rather a different way of analyzing the contents of the urn. By removing the blindness that existed during random sampling, we can better determine whether there are any black balls in the urn or not. The real power of the technique manifests itself when we combine its results with the results of random black-box testing. If we don't *see* any black balls nor *sample* any black balls, we greatly increase our confidence that all the balls are white.

So how can we do this? Suppose that we knew that black balls somehow "bubbled" up to the top of the urn—that is, they did not stay homogeneously mixed in with the white balls. And suppose that when they bubbled they often stuck together in big clusters and thus were not individually distributed throughout the urn. With such information and observing no black balls as we peered down into the urn, we begin to believe that there are no black balls. Furthermore, if blind sampling produced only white balls, we have a complementary piece of evidence supporting the hypothesis of the urn only containing white balls.

Let C be the number of balls in the urn. Then the true probability of selecting any particular ball is just

$$\frac{1}{C}$$

and the true probability of selecting a particular input value from the urn is

$$\frac{e}{C}$$

where e is the number of balls representing the input value. As you see, in terms of probability theory, this is a very basic model.

In Figure 1-2, there are two different colors of balls. A ball that is clear represents an input value on which the program P computes the correct value, and a black ball represents an input value on which the program does not compute the correct output value. In this model, we ignore the situation where we are not able to tell whether a particular output is correct or not with respect to the input value used. The coloring of the balls is a function of "whatever" stands as the deciding authority concerning correctness, which will be the specification or requirements for P. Recall that one of the criticisms against software testing is the issue of deciding whether all outputs are correct, which in this model is the process of coloring balls. Because of this and other problems, the balls and urn model is purely conceptual, and not an entity that we will ever have access to. We are only using this model for illustrative purposes in our discussion of testability, and not relying on it for actual sampling.

In the model, we assume that if one of the balls for some input value is clear, all of the balls representing that input are clear, and the same is true for black balls. Hence if the program works correctly for some input value y, then it always works correctly for input value y. We do not allow for nondeterminism in the process of ball coloring, and we assume that for each legal input value a color can be determined during testing for the ball(s) that represent it.

Software testing is simply the process of sampling balls from an urn, determining their color, and, if clear, sampling again and again until testing is halted. Because exhaustive testing is not feasible, any sampling from the urn is a minuscule reflection of what the contents of the urn truly look like. Furthermore, even if all of the balls that are selected during testing are clear, how do we assess the likelihood that the remaining balls that were not selected are also clear?

We now present what we consider are the three main classes of software urns. In the first urn in Figure 1-4, we have all black balls, which represents a program that is totally incorrect. This is a program for which there are no inputs that would enable the program to produce correct output. Although it may seem to the reader that this urn is a problem, it is only a problem for the development team, not the testing team, because no testing team would ever release code that is represented by this urn. In the urn in Figure 1-5, we see a correct program, which is not a problem for the development team, but will be a "nightmare" for the testing team, since the testers cannot exhaustively test, and they cannot know for certain whether they are in this situation or the situation shown in Figure 1-6. This is the case where we have achieved much higher quality than we can assess.

The situation shown in Figure 1-6 is the most troubling situation for software testers and developers. This is a situation where most of the balls in the urn are clear, however, notice that there are a few black balls scattered throughout the urn. This urn reveals that the development team has produced software of "good" quality; however, this urn is one which may cause the testers to overestimate the quality of

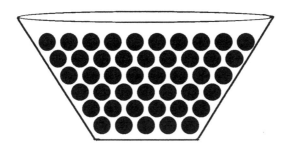

Figure 1-4. Scenario 1.

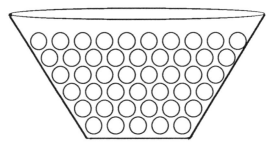

Figure 1-5. Scenario 2.

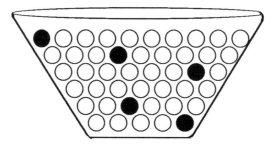

Figure 1-6. Scenario 3.

the software. The testers may report that they believe that there are no black balls in the urn, when that assumption is incorrect, and there *are* black balls in the urn. And if this happens, the development team will not be given the opportunity to correct the undetected faults. This shows that software that has not failed during nonexhaustive testing is "good" software but not necessarily correct software.

Because this is the most troublesome scenario of the three, we will attempt to produce information that would hint to the testers as to whether the code that they have tested is represented by the urn in Scenario 2 or Scenario 3. If we suggest Scenario 2, then they may consider the testing already performed to be thorough enough; however, if we suggest that they are likely to be in Scenario 3, then they may have a problem on their hands that requires more testing. The only "easy" solution to this problem is more testing, which may be too costly, and hence not easy after all.

TESTER'S UTOPIA

In the balls and urn model, we consider that each ball has an equilikely chance of being selected. There is no notion of depth within the urn, or of a ball being more likely to be selected than another by being closer to the top of the urn. For just a moment, consider the urn in Figure 1-7. This urn is actually a tennis ball canister, and note that in this urn there is the notion of only being able to select from the top. Also, this urn has mysteriously "bubbled" all of the black balls to the top, leaving the clear balls at the bottom. We term this scenario the "tester's utopia," a mythical state in which your program is unable to mask faults from you. In this scenario, any black ball will be at the top of the canister.

This is the "ultimate" testability, and hence it is an unrealistic state for a tester to expect to be in. Formally, the ultimate means a true testability of 1.0, not just a testability prediction of 1.0. In this state, the first clear ball selected provides a proof that the code is correct, which is far away from the typical day in the life of a tester. Imagine if you were to run down to your manager and say: "We tested once and produced the correct output, and therefore it is correct." But nonetheless, the tester's utopia represents the way in which we would like for our systems to be designed. We would like our systems to have as much trouble hiding faults from us during testing as possible.

WHY BALLS ARE BLACK

Before we can begin to determine whether we are in the Scenario 2 or Scenario 3, we need a complete understanding of why a ball is either clear or black. Many practitioners may mistakenly believe that if a ball is clear, then it did not cause any faults to be exercised during its execution; this is completely false!

There are three necessary and sufficient conditions that must occur in order for an input to cause the output to be incorrect (failure occurring). We refer to these three conditions as the *fault/failure model*, because this model relates the sequence of events that must occur in order for a fault to cause a failure:

1. The program input must exercise a fault.
2. The exercised fault must cause the program state to become *infected*.
3. The infected program state must *propagate* to the output and cause the output to also be infected (incorrect).

Figure 1-7. The tester's utopia.

(An infected program state is sometimes referred to as a *program state error.*) If any of these conditions fail to occur, then that input will be clear in the urn, which is different than saying that the input did not encounter any faults in the program. For this reason, we say that the three conditions are *necessary and sufficient*; nothing else needs to occur in order for failure to result.

We say that *data state error cancellation* has occurred when the third condition fails to occur, even though the first two conditions did occur. One special type of data state error cancellation is *coincidental correctness*, where the program gets on the wrong subpath during an execution but still manages to produce correct output. This is the situation where the program counter was an incorrect variable in the data state, and possibly remained incorrect through many data state transitions, but was unable to transfer its incorrectness to any output variable.

During testing and debugging, it is our hope that if there are any faults in the code, these three conditions will occur. Why? Because of the goal of testing and debugging, to achieve higher quality via defect removal. It is interesting to note that during deployment of the code, suddenly we want the opposite to be true: If faults remain, we don't want them to cause failure. The software mechanisms that enhance testability are those that will decrease fault tolerance, and thus assessing testability is also a way of indirectly assessing fault tolerance. (We will discuss more about this dichotomy later.)

As you can see, the relationship between input values, faults, and software failures is very simple. This simple relationship is tightly coupled to the computation model that we described earlier: $I \rightarrow S \rightarrow O$. Recall in the computation model that the output space is just the result of the transformations of program states during execution. For a member of I to result in a failure, we need the proper set of transformations between program states to ensure that an infected program state continues to remain infected until the output is produced. And when this "incorrectness" is preserved and failure occurs, we color the ball(s) representing that input value black. (Recall that there may be many black balls in the urn for a single input value if that value has a higher probability of being selected in D.)

From a statistics standpoint, Scenario 1 is the only one of our three scenarios where the program is incorrect and we are guaranteed not to be fooled into believing that the program is correct when it is not. That is why we said that from a development standpoint, Scenario 1 is bad, but from a testing standpoint, Scenario 1 is not a problem. Scenario 3 is the problematic scenario, because probabilistically, it is unlikely that we will select those few black balls during testing. Hence limited random sampling, given the urn in Scenario 3 with an enormous number of clear balls, will fail to reveal the black balls.

This highlights that a large problem in software testing exists when we are probabilistically incapable of selecting the inputs that will reveal the existence of a fault. Note that this situation only occurs in Scenario 3, not Scenario 1; hence the astute reader will realize that it is the clear balls in Scenario 3 that are causing the problems for testers. How strange it is to say that testing a program and never having it result in a failure is a problem, but indeed that is exactly what we are saying.

FAULT SIZE

Besides single black balls scattered throughout large groups of clear balls, there is another culprit at work here that must be addressed—namely, the concept of "fault size." A fault's *size* is the number of balls in the urn that are black as a direct result of that fault, meaning that the three necessary and sufficient conditions do occur for the (input, fault) pair. This is not an easy piece of information to ascertain, but it is very important to understand how different fault sizes affect our ability to determine whether there are any black balls in the urn during testing. Why, you ask? Because the greater a fault's size, then the more likely it is that we will catch that fault during testing. As we previously showed, Scenario 1 was not a problem for the testing team because we were guaranteed that we would select a black ball, and hence we would know that there was at least one fault in the code. In terms of fault size, large-sized faults will not be a problem for the testers, since they will be caught early in the testing phase. It is the small-sized faults—for example, like a fault that only causes failure once in every one million executions—that will be difficult to detect.

ESTIMATING FAULT SIZES VERSUS PREDICTING FAULT SIZES

In mathematics, there are often few exact solutions; most solutions are either estimates of some exact quantity or predictions of it. For example, for a fair coin, the probability of getting heads is exactly 0.5, but if we toss the coin 100 times, we may or may not get heads 50% of the time. Sampling (and testing) are methods of estimating the proportion of time that the event of interest occurs. There are other events of interest that we cannot estimate, because there exists no means of estimating them. For instance, before an election, polls (estimates) are taken and used to predict (a future event) the winner. In this case, we cannot estimate the winner, because the real ballots have not been turned in. In this manner, estimated information available now is used to "guess" how events will turn out in the future.

Fault sizes suffer from a similar problem as occurred in the voting analogy. One difficulty in directly estimating fault sizes is in first determining exactly what the fault is in a program when failure occurs. For example, suppose we programmed $x = x + 1$ instead of $x = x - 1$. You might immediately assume that the fault is using the wrong operator. However, someone else could argue that you have missing code and should have programmed $x = x + 1; x = x - 2$. Determining exactly what is incorrect and constitutes the fault is nontrivial. So before you can start calculating fault sizes, you must first define the set of all faults in your program. But even if you knew where each fault was in the program and you could uniquely identify them, why do so? Wouldn't you rather get them out, not estimate their sizes? Thus the notion of directly estimating fault sizes is not very useful; it is plausible to predict fault sizes, not directly estimate them.

Another problem here is that for a specification, there may be an infinite number of syntactically unique programs that implement that specification correctly. Now

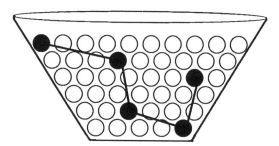

Figure 1–8. A fault of size 5.

think about the infinite number of incorrect programs that are "mutants" of just one of those correct programs. Given an incorrect program then, how can you determine which of those correct programs the incorrect program most resembles in order to determine what and where the fault is? Not an easy problem indeed!

Even though we will not directly estimate fault sizes, you can take what we term the "pessimistic approach" to fault size estimation and say: "I'll just assume that the smallest-sized fault in my program is of size 1." If you do so, you are suggesting the possibility of a failure probability of $1/C$. To test to the level required to be sure that a fault of size 1 is not hiding in your code when C is large will essentially require that you sample all C balls, which is exhaustive testing. So although the pessimistic approach to fault size estimation is allowable in the balls and urn model, it is useless in practice when C is large, which is the case that we are concerned with.

As we have said, faults with larger fault sizes are more likely to be detected during software testing than are faults of smaller fault size. Because we cannot directly estimate fault sizes, we instead "predict" fault sizes. To do so, we introduce a notion that we term "ball chaining." Ball chaining is a way of linking together all of the balls in the urn that are black and associated with a specific fault. Each unique fault in a program will have its own unique chain of black balls in the urn. The longer the chain, the greater the fault size, and the less worrisome that fault will be for testers because it is less likely to escape detection. In Figure 1-8, we show a fault of size 5; to detect this fault during testing, you need to select only one of the balls that are linked in the chain. In Figure 1-9, we are showing a program that has 5 faults, each of size 1. To detect these faults (which are of smaller size than the single fault in Figure 1-6), you will need to select each of these black balls during software testing, which probabilistically will be difficult to do, unless of course you do an enormous (and possibly exhaustive) amount of testing.

TESTABILITY, FAULT SIZES, AND BALL CHAINING

Software testability, when it is defined as a prediction of the probability that software testing will reveal any existing faults and the urn is ordered according to the test distribution, is a way of predicting how long the chains will be in the urn if black

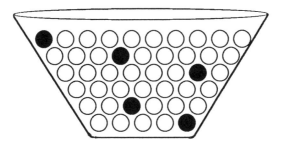

Figure 1-9. Five faults of size 1.

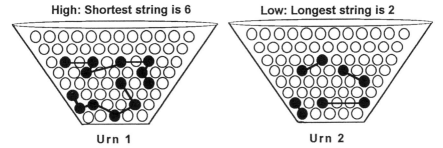

Figure 1-10. Two different urns.

balls exist. This presents an interesting situation, because as we have said, chains are related to specific faults, and we do not know where any faults are in our program; we have tested the program and observed no failures, so we have no direct information concerning where faults are. Hence we cannot estimate how long the chains are in our "conceptual urn," but we can simulate the effect of faults in our code, estimate the length of those chains, and then use that information to predict how long the actual chains, if any, are in the urn.

In Figure 1-10, we are showing two different urns: Urn 1's shortest string is of size 6, and Urn 2's shortest string is of size 2. What this tells us is that if both urns have the same number of balls, then it will be harder to catch the fault in Urn 2 associated with the chain of size 2 than the fault in Urn 1 with the chain of size 6. Thus the relationship between software testability, fault size, and ball chaining is as follows: Balls that are chained together represent a particular fault in the program. The length of the chain is the size of the fault. Software testability is a prediction of the probability that if a fault existed, and hence that there is at least one black ball representing that fault in the urn, then it would be revealed during testing according to D over I. Clearly, longer chains in the urn represent faults that are more likely to be caught during testing, and shorter chains represent faults that are more likely to remain hidden.

Testability, then, is a prediction of the shortest chain that we believe can be in the urn. However, since the length of the chain is not as important as the length of the chain with respect to the number of total balls in the urn, we typically consider the testability to be the prediction of the length of the shortest predicted chain in the urn divided by the total number of balls in the urn:

$$\text{Urn testability} = \frac{\text{shortest \_ predicted \_ chain}}{C} \qquad (1\text{-}1)$$

Given an urn with C balls, the probability of detecting a fault j of size n is roughly

$$\text{Prob[detecting } j] \cong n/C \qquad (1\text{-}2)$$

(This assumes sampling from the urn is *with replacement*, which is a reasonable assumption, since the likelihood of reselecting the same ball twice is so tiny given large C). Then the probability of failure of program P with N distinct faults, $\{n_1, n_2, \ldots n_N\}$, is simply

$$\text{Prob}\{P \text{ failing}\} \cong \sum_{i=1}^{N} n_i/C \qquad (1\text{-}3)$$

In Musa et al. (1987), a simple model is proposed that predicts the impact that faults have on the failure probability of a program. This model does not attempt to find minimum fault sizes, but rather average fault sizes. The *initial failure intensity* parameter of a program λ_0 at time 0 is

$$\lambda_0 = fK\omega_0 \qquad (1\text{-}4)$$

where f is the linear execution frequency of the program, K is the fault exposure ratio, and ω_0 is the number of inherent faults at time 0. The *linear execution frequency* is the number of times the program would be executed per time unit if the program was straight-line code (no branches or loops). The *fault exposure ratio* represents the fraction of time that the passage results in a failure; it accounts for the possibility that the program is not straight-line code. (You can think of the fault exposure ratio as being the same as the average length of all chains of black balls.) $f\omega_0$ is the *fault velocity*, which is the average rate at which faults in the program would pass by (meaning be executed) if the program were executed in straight-line fashion; this is just the probability of executing a fault (1.0) with respect to time. For example, if there are 10 faults in the code, and the code is executed once per second, then the fault velocity is 10 faults per second. The average initial failure intensity is the product of the fault velocity and the fault exposure ratio. For example, if the initial failure intensity is 0.01 failures per minute, and the fault velocity is 10 faults per minute, then the fault exposure ratio is 0.001 failures/fault on average.

To give the reader a feeling for what types of values K has taken on in previous experiments, Musa et al. (1987) provide data for different values of K for different projects, of which the average is 4.2×10^{-7}. To our knowledge, there are organizations that use this value in actual projects instead of trying to estimate the value for the individual projects. In our model, a value for K of 4.2×10^{-7} would represent very-small-sized faults. To find K, there are four pieces of information that are needed:

1. B, the fault reduction factor
2. f
3. λ_0
4. v_0 is total failures

K is given by

$$K = (1/Bf) \, (\lambda_0/v_0) \tag{1-5}$$

For example, if B is 1, f is 100 executions per minute, λ_0 is 10^{-3} failures per minute, and v_0 is 20 failures, then K is 5.0×10^{-7} failures/fault. Chapter 2 introduces a model for finding the minimum fault exposure ratio for the smallest-sized fault, which is quite different than Musa's K factor here. Chapters 7 and 8 discuss software reliability modeling in detail.

ESTIMATING A FAILURE PROBABILITY

There are two means for estimating the failure probability of a system. You can measure it directly (like sampling balls from the urn repeatedly) according to D, or you can calculate it from failure probability estimates for its components. To calculate a system's failure probability from its components, there must be information on how the components are interconnected. This approach is often performed via stochastic Markov models. One method for estimating the component failure probabilities is partition testing, or possibly unit testing of the components, assuming that the unit testing of a subcomponent is with respect to the internal distributions that are associated with D.

Direct sampling to quantify a failure probability is not a problem unless we are trying to demonstrate failure probabilities in the low orders of magnitude, namely, 10^{-4} to 10^{-12}; in this range it is very difficult, particularly if any failure occurs in this process which will require code repair and regression testing. And the problem with Markov models is that we have to show independence between the components in order to apply them; it is difficult to show that software components are completely independent. Hence both classes of schemes are limited.

We have said that we are not interested in estimating fault sizes for two reasons:

1. If there were a fault, we'd remove it, not estimate its fault size.
2. We doubt we'll ever detect one during testing, because we have assumed that we've had a long string of clear balls, and we expect that to continue if sampling continues.

We have just shown the relationship between fault sizes and the true probability of failure of a program. If we were able to estimate fault sizes, we could use Equation 1–2 to estimate the failure probability, so that method for estimating the failure probability does not exist for us. If we could get the program to fail at least once, then we could use that information to estimate the failure probability, but not necessarily the fault sizes; we would still need a set containing each distinct fault to do that.

By the way, research has been performed concerning the difficult problem of estimating a probability of failure when a program does not fail. Classic work on estimating a probability of failure when only clear balls are drawn can be dated back to Laplace, who derived the formula (termed Laplace's rule of succession)

$$1/(t + 2)$$

where t is the number of clear balls that have been drawn (Feller, 1970). Miller et. al. (1992) introduced formulae for this problem based on the *Beta (a, b)* distribution, since $(1/(t+2))$ is a special case *(a = b = 1)* of the expected value of a *Beta (a, b)* distribution. *a* and *b* are chosen consistent with prior knowledge about the failure probability. The formulae incorporate random testing results, information about *D*, and prior assumptions about the probability of failure. The formulae were based on a discrete sample space statistical model of the software including Bayesian prior assumptions.

THE THREE URNS

In our balls and urn discussion to this point, there have actually been three urns. The first urn is just the urn that we have been talking about; it contains every legal input to the program with the appropriate coloring and number of corresponding balls. Also, in this urn, you can think about the balls being chained for each specific fault in the program if you so desire, but this is not necessary. Because this urn does not really exist, we call it the "conceptual" urn. Figure 1-8 showed an example of this urn, with one fault of size 5.

After we have performed some number of tests, we begin to gather a feeling for what the contents of the conceptual urn looks like. This "feeling" might look like Figure 1-11 after we have tested our program seven times. In this example, we'd estimate a probability of failure of 1/7 with a large confidence interval (because 7 is a small sample size). And from testability analysis, we will have an urn that represents our predictions of how black balls might be chained in the conceptual urn. Our prediction might look like Figure 1-12. Notice in this figure that we purposely exclude the white balls. Why? Because in testability analysis, we do not care about white balls; we care about chains of black balls. Also, notice that our predictions for fault sizes in this urn are 2, 3, and 5. The benefit of that information is that we can statistically estimate how much testing is needed to detect faults that have those fault sizes. Less testing will be needed to detect faults of size 5 than of size 2. This pro-

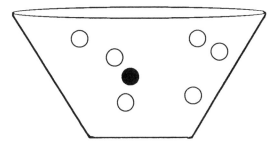

Figure 1-11. An "estimated" urn from testing.

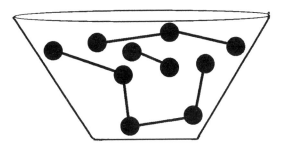

Figure 1-12. The "predicted" urn from testability.

vides a better understanding of what it means to test our code and not observe a failure. In this urn, we have a testability of $2/C$.

Looking back, we referred to testability as the ease with which some testing criteria could be satisfied. As mentioned, cyclomatic complexity suggests the difficulty in coverage testing schemes such as path testing. When testability is viewed in this manner, you lose the ability to predict the chaining within the urn. Why? Because this perspective on testability ignores the second and third conditions of the fault/failure model. Furthermore, because cyclomatic complexity is not dependent on D, there is no meaningful way of estimating the first condition of the fault/failure model either.

Cyclomatic complexity does represent an interesting measure of whether a programmer or designer has followed "good" structured programming and modularity practices. It is a terrific way of measuring "spaghetti code." The trouble, however, is that we are facing a harder problem than simply assessing the quality of the structure. We are interested in whether the urn is hiding faults during testing. As an example of how the structural definition of testability differs from the predicted fault size model, consider Figure 1-13. This is a program with two branches, and we have a fault in one of the branches: "−" instead of "+". We are always off-by-2 in the value of x after the fault is executed. Assume that we execute the fault 25% of the time. We always infect the data state after the fault is executed. But we only propagate the infected data state to the output 0.00666% of the executions of the

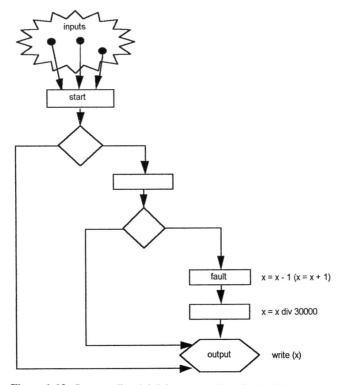

Figure 1-13. Structurally trivial, but an excellent fault hiding program

fault. This means then that the probability of observing the fault in this syntactically trivial program is

$$0.25 * 1.0 * 0.000066 = 0.0000166.$$

So although this code has low cyclomatic complexity, it has an enormous ability to hide a fault in that particular statement. There are cases where these two different perspectives agree, but in general they are not interchangeable.

ROLE OF *D* AND *I* IN TESTABILITY ASSESSMENT

In our definition for testability, we always preface our probability predictions on having *I* and *D*. Thus you might ask whether a change to *I* or *D* affects our testability assessments. Because software testability is trying to predict how *any* black balls might be distributed in the urn, then obviously when *I* or *D* change, it is very likely that our predictions will also change, but not always. It might be that even when the contents of the urn change (meaning the input values that the balls represent), the coloring and distribution of the black balls do not change; hence a change to *D* or *I* does not automatically guarantee a different testability prediction. However, this will be the exception, not the rule.

Unlike static complexity metrics, whose assessments only change when the code changes, dynamic assessments of the behavior also change when the dynamic components, the input space and distribution, change. This is intuitive; we all know that different test distributions are better or worse for finding defects, and hence different distributions and input spaces will cause a program to have different testabilities. Although we do not know how, we would like to find a distribution that truly gives us the greatest testability when we are testing for defect detection. We have access to the subsumes hierarchy, which suggests that if C_2 subsumes C_1, then C_2 will be of greater testability than C_1. But research has not been done to confirm this hypothesis, and, if true, to what degree the testability of C_2 is greater than the testability of C_1. We know that in terms of the coverage factor of the testability equation, C_2 will be of greater testability than C_1, but from the fault/failure model we recognize that there are two factors that must be accounted for. And whether these two other factors will also suggest that C_2 is of greater testability than C_1 needs to be researched.

In terms of software reuse, it may be the case that under the original environment, D_1, the code is of lower testability than under the new environment, D_2. Of course the same is true of reliability; the common myth that a software component that worked correctly in D_1 will automatically work as well in D_2 is absurd. In terms of maintainability, a lower testability region of the software under D_1 will suggest that if that region is modified, more regression testing will be needed, because that region has been shown to have a lesser impact on the code's behavior. During maintenance, if the input environment remains fixed, and a region of high testability is modified, then less regression testing should be needed. Why? Because as you will see in Chapter 2, the testability of a code region is more a function of the other code regions and D than it is a function of itself.

RELATING TESTABILITY TO RELIABILITY AND PROBABILITY OF FAILURE ESTIMATION

Software reliability assesses the likelihood of software failure occurring under the assumption that the program contains faults under D and I. When D and I change, so too may the assessed reliability. Recall that we are assuming that the program only fails from software faults, not hardware or system problems. Of course we know in practice that these "other" problems can cause failure, but we are not concerned with that here. That is a problem for the embedded system test team, and hence requires an integrated hardware/software testability theory, which is outside the scope of this book and, to our knowledge, does not exist.

Software testability takes a different perspective, asking the likelihood of a faulty program *not* failing, rather than asking the likelihood of a faulty program failing. By answering this question instead, we are able to assess the likelihood of our being fooled into believing that an incorrect program is correct, after testing that program repeatedly and not observing a failure. This shows how software testability and software reliability estimation are distinct yet related. Also, reliability is typically defined with respect to time, and testability does not directly have the time component in it. Testability could have time included in its definition, by simply adding some "mean" number of balls selected per unit time, giving us the likelihood of failures not occurring during a time interval given that faults exist.

We have defined both software reliability and software probability of failure. The relationship between these two is straightforward: Probability of failure is defined with respect to the *next* input selected, and reliability is defined with respect to an interval of time. Note that these are both defined with respect to *D*. A high probability of failure implies low reliability, and low probability of failure implies high reliability.

One question that is frequently asked is whether high reliability or high testability is more important. Such a question has no answer, because it is an "apples and oranges" comparison. From a customer's perspective, high reliability is the quality they want. Consider six scenarios for a system:

1. Low reliability, low testability
2. Low reliability, high testability
3. High reliability, low testability
4. High reliability, high testability
5. Correct, low testability
6. Correct, high testability

If a program has low reliability, then its testability, whether high or low, is really not an issue; its lack of reliability is the issue! If a program has high reliability, testability becomes a concern in the situation where we would like to make a "leap of faith" that the code probably contains no faults. If we have an acceptably high reliability and do not wish to make the "leap," then testability is not an issue. And if we have shown, or know, that the program or some part of the program is correct, then a testability assessment for the "correct" code is not meaningful. To truly know that the code is correct requires either exhaustive testing or a proof-of-correctness, neither of which are practical. There are two issues here: (1) being fooled into accepting software as correct when it is not (a potential for liability suits) and (2) being fooled into doing too much testing when the code is correct (wasted additional costs).

In summary, testability is only important to reliability assessment if we want a confidence that the quality of the software is even greater than our reliability estimate suggests. We are not implying that the only application of testability is assessing a confidence in software correctness. But we are saying that if a system has a reliability goal and meets the goal, then testability analysis may not be necessary.

TESTABILITY AND PARTITION TESTING

We have previously mentioned various partition testing schemes, such as branch testing and data flow testing, and whether partition testing is worth the additional costs beyond classical random testing. It is interesting to note the relationship that exists between a partition and the testability of that partition. Furthermore, it is interesting to note that if you have the testability of a partition, meaning some prediction of the shortest chain of black balls for that partition, then you can immediately assess the minimum number of tests needed for that partition for a confidence that there are no black balls in that subdomain.

Howden and Huang (1993) consider the situation where we have I partitioned into n subdomains, and each subdomain i has a testability t_i. Then there is an integer N that is *an adequate number of tests for supporting a level of confidence c in the program* if there is a test distribution vector **N** for N such that

$$c \leq 1 - \max_{1 \leq i \leq n} \{ (1 - t_i)\, Ni \} \tag{1-6}$$

N is an *optimal number of tests for supporting a level of confidence c* if it is the minimal adequate number of tests for supporting that level of confidence, that is, it is the smallest integer with a test distribution vector N satisfying Equation (1-6).

As an example, suppose that we have two partitions with $t_1 = 0.1$ and $t_2 = 0.5$. And suppose that we have tested with three inputs from the second partition ($N_2 = 3$) and one input from the first partition ($N_1 = 1$). Then our confidence is less than or equal to $1 - \max(0.9, 0.125)$ which is 0.1, meaning that we are less than 10% confident in our code. The interesting thing to note here is that we used four test cases, for roughly 10% confidence; according to our formula, all we really needed were two test cases for this level of confidence. We could have merely selected one test case from the second partition, because the max operator dominates Equation 1-6. So in this scenario, two was the optimal number of test cases needed for $c \leq 0.1$. This example shows how testability can be used to assess the amount of testing that is needed relative to the shortest chain in a partition of I. This scheme allows for better optimization of partition testing, which is performed at the unit testing level.

SUMMARY

Software testability can be viewed in many different ways; and until a universal perspective on it is adopted, it will be used in different ways and carry different meanings. We have generally classified testability along three boundaries: (1) as a source code complexity metric such as the number of expression operator occurrences, (2) as a measure of the ease with which some structural coverage criteria can be satisfied, and (3) as a measure of the likelihood that faults are hiding from a particular testing scheme D. Because this third perspective is the only one of the three that is based on all three conditions of the fault failure model, we opt to make it the definition for testability that we use throughout the remainder of this book. We hope that someday this definition will be considered by the Institute of Electrical and Electronics Engineers in future revisions to IEEE (1990). This perspective on testability can be thought of as a prediction of the smallest nonzero software probability of failure. This is the shortest chain of black balls in our third urn, the predicted urn. It is clear that the longest predicted chain could be all of the balls strung together, and the shortest predicted chain could be a single ball. But unfortunately neither of these predictions is particularly useful, and we need a "smarter" way to predict the shortest chain than to take the pessimistic perspective. Amazingly, the semantic perspective is going to allow us to predict many characteristics that are of interest to the software engineering community today, such as safety, fault tolerance, a testing stoppage criteria, where to emphasize validation activities other than testing, when inspections should be applied, how expensive maintenance activities will be for various regions of the code and the level of regression testing effort required. The information associated with a prediction of the shortest chain of black balls in the urn is applicable to many activities in the software engineering life cycle, and hence it is a very powerful notion.

EXERCISES

1. Can you find an example where two high-reliability components, $g(x)$ and $f(y)$, have a low reliability when they are composed, $g(f(y))$? Can you find an example where two software components, each with 0.00 reliability, form a correct composition?

2. Other than software testability and probability of failure assessments, what other semantic characteristics might be worth the cost to quantify?

3. Write a program that is incorrect, where one urn for the program is all black balls and the other is all clear? Show the different I values that allow this to be true.

REFERENCES

B. Beizer. *Software Testing Techniques*, 2nd Edition. New York: Van Nostrand Reinhold,1990.

B. W. Boehm. *Software Engineering Economics*. Englewood Cliffs, NJ: Prentice–Hall, 1981.

B. W. Boehm. "A Spiral Model for Software Development and Enhancement." *IEEE Computer* 21(5), 61–72, May 1988.

R. Butler and G. Finelli. "The Infeasibility of Experimental Quantification of Life-Critical Software Reliability." In: *Proceedings of SIGSOFT '91: Software for Critical Systems*, December. 1991.

L. A. Clarke, A. Podgurski, D. Richardson, and S. J. Zeil. "A Comparison of Data Flow Path Selection Criteria." In: *Proceedings of the 8th International Conference on Software Engineering*, London, August 1985. IEEE Computer Society, pp. 244–251.

A. Comte. *Principes de Philosophie Posive*. Paris: J. B. Ballière et Fils, 1848.

R. DeMillo, R. Lipton, and F. Sayward. "Hints on Test Data Selection: Help for thePracticing Programmer." *Computer* 11(4), 34–41, April 1978.

J. W. Duran and S. C. Ntafos. "An Evaluation of Random Testing." *IEEE Transactions on Software Engineering* SE-10(4), 438–444, July 1984.

W. Feller. *An Introduction to Probability Theory and Its Applications*, Volume I, 3rd edition, New York: John Wiley & Sons, 1970.

P. G. Frankl and E. J. Weyuker. "An Applicable Family of Data Flow Testing Criteria." *IEEE Transactions on Software Engineering*, 14(10); 1483–1498, October 1988.

M. H. Halstead. *Elements of Software Science*. Amsterdam: North-Holland, 1977.

D. Hamlet and R. Taylor. "Partition Testing Does Not Inspire Confidence." *IEEE Transactions on Software Engineering* 16(12), 1407–1411 December 1990.

J. C. Huang. "An Approach to Program Testing." *ACM Computing Surveys* 8, (3), 113–128, September 1975.

W. E. Howden and Y. Huang. "Analysis of Testing Methods Using Failure Rate and Testability Models." Technical Report CS93-296, Department of Computer Science, University of California, San Diego, June 1993.

Institute of Electrical and Electronics Engineers. *IEEE Standard Glossary of Software Engineering Terminology*, ANSI/IEEE Std. 610.12-1990. New York: IEEE, 1990.

S. C. McConnell. *Code Complete*. Richmond, WA: Microsoft Press, 1993, p. 395.

K. Miller, L. Morell, R. Noonan, S. Park, D. Nicol, B. Murrill, and J. Voas, "Estimating the Probability of Failure When Testing Reveals No Failures." *IEEE Transactions on Software Engineering* 18(1), 33–43, January 1992.

L. J. Morell. "A Theory of Fault-Based Testing." *IEEE Transactions on Software Engineering*, 16(9), 844–857, August 1990.

G. J. Myers. *The Art of Software Testing*. New York: John Wiley & Sons, 1979.

J. D. Musa, A. Iannino, and K. Okumoto. *Software Reliability Measurement, Prediction, Application*. New York: McGraw-Hill, 1987.

Robert L. Probert, "Optimal Insertion of Software Probes in Well-Delimited Programs." *IEEE Transactions on Software Engineering* SE-8(1), 34–42, January 1982.

S. Rapps and E.J. Weyuker. "Selecting Software Test Data Using Data Flow Information," *IEEE Transactions on Software Engineering* SE-11(4), 367–375, 1985.

W. W. Royce. "Managing the Development of Large Software Systems: Concepts and Techniques." In: *Proceedings of WESCON*, August 1970.

J. Voas, J. Payne, C. Michael, and K. Miller. "Experimental Evidence of Sensitivity Analysis Predicting Minimum Failure Probabilities." In: *Proceedings of Eighth Annual Conference on Computer Assurance*. Gaithersburg, MD: NIST, 1993, pp. 123–133.

S. N. Weiss. "What to Compare When Comparing Test Data Adequacy Criteria." *ACM SIGSOFT Notes* 14(6):42–49, October 1989.

E. J. Weyuker and B. C. Jeng. "Analyzing Partition Testing Strategies." *IEEE Transactions on Software Engineering*. SE-17(7), July 1991.

L. J. White and E. I. Cohen. "A Domain Strategy for Computer Program Testing." *IEEE Transactions on Software Engineering* SE-6(3), 247–257, 1980.

M. R. Woodward, D. Hedley, and M. A. Hennell, "Experience with Path Analysis and Testing of Programs," *IEEE Transactions on Software Engineering*, SE-6(3), 278–286, May 1980.

S. Zeil, "Testing for Perturbations of Program Statements." *IEEE Transactions on Software Engineering* SE-9(3), 335–346, May 1983.

S. Zeil, "Selectivity of Data-flow and Control-flow Path Criteria." In: *Proceedings of the Second Workshop on Software Testing, Verification, and Analysis*. Washington D.C.: IEEE Computer Society Press, 1988, pp. 216–222.

CHAPTER 2

The PIE Assessment Model of Software Testability I

FAULT-BASED METHODOLOGIES

Chapter 1 has set up the problem that we wish to solve: *What are the predicted sizes for faults that may reside in the code*? A second problem that we will be able to solve without any additional effort, once this problem is solved, is: *Where in the code are the predicted fault sizes coming from, particularly the tiny ones?* Answering these questions allows testers to determine (1) how much testing to perform (based on predicted fault sizes) and (2) where to emphasize testing resources or other validation resources (in those regions that have suggested the smallest predicted fault sizes). For example, manual inspections might be a prudent technique to employ in those regions where we predict such tiny fault sizes. These are regions where testing is less powerful at catching such faults. Or a formal verification might be possible if a small [in source lines of code (SLOC)] function has a particularly low testability.

Because direct estimation of fault sizes is not an alternative, we will rely on the ability to "simulate" faults and measure the impact that the simulated faults have on the program. There are different ways to decide *whether* an impact has occurred, and these methods will be based on the fault/failure model. The estimates of the impact that simulated faults demonstrate will then be used to predict the fault sizes of "actual" faults, not simulated ones. Hence we will heavily rely on some of the concepts that are used in fault-based testing methodologies without any interest in the testing aspects of those ideas (recall the distinction between testing and testability).

Chapters 2 and 3 introduce the PIE assessment model for software testability. Note that these chapters are dedicated to describing this *one* model for assessing testability; recall earlier discussions about different perspectives on what testability means. In the PIE model, testability is the probability of revealing faults during testing and thus is a semantically based testability model. Other models for assessing testability in the more classical (syntactic) manner can be described in most software engineering texts.

Chapter 1 defined fault-based testing and mentioned several different types. The PIE testability assessment model is not directly related to fault-based testing, but rather indirectly related to several of the concepts that fault-based testing methods (such as mutation testing) employ. Recall that fault-based testing is the class of testing techniques that seeks to show that particular classes of faults do not exist in a program. That is, the actual fault sizes for faults represented by these classes is zero. Hence we classify PIE as a *fault-based analysis* method.

The problem with fault-based testing, regardless of method, is that once the program is completed and successful (meaning that no faults of those classes have been shown to exist), the tester only knows that it is fault-free for the classes considered, not for all fault classes. Fault-based testing does not provide a demonstration that the program is correct. But even the ability to eliminate certain classes of errors from concern is a useful capability.

FAULT SIMULATION

Fault injection is the process of physically inserting a fault in a program, where an oracle or specification is available that is able to assert that what was modified was made incorrect. *Fault simulation* is different, in that what is modified in the code may or may not have been incorrect. This may seem strange, but in fault simulation you may actually modify an incorrect statement in your code and turn it into a correct statement. It is more likely, however, that your modifications will change correct code into incorrect code, but without an oracle or specification, this cannot necessarily be determined.

Fault seeding is a statistical fault injection method that is used to estimate the number of faults residing in a program after testing has been performed (Mills, 1983). In fault seeding, faults are injected into a program and the program is tested. The number of "injected" faults that are found is used to estimate the number of actual faults in the code that are yet to be caught. For instance, suppose that our testing revealed half of the seeded faults, and our testing had uncovered 100 actual faults in the code. Then we would estimate that there are still 100 actual faults remaining in the code yet to be found. A criticism against this technique, as with all fault injection schemes, is that the faults that are injected must be representative of the faults that are hiding in your program. If faults are injected that are easily caught, but the actual faults in the code are very difficult to detect, then you will gain an "inflated" opinion of the quality of your code. If faults are injected that are not easily caught and few of them are caught, but the actual faults in the code are easy to detect, then you will be left with a "pessimistic" opinion of the quality of the code. In short, it is important that the faults that are injected with a fault injection scheme be representative of the faults real programmers make. Because no one really knows how to do this, criticisms against techniques that are based on injected faults are defensible and justified. Because fault-based techniques are more advanced than simple coverage techniques, and in certain cases fault-based techniques can be shown to subsume simple coverage techniques, fault-based methods are receiving more interest from the testing research community.

This brings us to an interesting question: "Is it more important that injected faults *look* like the faults that real programmers would make, or is it more important that injected faults *behave* like the faults that real programmers would make?" (Note that "behaves" suggests a semantic perspective, and "looks" suggests a syntactic perspective.) The obvious answer is "behave," but quantifying behavior is at best a fuzzy notion, and we do not have many metrics to do this. An example of a behavioral metric is the probability that the software fails. Once again, we see a possible conflict between the semantic perspective and the syntactic perspective on software. And once again it will turn out that taking the syntactic perspective is easier than the semantic.

It is intuitive that we should prefer the semantic perspective, meaning inject faults that behave like real faults regardless of how they look, but it is unclear as to how we determine whether a fault behaves in this manner. What does a real programmer fault behave like? And for that matter, what does a real programmer fault look like? It is far easier, from a practical standpoint, to inject faults based on some loose notion of how they look. For instance, substitute an operand or operator, regardless of whether that change reflects in any way the type of fault a real programmer would make at that point.

There's not enough historical information that is publicly available to know what "common" programmer faults are. There are small repositories of publicly available code that contain documented faults, but these sets of faults are frequently language-dependent problems, and often for languages that are used less today than in past years, such as the FORTRAN faults noted in the "Common Blunders" chapter in *The Elements of Programming Style* (Kernighan and Plaugher, 1974). This failure to publicize software problems within commercial organizations is mainly because companies that write commercial code do not want either their customers or competitors to know the types of problems they have; why hang out your dirty laundry for everyone to see? University studies that employ student programs that result from 2–3 years of education (but no real experience) do not represent the types of systems that are built commercially. Hence any conclusions from such studies are often dismissed as too preliminary or too clinical.

Given the obvious difference between the syntactic and semantic perspective on faults, it will be useful for us to differentiate fault classes in the same manner. A *class of faults* is simply a group of faults that have a similar property. Examples of classes of faults that are defined syntactically would include (1) missing code faults, (2) incorrect operator, (3) incorrect operand, and (4) substituting a constant for a variable. A semantically defined class of faults would include off-by-one faults, off-by-two faults, off-by-three faults, and so on. Notice the relationship here between the syntactic and semantic class types: There could be a syntactic fault from the missing code fault class and incorrect operator class that both cause a fault in the semantic class, off-by-one. But there might not be any fault from the incorrect operand class that could cause an off-by-one problem at some statement. Hence semantic fault classes can be related to the syntactic fault classes, but only on a case-by-case basis (i.e., with respect to the code and D and I). This presents problems in generalizing that certain syntactic fault classes are equivalent to other syntactic fault classes. This is only true if for all programs the semantic effect of these classes is equivalent—for example, $1 + \mathbf{x}$ is semantically equivalent to $1 + \mathbf{x}$.

There are basically two types of faults that we can simulate: single and distributed. A *single* fault only exists in a single location, whereas a distributed fault exists in more than one location. For a fault to be distributed (versus being many individual single faults), the fault must require that all of the locations throughout which the fault is distributed are executed for some test case in order for that fault to cause a failure. The combinatorics of simulating distributed faults becomes intractable immediately, and to our knowledge there are no tools that perform distributed fault simulation.

In a listing of computer failures, The Association of Computing Machinery's Special Interest Group on Software (SIGSOFT) detailed over 500 computer failures (Neumann, 1989). A close examination of this listing reveals that many of the failures were caused by simple mistakes, not necessarily complicated ones. If common faults can cause consequences as serious as those of complex faults, then methods for researching and avoiding common errors can be very beneficial to software quality. This suggests that simulating single faults and studying their impact can reveal useful information, even if it is very difficult in practice to handle distributed fault simulation.

SOFTWARE MUTATION

Mutation analysis (DeMillo et al., 1978; DeMillo et al., 1988; Hamlet, 1977a; Hamlet, 1977b) is a fault-based methodology that is similar to fault seeding, except that mutations to program statements are made in order to determine properties about test cases. Mutation testing is a fault-simulation technique. In this technique, multiple copies of a program are made, and each copy is altered; this altered copy is called a *mutant*. A mutant is a simulated fault, and in many cases the mutant is also a fault. Mutants are executed with test data to determine whether the test data are capable of detecting the change between the original program and the mutated program. (We later talk about the three types of mutation testing, and how each of these decides whether the change is detected.) A mutant that is detected by a test case is termed "killed," and the goal of mutation analysis is to find a set of test cases that are able to kill groups of mutant programs.

Mutants are produced by applying *mutant operators*. An operator is essentially a grammatical rule that changes a single expression to another expression. The new expression is hopefully syntactically legal according to the language. (A mutant that is not syntactically legal is sometimes referred to as "stillborn.") A finite set of mutant operators are applied to a given type of expression in the code. For example, an expression might be deleted or a referenced variable name in an expression might be replaced by a variable name of another variable of the same type. If one or more mutant operators are applied to all expressions in a program, the result is a large set of mutants, all of which must be killed by the test cases or shown to be equivalent to the original expression (and hence not a mutant in the first place).

When you mutate code, there needs to be a way of measuring the degree to which the code has been modified. For example, if the original expression is $x + 1$ and the mutant for that expression is $x + 2$, that is a lesser change to the original code than a mutant such as ($c * 22$), where both the operand and the operator are changed. In mutation analysis, there is a ranking scheme, where a *first-order* mutant is a single change to an expression, a *second-order* mutant is a mutation to a first-order mutant, and so on. As you can see, the combinatorics of all possible mutants becomes intractable as the orders get higher, and thus in practice only low-order (i.e., first- and second-order) mutants are used.

For examples of the 22 different mutant operators used by MOTHRA (SERC, 1987), the first full mutation testing tool for Fortran-77, see Table 2-1. These mutant operators were derived from studies of programmer errors and correspond to mistakes that programmers typically make, and enforcing common structural testing criteria (e.g., executing each statement). This set of mutant operators represents over 10 years of refinement through several earlier mutation systems. The operators in this set not only require that the test cases meet statement and branch coverage criteria, extremal values criteria, and domain perturbation, but they also directly model many classes of faults. Each of the 22 mutation operators is represented by the three-letter acronym given on the left. For example, the "array reference for array reference replacement" (AAR) mutation operator causes each array reference in a program to be replaced by each other distinct array reference in the program. For additional information on this list see King and Offutt (1991).

Given that error-based techniques are limited according to the class of errors that they consider, several assumptions are made by mutation testing advocates. The first is called the *competent programmer hypothesis*, which says that most actual faults are of a class that can be corrected by simple syntactic transformations. The *coupling effect* assumption states that test data that can detect simple faults (low-order

TABLE 2-1. MOTHRA Mutant Operators

Type	Description
AAR	Array reference for array reference replacement
ABS	Absolute value insertion
ACR	Array reference for constant replacement
AOR	Arithmetic operator replacement
ASR	Array reference for scalar variable replacement
CAR	Constant for array reference replacement
CNR	Comparable array name replacement
CRP	Constant replacement
CSR	Constant for scalar variable replacement
DER	Do statement end replacement
DSA	**DATA** statement alterations
GLR	**GOTO** label replacement
LCR	Logical connector replacement
ROR	Relational operator replacement
RSR	**RETURN** statement replacement
SAN	Statement analysis (replacement by TRAP)
SAR	Scalar variable for array reference replacement
SCR	Scalar for constant replacement
SDL	Statement deletion
SRC	Source constant replacement
SVR	Scalar variable replacement
UOI	Unary operator insertion

mutants) will likely detect complex faults (high-order mutants); this assumption was reported to be true 99.9% of the time by (Offutt, 1989) for *compound faults*—that is, faults created by repeated application of simple fault transformations.

Mutation analysis is not without controversy, as you might expect given the coupling effect assumption and the competent programmer hypothesis. Also, there are many issues yet to be resolved. Another problem surrounding mutation analysis is the problem of "semantic equivalence." A mutant is *semantically equivalent* to the original program when there is not a test case in I that could ever distinguish the mutant from the original program. When a mutant is proven to be semantically equivalent, it is discarded from the mutant set, however, proving semantic equivalence is typically done manually, which limits the applicability of mutation testing to large systems. For example, **x := x mod 2** is semantically equivalent to **x := x mod 4** for incoming values of **x** that are a power of 2. Note in the definition of semantic equivalence that *one* test case is all that is needed to decide whether equivalence has occurred. Thus equivalence is a dynamic phenomenon, rather than static.

One difficulty associated with whether mutants will be killed is the problem of reaching the location; if a mutant is not executed, it cannot be killed. To show whether a mutant can be reached, *static reachability constraints* (on the input variables) can be derived for the location in order to try to determine whether any member of I could satisfy those constraints. For example, suppose that we have the code

```
read (a,b,c);
if (a > b) and (b = c) then
    x := a * b * c;   {make mutants: m1, m2, m3, . . .}
```

The static reachability constraint shows that I must contain a value such that **a** is greater than **b** and **b** equals **c**. If I does not contain such a value, then all mutants made at this location should be considered equivalent, because the statement **x := a * b * c** is dead code (code that cannot be reached during execution).

Thus, determining dynamic semantic equivalence is a difficult issue. Consider four possibilities for a mutant and whether it is equivalent: (1) not syntactically equivalent nor dynamically equivalent; (2) syntactically equivalent and dynamically equivalent; (3) not dynamically equivalent but statically equivalent; and (4) dynamically equivalent but not statically equivalent. The first case represents an acceptable mutant, while the second case represents no mutant at all. It is the third and fourth cases that are more interesting. The third situation is not possible, since statically equivalence implies dynamic equivalence. The fourth situation is the problem, because we are unable to statically show equivalence, but we are also probably unable to show dynamic equivalence, particularly if it is true that there is only one member of I that will kill the mutant. An example of dynamic equivalence but not static equivalence would be the mutant **a ≥ 5** for **a > 5**. Here, if all values for **a** according to I cause **a** to be greater than 5, then there is no dynamic nor static equivalence. But showing this will likely require manual effort.

In general, dynamic semantic equivalence is too difficult to resolve, so syntactic analysis is the manner by which we attempt to resolve this issue for a particular mutant. Besides manually tracing through the code, an alternative technique is to find the static constraints that must be true in order for the mutant to be killed; for instance, if we make the mutant **x + y** for **x + 1**, then we know that the condition that must occur for a data state change to occur is y ≠ 1. We can also find the static constraints that will cause the mutant to be executed, and we can statically derive the constraints that must occur for propagation to occur. Note that some of these constraints may only be *partially* derivable.

It has been reported that, on average, the number of mutants made of a program is v^2 for the MOTHRA tool, where v is the number of occurrences of variables in the program (Weiss and Fleyshgakker 1993). For a program with 100 variable occurrences, there would be on the order of 10,000 mutants, which is a large number of mutants. For a larger module, with say 1000 variable occurrences, there would be approximately 1,000,000 mutants created, which clearly limits the practicality of this technique. *Selective mutation* is the process of decreasing the number of mutant operators applied when redundancy can be shown to occur in a mutant set. Experiments have shown that particular mutant operators are disproportionately applied when compared to other operators (Offutt et al., 1994). In selective mutation, the operators that are "overused" are applied less often or possibly not at all, producing fewer total mutants. This optimization greatly reduces the number of mutants produced while still maintaining the fault revealing ability of the test suites. Research into creating a minimal set of mutant operators is ongoing by Offutt and, if successful, may substantially improve the effectiveness of this technique (Offutt et al., 1994). However, recall our prior discussion of the syntactic versus semantic perspective on fault classes. It may be true that two distinct syntactic fault classes have the same semantic impact and thus one can be eliminated for consideration for a *specific* program. But to show that for all programs this is true is not possible. The benefit of selective mutation is that it does improve the practicality of mutation testing. However, it also has a negative impact on the theoretical foundation of mutation testing: It assumes that certain classes of mutants will automatically be caught if other mutant classes are caught, and hence it avoids generating these classes. Although this may be partially true, it will not always hold. The real question then is, "What is lost by using selective mutation versus not using selective mutation?" If little is lost, then selective mutation may make mutation testing viable and practical.

A large problem for mutation testing proponents has been that there is only one commercial tool for performing mutation testing, which is part of the *PiSCES Software Analysis Toolkit* ™ 1.2. (We will talk more later about this toolkit.) This mutation testing tool operates on C and F-77 source code, and it is expected to handle Ada and C++ by the time this book is published. There are also two public domain tools available, MOTHRA for FORTRAN-77 (SERC, 1987) and GCT for C; however, neither tool is supported. To make mutation testing into a commonly used unit testing scheme, many of the practicality issues of building a fault-based tool must be resolved. For instance, what if a mutant creates a run-time error or infinite loop? How can mutation analysis be applied to real-time code with serious timing constraints, and so on? These are issues and classes of systems that fault-based methodologies must find solutions for before these methodologies become mainstream.

We mentioned earlier that there are different heuristics for deciding if a mutant has been killed. There are three types of mutation testing, two of which will be of interest to us when we try to approximate the likelihood of the second and third conditions of the fault/failure model occurring (for predicting fault sizes). *Strong mutation testing* (DeMillo et al., 1978) determines whether a mutant has been killed by comparing the output of the original program and the mutant program. *Weak mutation testing* (Howden, 1982) compares the data state that occurs immediately after the original statement is executed and the mutated statement. *Firm mutation testing* (Woodward and Halewood, 1988) does not compare program outputs, but internal data states after some point later on during execution. Firm mutation testing is essentially a compromise between weak mutation testing and strong mutation testing; instead of checking at the output state or the state that immediately succeeds the mutant, a data state somewhere in between these extremes is chosen. The benefit of weak mutation is twofold: (1) Less code is executed, and (2) it is easy to check the exact portion of the data state that might have been affected. The benefit of firm mutation testing is again that less code is executed, but the entire data state will need to be checked. The benefit of strong mutation testing is that the output space can be easily compared using an operating system file compare command, but the cost of executing all of the program for every mutant is expensive. Also, from a theoretical standpoint, a strong mutation adequate set of test cases should be better at revealing faults than a weak mutation adequate test suite.

We stated earlier that in certain cases, we can show that a fault-based technique subsumes a coverage-based technique. As an example, consider weak mutation testing and branch coverage. Weak mutation testing can be coerced into finding sets of test cases that are branch coverage adequate. What is needed is to create two mutants for each decision point in the code: **if (decision = TRUE) then mutant1 := 'killed';** **if (decision = FALSE) then mutant2 := 'killed'.** When each of these mutants have been "killed," we know that both branches have been traversed. By instrumenting the code with these mutants and other mutants for nondecision statements, when our test set has killed all mutants, we have at least covered all branches and we may have partially satisfied a higher-order coverage such as condition coverage. This demonstrates that fault simulation of a broader class of faults can provide coverage adequate test sets. We leave it to the reader to find the mutant operators that will satisfy higher-order coverages in the exercises.

The manner by which a test suite is evaluated (scored) via mutation testing is as follows: For a specific test suite and a specific set of mutants, there will be three different types of mutants in the code (*killed* (or dead), *live*, *equivalent*). The sum of the number of live, killed, and equivalent mutants will be the total number of mutants created. The score associated with a test suite T and mutants M is simply

$$\frac{\text{\# killed}}{\text{\# total} - \text{\# equivalent}} \times 100\%$$

This equation allows us to determine the likelihood that a particular mutation adequate test suite will catch real faults based on how well the suite killed mutants. Note that this scheme does not penalize a test suite if it is of a larger size than a different test suite. For instance, suppose that test suite A with 100 test cases had a score of 50%, and test suite B with 25 test cases had a score of 49%. Although A has a better mutation score, it is also four times as large as B, and for the small increase in mutation score there is a large increase in testing costs.

ISOLATING UNIQUE PARTS OF A PROGRAM

Because there are three conditions that must occur before a fault can cause a ball to be colored black, before you begin simulating faults, you should ask: *How likely is a simulated fault to cause the three conditions to be true?* The answer can be found by simulating a fault in the code and determining how likely these three conditions are to occur for the simulated fault. But before we can do so, our first task is to determine what in a program we consider to be a syntactic unit that could contain a programmer fault. Any part of the code can be faulty, but there are time and space limitations to the classes of faults that we will be able to simulate. Then we will determine how likely it is that the syntactic unit would have each of the three conditions of the fault/failure model occur in it. To do this, we need to determine the following:

1. How likely it is that the syntactic unit is executed according to D (*execution probability*).
2. How likely it is that if the unit has its syntax altered, the data state of the program immediately succeeding the unit will be altered when executed according to D (*infection probability*).
3. How likely it is that if the data state that results from the unit is corrupted, the output of the program will be altered (*propagation probability*).

Answers to these three questions will allow us to predict fault sizes. If these "likelihoods" are large, we will predict large fault sizes. If they are small, we will predict smaller fault sizes. Note that there is no notion of a "good" predicted fault size versus a "bad" predicted fault size. Good and bad can only be assessed relative to the amount of testing resources available; after all, if you have enough testing resources to exhaustively test, then no matter what the predicted fault sizes are, they are good.

   Of particular interest for testability predictions are those faults that will compile into the code; thus, we are not interested in simulating syntax errors because a compiler will usually catch those. Why? Because a fault that will not even compile is not a fault that is going to escape detection and hide in the urn. Furthermore, simulating faults that lead to run-time failures may occur, however, if some fault continually causes a run-time failure, it should no longer be used and should be deleted. Static detection of such faults is prudent when possible. We are more interested in logic errors than in data structure errors (structures that have been improperly defined), and thus we will not simulate improperly defined structures. The true purpose in fault simulation is to simulate those classes of faults that a programmer is likely to make. Our purpose is even more specific: to see how small the smallest-sized fault is that we can inject into P. It is meaningless to simulate such a fault as a programmer writing a compiler when they should have written an operating system. Clearly such a fault is "big," probably equal to the size of C, and that is not the type of fault whose size we are interested in predicting. We are interested in typical programmer faults, which obviously includes large and small faults, but we must pay special attention to simulating smaller-sized faults if possible, because recall we want the smallest-sized chain. A real bonus will occur if we attempt to simulate small-sized faults, but discover that for our program, those faults turn out to have a larger size than we originally thought they would. This suggests a higher testability than we might have expected.

The syntactic unit of code that a programmer fault can reside in is called a "location." A *location* is any statement that directly affects either the contents of a programmer defined variable (either static or dynamically allocated) or program counter. Examples of locations that affect programmer defined variables are assignment statements or read statements; conditional expressions, **returns**, **goto**s, and exceptions are examples of locations that affect the program counter. A program *data space* is the collection of all data states that can occur between two sequential locations according to I and D. As you will see later, it is in the data space that faults actually develop the ability to mask themselves for long periods of time (long sequences of executions).

A variable is termed *live* at a location if the potential exists for that variable to make an impact on the output of the program. A variable is termed *dead* at a location if it is not live. The value of the notions of live and dead will become more obvious later, but for now a dead variable has no ability to affect the output of the program, and that means more ability to hide any incorrect value that it contains. Here we are assuming that the dead variable was previously live; if a variable is always dead, then it represents dead code, and any fault in dead code is a meaningless notion and therefore not a concern. Note also that there is a difference between "statically live" and "dynamically live." Any variable that is statically live is also dynamically live, but the reverse is not true. In applying these definitions, it makes sense to determine static liveness, not dynamic liveness, since we would have to exhaustively sample I to actually prove dynamic deadness if the variable is statically live.

Note that once we have an equivalence class of all locations in a program, then we can begin the task of simulating faults for each individual location. There will need to be specific rules for how each different type of location is handled. We will also need rules for the different operators and operands within a particular type of location. For example, we would perform a different type of mutation for the expression $x + 1$ than we would for the expression $(x * 100) + (x = 100)$.

VARIABLE CORRUPTION

An *execution trace* is the sequence of locations that are encountered during a program execution; there can be a unique execution trace for each input in I. Given an execution trace and input value, we should be able to determine the sequence of data states that are created after each location of the trace; we call this sequence of data states a *state chain*. If an execution does not terminate, the state chain is of infinite length.

A live variable is termed *infected* if the program has encountered a fault during an execution trace and that variable has a value at that point in the program that it should not have. It is difficult to determine whether infection has occurred without having some notion of a "mini-specification" for each statement in a program, because simply reversing the order in which statements are executed when the execution ordering is not important can make it appear as though some variables have an incorrect value. When a variable is infected, we say that we have a *data state error*. If a variable is not infected, we refer to it as being *clean*, and the data state is also referred to as being clean.

HIDING FAULTS

We consider a fault to be "hiding" in a program if we have tested the program and observed no failure caused by that fault. The more testing that has been done that has not resulted in a failure, the better the fault is at hiding. The reason that a fault can hide at a location has less to do with the location where it resides than with the locations that precede and succeed the incorrect location. Also, the data states that succeed it (and are directly related to D) play a large role in a location's ability to hide a fault.

Recall our example from Chapter 1, where the correct statement **x := x div 30000** was the reason that our off-by-two fault (in an incorrect statement that preceded the division expression) virtually never caused failure. It was a correct statement that was actually causing an incorrect statement to hide a fault. Although this may seem troubling, it is unavoidable. Incorrect statements can also mask other incorrect statements, so it is not only correct statements that can allow faults to hide.

A location that is considered as having a greater likelihood of hiding faults receives this distinction for one of three reasons:

1. This location will be unlikely to
   (a) be executed,
   (b) cause an infection, or
   (c) have its data state error propagate to the output if the location is incorrect.
2. This location will not cause an additional data state error (i.e., will not infect a live variable that is currently clean) when given the opportunity.
3. This location will not propagate a data state error across it; that is, this location will likely make infected variables into clean variables.

If any of the three reasons are true, then we label this location as having a greater ability to hide faults during testing. As you will see, the second and third of these conditions is harder to quantify, and most of our effort will be focused on predicting the first condition.

The tester's utopia state represented the scenario with no faults hiding during testing and our ability to know this after one test case, and we considered this to be impossible. As you will discover in Chapter 4, different function classes lend themselves to being closer or farther away from the utopia. For example, **onto** (one-to-one) functions, those for which there is a unique output for each unique input, generally have the greatest testability, while Boolean functions, those for which each unique input has only two possible outputs, tend to have the least. Many-to-one functions, those that produce a fixed output value regardless of input, *are* represented by the tester's utopia. For example, consider the function: $g(x) = 1$ for all x. The following program can be shown to be correct from a single test case:

```
Program dummy;
     x:integer;
     read(x);
     write('1');
end dummy.
```

This is because no matter what is read into the program, the program only produces a '1' as output. Of course, many-to-one functions are hard-wired and are either always correct or always incorrect, and so we consider the tester's utopia to be unrealistic for all other classes of functions. This means that initialization statements at the beginning of a program, if they produce correct results once, are always correct.

Different faults have enormously different impacts on the failure probability of a program, and thus they have different fault hiding abilities. Using data from IBM, Currit et al., (1986) showed that one-third of the faults have a mean time-to-failure (MTTF) of over 5000 years, while 2% of the faults in this study cause 1000 times more failures than 60% of the faults that had the least impact. This suggests that reliability improvement techniques will get the faults associated with long black chains, but the short-chained faults will likely slip past these techniques for longer periods of time. Quality improvement techniques are needed that are aimed specifically at the shorter-chained faults, even though shorter-chained faults have little impact on the system's reliability. This is particularly important if the short-chained fault leads to failures that are classified as catastrophic, a subject that we will discuss later.

FAILURES

Hardware and software failures can be classified as either *systematic* or *random*. An example of what causes a random failure would be fatigue or aging of a physical system. An example of what causes a systematic failure would be a fault in the logic or system design. Random failures can be measured by classical hardware reliability theory—that is, MTTF models. For example, to get the average life expectancy of a light bulb, take a sample, turn them on at time t_0, record when each bulb burns out, and calculate a mean time to burnout (failure). Because systematic failures are not random, they will occur every time the inputs that lead to them are fed into the system. Because of this determinism, systematic failures can be modeled as stochastic processes.

Our focus in software testability is on failures that are systematic; we are concerned with programmer faults and how legal inputs to the system (I) interact. The reason we limit the scope is that we do not yet know how to predict testability at the embedded system level. (This requires a theory to handle the software, hardware, and hardware–software interface.) In Chapter 4 we will discuss hardware design-for-testability heuristics, and in Chapter 3 we present a model for studying the impact of random hardware failures on the performance of the software. Previous work in this area is vague, mainly because the size of the space that contains "faulty" inputs can be of greater size than I, and we already have enough trouble sampling from I.

APPROXIMATING THE FAULT/FAILURE MODEL AT A LOCATION

Recall Musa's basic execution time model and his fault exposure ratio K, which represented the average number of failures exposed per fault given certain assumptions about the execution frequencies of the program. This model has admitted weaknesses, the most important of which is that it treats all faults and the likelihood of a fault being revealed with an average-case analysis. Some faults are harder to catch than others, and the very-difficult-to-catch faults are the ones we are concerned with. Suppose that a program had 100 faults, 99 of which caused frequent failure. Musa's model will let these 99 "easy-to-catch faults" suggest that there were 100 easy-to-catch faults, when in fact there is one difficult-to-detect bug. It is the troublesome fault that our model is concerned with, and we will now present a different scheme for predicting the likelihood of such existing at a specific location. This scheme is directly tied to the reasons that a fault can hide in a location, and this scheme treats each location uniquely, instead of finding some average statistic over all faults.

The reason that a chain of black balls can either be long or short is directly related to how many balls cause all three conditions of the fault/failure model to occur for that fault. If the fault has few balls that are able to cause all three conditions to occur, that chain will be short; if the fault has many balls that trigger all three conditions, the chain will be longer. As we have stated, if given a choice as testers, we would prefer long chains to short chains; that is, we would prefer programs that failed frequently when there were faults to programs that failed infrequently when faults existed.

Without knowledge of where the faults are, we are left with no way to estimate fault chain lengths. However, the use of fault simulation will allow us to estimate "simulated fault chain" lengths. And estimates of simulated fault chain lengths can be used to predict actual fault chain lengths.

Estimation of the length of chains for simulated faults is accomplished by first answering three questions that are related to the three conditions of the fault/failure model. The first question is trivial and does not require fault simulation: **What is the probability that this location is executed according to D?** The answer to this question has nothing to do with whether there is a fault in the location. Hence, we do not need to simulate faults. The second question is: **What is the probability that if the location is incorrect, the data state will become infected?** This question requires fault simulation. We will apply techniques that are similar to the techniques of weak mutation testing; however, instead of creating a set of test cases, we will assess how likely it is that a fault in a location will affect the data state that immediately succeeds the location. The third question, which also requires fault simulation, is: **What is the probability that if the location is incorrect and causes an infected data state, then the program will produce different output than would have been produced?** To answer this question, we will apply an analysis similar to strong mutation testing, however we will not use mutants, instead simulating the data state effect that a mutant would make to determine the likelihood of propagation occurring.

To estimate the first condition of the fault/failure model for some location l, all that we need to do is to execute the code some number of times N according to D. The proportion of times that l is executed is the answer to the first question. This process is termed "execution analysis," and an algorithm for performing execution analysis follows:

Execution Analysis Algorithm:

1. Set **counter** $\leftarrow 0$.
2. Increment **counter** each time location l is executed; make sure that **counter** is incremented at most once per input, hence if l is repeatedly executed for the same input, **counter** is only incremented once.
3. Execute the code with N test cases according to D.
4. The execution estimate for location l is $\dfrac{\textbf{counter}}{N}$.
5. Perform steps 1–4 for all locations in code.

Although this process is very simple, you should realize that locations that are rarely executed immediately suggest to you that the possible length of their black ball chains is short, since there are few balls associated with those locations. This is very intuitive: *If a fault is in a location that is rarely executed, then the likelihood that testing will discover that fault is reduced.* This observation is related to the argument for why *boundary-value testing* should be used. Boundary-value testing uses test cases that are near domain boundaries. For example, suppose that you have a condition **if (a > = 0) then**. In boundary-value testing, you would try the case where **a = 0**, which might be a rare condition according to D, but boundary-value testing argues that rare conditions should be exercised using special test cases. Rare input conditions often trigger less frequently executed portions of the code to be exercised. Approximating the first condition of the fault/failure model is a simplistic procedure that is crucial for predicted minimum fault sizes.

As an example of the execution analysis algorithm, consider the following code segment, and assume that the distribution of values for **x** is uniform in [0,99]:

```
read(x)
if odd(x) then
   x := x * 2 - 1   {A}
else
   begin
   if x = 2 then
        x := 0    {B}
   else
        x := x * 2 + 1;   {C}
```

We now find the execution estimates for locations A, B, and C. For location A, we reach it approximately 50% of the time, so its execution estimate is 0.5. For location B, we know that **x** will equal 2 only 1% of the time, so its execution estimate is 0.01. And for location C, we will reach it 49% of the time (since 1% of the time we reach location B and 50% of the time we reach A), so its execution estimate will be 0.49.

Approximating the second condition of the fault/failure model is slightly more complicated than approximating the first. To do so, we play a "what-if" game: We apply fault simulation techniques similar to those applied in mutation testing. A set of mutants is created at the location for which we are determining the following: *If the location has a fault and is executed, will the location cause the data state to become corrupted?* Once we have created a set of mutants, we execute the original code and one of the mutants with one input selected according to *D*. As is done in weak mutation testing, if we notice that the resulting data state is different for the mutant than it is for the original location, we will increment a counter for that mutant at that location. The algorithm for performing this analysis follows:

Infection Analysis Algorithm

1. Set **counter** ← 0.
2. Create a mutant *M* of location *l*.
3. Execute the location *l* and mutant *M* on a randomly selected data state that occurs before *l* according to *D*.
4. Compare resulting data states; if different, increment **counter.**
5. Repeat steps 3 and 4 *N* times.
6. The infection estimate for mutant *M* at location *l* is $\dfrac{\text{counter}}{N.}$
7. Perform steps 1 and 6 for different mutants.
8. Perform step 7 for different locations.

Note, however, that before we can make the comparison between the data state produced by the mutant and the data state produced by the original code, we must know that the selected input executes the original location. If the location is not executed during execution analysis on the location, then it is quite unlikely that infection analysis can be performed at the location, unless we used a very small *N* during execution analysis and there is actually a reasonably large likelihood that *l* will be executed. If it is unlikely that *l* will be executed even with large *N* according to *D*, then essentially two choices are available:

1. Continue to increase N until l is executed on some n test cases ($n << N$), or
2. Force the program to execute l by injecting a **goto** l statement after the statement that is currently sending control to some statement other than l. This will force l to be executed, but the program will be in some artificial program state that is not proper for the specific program input value. This may greatly bias the infection results to the point that they are considered to be too contrived to be believable. Because the first alternative could take an extremely long time, and the second alternative could be argued as creating nonsense results, both alternatives are unacceptable. The unfortunate reality is that locations that are rarely executed are not candidates for infection analysis, and the testability of such locations will be solely based on the small execution estimates.

If a reasonably large N causes the location to be executed often, then this process is repeated for this location and mutant for N test cases selected according to D. After the N trials are done, we divide the value of the counter by N to estimate the likelihood that we would discover that mutant during testing. This likelihood is termed an *infection estimate*. This is done for all the mutants in the set for this location and for all locations in our code.

Step 3 of the algorithm presents us with an interesting challenge, which we will also see when we present the upcoming propagation analysis algorithm. The algorithms randomly select a data state (that would normally be seen when the testing distribution is used) that occurs before l in this algorithm or after l in the propagation analysis algorithm. The notion of randomly selecting a data state is according to the distribution of data states that normally occur at these data spaces, and that is with respect to D. In practice, there is no data space entity that is distributed in this manner from which these algorithms can sample. Thus it is necessary to sample according to D; when l is reached, consider that data state as the randomly selected data state, and proceed with the algorithm from that point on. Note that if l is executed more than once for a single input, then any data states may be used, because infection could occur on any iteration of l.

As an example of the infection analysis algorithm, consider the original expression $(\mathbf{a} + \mathbf{b}) * (\mathbf{a} + \mathbf{1})$ and the five mutants:

1. $(\mathbf{a} - \mathbf{b}) * (\mathbf{a} + \mathbf{1})$
2. $(\mathbf{a} - \mathbf{1}) * (\mathbf{a} + \mathbf{1})$
3. $(\mathbf{b} + \mathbf{b}) * (\mathbf{a} + \mathbf{1})$
4. $(\mathbf{a} + \mathbf{b}) + (\mathbf{a} + \mathbf{1})$
5. $(\mathbf{a} + \mathbf{b}) * (\mathbf{a} - \mathbf{1})$

And consider the five following $(\mathbf{a}, \mathbf{b})$ pairs: $(\mathbf{0}, \mathbf{0})$, $(\mathbf{0}, \mathbf{1})$, $(\mathbf{1}, \mathbf{0})$, $(\mathbf{1}, \mathbf{1})$, $(\mathbf{1}, \mathbf{2})$. We get crude infection estimates (since five is a small sample size) of 0.6, 1.0, 0.6, 0.8, 0.8, respectively, for the five mutants.

Approximation of the third condition of the fault/failure model is more complicated (and computational) than execution analysis or infection analysis. This process termed *propagation analysis* applies a fault simulation technique to the data state of the executing program, without using syntactic mutants. Formally, *propagation* occurs whenever the effect of an infection is evident at a time later than when the infection first occurred. Propagation can be observed to have occurred both in the output or in a data state. Propagation analysis restricts its observations to the output space. In propagation analysis, the algorithm mutates the internal data state (which is a dynamically created entity) and estimates the impact of this on the output of the program. By doing so, it answers the following question: *Will a fault that is executed and infects the data state actually cause the program to fail?* Because we cannot know what type of fault might be in the location, there will need to be a mechanism for *perturbing* the internal data states that are representative of syntactic faults that could reside in the location. We again have the same problem as occurred in infection analysis: If the location is not executed during execution analysis, then the location is not considered as a candidate for propagation analysis. The algorithm for performing this analysis follows:

Propagation Analysis Algorithm

1. Set **counter** $\leftarrow 0$.
2. Randomly select a data state that occurs after l according to D.
3. Perturb the data state for some variable a and continue execution; also perform a different execution using that data state without perturbing it.
4. Compare resulting outputs; if different, increment **counter**.
5. Repeat steps 2–4 N times.
6. The propagation estimate for variable a at location l is $\dfrac{\textbf{counter}}{N.}$
7. Perform steps 1–6 for different variables
8. Perform step 7 for different locations in code.

The software mechanism that we use to perturb data states is termed a *perturbation function*. This function inputs the current value that the variable has during an execution, assuming that it has already been defined, and modifies that value to a similar yet different value. Research into how to modify values is ongoing; however, preliminary results have indicated that, in general, the degree to which a value is modified is a small factor in whether propagation occurs. This suggests that once a value is altered, whether it is modified enormously or just slightly from the original value, propagation will either occur often or not occur at all, regardless of the severity of the modification. Why? Because as we have said, it is all of the other locations that will either let propagation occur or not. This is analogous to a dam on a river: Either it will let the water pass or it will hold it back. Other locations will either stop the third condition or allow it to occur.

Examples can be found, however, where a large change to a value has a lesser impact on propagation than a smaller impact. For example, suppose that the current value is 50 and that is modified to 4050. Then at the later statement, **x := x mod 49**, x still is assigned a value of 1; it is not at all affected by this large change to x. Had the change to x been 49 instead of 4050, there would have been propagation. Hence there is no direct link between the degree of the change and the likelihood that propagation occurs. Note that if a variable has no current value on which to base a perturbed value, a random value can be assigned. This simulates the class of faults known as *missing location faults*. This simulates the existence of code that is not there when we assign a value to a variable that may or may not be currently undefined.

Before perturbing a data state, there are two questions that must be answered: Which variable in the data state is going to have its value modified, and will we repeatedly modify the value of that variable in the data space if the location is executed more than once for a single input? In general, we perturb only on the variable that is being affected at l. If l affects control flow, then we would modify the program counter; if l affects a programmer-defined variable, then that variable would be modified, which is usually on the left-hand side of an assignment statement (depending on the language). To answer the second question, we should first answer this question: *Do faults that infect only infect during an execution or are they likely to repeatedly infect if the location is executed more than once on a single execution?* Experience here has been limited, but what has been shown is that if infection occurs once, then it occurs frequently, so because we want to simulate faults that behave like real faults, we will perturb on each additional execution at the same location.

Types of members of a data state that can be perturbed include: integers, reals, Booleans, characters, pointers, strings, and the program counter. The first five of these are variables that the programmer has direct access to; the programmer has a more indirect way to control the program counter if structured program design is employed, because direct **gotos** are strongly discouraged. Generally the program counter is modified by decision points in a program. To perturb a decision point like **(a > b)** and force the program counter to always have a different outcome requires directly changing the logic to **(a ≤ b)**, which always will force the program counter to be perturbed. Simulating a fault class such as this allows for the study of whether coincidental correctness occurs; coincidental correctness is detrimental to propagation.

In an earlier discussion on what constitutes a data state, we argued that because a data state is a nonphysical entity, the user has control over what is considered to be a part of the data state. Because perturbing occurs to a variable, it is only useful to perturb data state variables that have the potential to affect the output of the code— that is, live variables. If the system undergoing propagation analysis is a parallel/distributed system, then time (or the ordering in which computations are performed between tasks) is an option here, and during propagation analysis you can perturb time to simulate timing faults in the system. We mention this because of one fascinating discovery that was made in a recent research project that involved perturbing time: *A time perturbation that propagates indicates that the code is not correct.* This is very interesting, because throughout the previous discussions we have been careful to explain that testability analysis and testing are distinct. In this particular situation, we are saying that testability analysis has the potential to indicate incorrectness just as testing does. Why? Because any timing perturbation that propagates to the system's output indicates that a programmer has failed to account for the variability of processor speeds and loads among different processes; that is, the programmer failed to put in the synchronization mechanisms to account for timing variations.

Once you decide how you wish to perform the data state perturbations at some location l, you will need to use some number of input cases selected according to D, and the resulting probability estimate is termed a *propagation estimate*. This estimate represents the probability that if a fault existed in l that caused the value of the perturbed variable to be incorrect, then the output would also be incorrect. Several issues that must be addressed in the propagation analysis algorithm that were not mentioned in infection or execution analysis include infinite loops and run-time errors that can be induced by changes to data states. Any time you modify code or data states, you run the risk of putting the system into a state that it cannot handle or get out of, and hence the system may crash or hang. Mechanisms must be built into the propagation (and infection) algorithms to keep this from occurring. These and other practical issues associated with propagation analysis are addressed in greater detail by Voas (1992).

We have been talking about "propagation to the output space," O. As it will turn out later, the definition of exactly what constitutes O will become very important when we turn our attention to assessing software safety via testability analysis. As an example, suppose that we have a program that has three output variables: $\{a, b, c\}$. It might be the case that a particular perturbation in a data state propagates to only variable a, not b and not c. Now suppose that variable a has been classified as a critical output variable, but b and c have not. The fact that the perturbations have propagated to a are important to know; this tells us that in the data space where those fault simulations occurred, we have been able to affect a critical output variable. Hence the definition of the output space employed during propagation analysis will greatly impact the benefit and number of ways that this technique can be applied.

Infection analysis and propagation analysis are subject to the same limitations as other fault-based techniques. Note the difference in how strong mutation testing and propagation analysis handle the third condition of the fault/failure model. In strong mutation testing, the likelihood of the third condition being satisfied is partially dependent on the mutant and whether the mutant causes an infection. In propagation analysis, a data state perturbation forces the second condition to be simulated and then estimates the third condition. Note that any modified value produced by a perturbation function in a data state can be mapped to some syntactic mutant, but this technique purposely uses random data state modifications instead of fixed syntactic mutants to increase the fault classes considered. By using a random perturbation, we are able to *increase* the fault classes considered beyond those of other fault-based methodologies. So although we are still restricted in the number of classes that we can consider, a random perturbation partially decreases this restriction.

One might wonder if any relationship exists between adjacent locations that might help shrink the costs of the analyses. For example, if there are two sequential locations—**statement1** and **statement2**—and **statement1** has an execution estimate of 0.1, does **statement2** necessarily have the same execution estimate? Given a block of K adjacent locations with no intervening decision locations or exceptions, the execution estimate for one of the K locations is also the execution estimate for the other locations, assuming no run-time errors occur within the block. Also, for two adjacent locations of the form $a := f(x)$; $b := f(y)$, the propagation estimate based on perturbing a at either location is the same, because the assignment to b is not a function of the value of a. So estimates from execution analysis and propagation analysis for location 1 may be the same information that would be produced for another location 2 if analysis was desired at 2, and hence analysis need not be performed at 2 to get this information (assuming analysis was performed at 1). Static analysis should be applied to determine these relationships.

The algorithms presented here are straightforward; in fact they may appear somewhat trivial. However, implementing these algorithms into a stable commercial quality tool is not a straightforward process. There are many difficulties that can arise when you apply fault simulation including run-time errors and infinite loops arising from perturbations. Infection analysis mutants can cause divide-by-zero and run-time errors, or if too many mutants are created in the instrumented file to be compiled, that can cause insufficient memory problems. Problems can arise when trying to compile instrumentation, not because the code is incorrect, but because the instrumentation may be too complicated for the compiler. We say this not to discourage the reader from implementing these algorithms, but to be aware that as the complexity of the code under analysis increases, the complexity of the instrumentation increases at a much greater rate, and this can lead to enormous problems. Because of problems such as these, fault-based methodologies have been regarded as too difficult to implement by many software tool developers.

In each of these algorithms, the resulting probability estimate has an associated confidence interval, given the particular N used in the algorithm. The computational resources available when PIE is performed will determine the value of N. For example, for 95% confidence, the confidence interval is approximately $p \pm (2\sqrt{p(1-p)/N})$, where p is the sample mean. If the N values used are significant, then $(2\sqrt{p(1-p)/N})$ will likely be small. It should be noted that PIE can suffer from qualitative errors and that confidence intervals play a minor role in any confidence in the technique. After all, rough approximations are made from a limited class of simulated faults. Justification for the benefit of the PIE technique is not based on 95% or 99% confidence intervals, instead, experimentation has shown that these approximations often reflect the effect of actual faults.

SUMMARY

In this chapter we have seen how the PIE assessment model can be used to determine the testability of the locations in a program. In the model, testability is a function of three characteristics: the likelihood of location execution, the likelihood of a fault at that location causing infection of the data state, and the likelihood of a data state infection at that location propagating to the output state. Execution analysis is performed by seeing whether the location is reached when executed in accordance with an operational profile. Infection analysis is performed by perturbing the source code statement at that location. Propagation analysis is performed by perturbing the data state at that location. Because execution analysis, infection analysis, and propagation analysis do not require an oracle, the analyses can be automated.

EXERCISES

1. Given the statement $x + 1$, how many first-order mutants are possible with $\{a, c, b\}$ as possible variable replacements, $\{-, *\}$ as possible operator replacements, and $\{2, 3, 4\}$ as possible constant replacements? How many second-order mutants are possible?

2. If the fault classes that are simulated are not representative of the types of faults that programmers make, is it still possible that we will be able to produce a meaningful predicted shortest black ball chain?

3. Would it make sense to make a hybrid mutation testing technique as follows: We perform weak mutation testing at those regions of the code where propagation analysis has suggested very high probabilities of propagation, and we perform strong mutation testing in those regions that have low probabilities of propagation occurring. Discuss the tradeoffs in terms of the test sets collected, and also discuss the additional cost of performing propagation analysis before mutation testing is applied.

4. If we perturb a value, making the current value of '100' into '1000', what fault class have we simulated?

5. What are the differences between *testability* and *reliability?*

6. Suggest ways of including timing faults in the PIE model.

REFERENCES

P. A. Currit, M. Dyer, and H. D. Mills. "Certifying the Reliability of Software." *IEEE Transactions on Software Engineering* SE-12(1), 3–11, January 1986.

R. DeMillo, R. Lipton, and F. Sayward. "Hints on Test Data Selection: Help for the Practicing Programmer." *Computer* 11(4), 34–41, April 1978.

R. DeMillo et. al. "An Extended Overview of the MOTHRA Software Testing Environment," *Proc. of the 2nd Workshop on Software Testing, Verification, and Analysis.* Washington, D.C.: IEEE Computer Society Press, 1988, pp. 142–151.

R. G. Hamlet. "Testing Programs with the Aid of a Compiler." *IEEE Transactions on Software Engineering*, SE-3(4) 279–290, July 1977a.

R. G. Hamlet. "Testing Programs with Finite Sets of Data." *Computer Journal* 20, 3 August, 1977b, pp. 232-237.

W. E. Howden. "Weak Mutation Testing and Completeness of Test Sets." *IEEE Transactions on Software Engineering* SE-8 (4) 371–379, July 1982.

B. W. Kernighan and P. J. Plauger. *The Elements of Programming Style.* New York: McGraw–Hill, 1974.

K. N. King and A. J. Offutt. "A Fortran Language System for Mutation-based Software Testing." Software-Practice and Experience 21(7), 685–718, July 1991.

H. Mills. *Software Productivity*. Boston: Little, Brown, 1983.

P. G. Neumann, "Letter from Editor.*" ACM SIGSOFT. Software Engineering Notes* 14(1), 3, January 1989.

A. J. Offutt. "The Coupling Effect: Fact or Fiction." *Proceedings of the ACM SIGSOFT/IEEE 3rd Workshop on Testing, Analysis, and Verification. Software Engineering Notes*,14(8), 131–140, December 1989.

A. J. Offutt, A. Lee, G. Rothermel, R. Untch, and C. Zapf. "An Experimental Determination of Sufficient Mutation Operators." Technical Report ISSE-TR-94-100, Dept. of Information and Software Systems Engineering, George Mason University, 1994.

SERC. "The MOTHRA Software Testing Environment." Software Engineering Research Center Report SERC-TR-4-P, Purdue University, 1987.

J. M. Voas. "PIE: A Failure-Based Technique." *IEEE Transactions on Software Engineering*, SE-18(8), 717–727 August 1992.

S. N. Weiss and V. N. Fleyshgakker. "Improved Serial Algorithms for Mutation Analysis." In *Proceedings of the 1993 International Symposium on Software Testing and Analysis,* ACM, Cambridge, MA, June 28–30, 1993.

M. R. Woodward and K. Halewood. "From Weak to String, Dead or Alive? An Analysis of Mutation Testing Issues." In *Proceedings of the ACM SIGSOFT/IEEE 2nd Workshop on Testing, Analysis, and Verification*, Banff, Canada, July 1988.

CHAPTER 3

The PIE Assessment Model of Software Testability II

PROPAGATION AND FAULT SETS

We now introduce a model for statically trying to produce a "crude" approximation to the propagation analysis algorithm. Given that the propagation analysis algorithm is computational, a static model that would lessen the number of locations requiring dynamic analysis would be welcomed.

A *fault set* is the set of variables that are infected in a data state. For a specific input and specific location, if a fault has been encountered prior to the location, this set may or may not be empty. If no faults have been encountered, this set must be empty. If a fault was exercised but the set is empty, either the infection or propagation condition has failed to occur.

A hypothesis exists that says the following: *As the size of a fault set increases, so does the likelihood of propagation; and if the size of the fault set reaches some threshold, then propagation is guaranteed to occur.* There is an intuition for this hypothesis and the hypothesis is probably true, but there is one large flaw if you try to apply the hypothesis, and that is finding the threshold. For example, suppose that for some program P the largest fault set to exist on any execution is size 10, and there are 10,000 live variables in the data state where this fault set existed. For a different program P' with the same maximum fault size, there are 11 live variables in the data state where this fault set was discovered. In practice, you would expect P' to be more likely to have propagation occur, but maybe the 10 infected variables in P might be the only output variables, and the one noninfected variable in P' is its only output variable. Thus the notion of a generalized threshold for all programs (other than an all live variables threshold) cannot be found. An alternative is the notion of a proportional threshold, where in general if some proportion of the live variables are infected, then propagation is probably guaranteed. For example, if 99% of the variables are infected, we suspect that propagation almost always occurs.

A second problem in applying this hypothesis is finding the fault set; it requires dynamic fault simulation at some location to start the set and then build up the set to determine its size. If you are already performing dynamic analysis to find these sets, why not go ahead and run the propagation analysis algorithm and find out exactly what the propagation estimates are? You could statically create fault sets if you assume that x is infected after some computation of the form $\mathbf{x} := \mathbf{f}(\mathbf{a})$, where $\mathbf{a}$ was infected before this statement. But assuming that fault sets always increase in size whenever the opportunity exists to infect a clean variable is similar to assuming that every fix to a program increases the program's reliability, which is known to not be true.

Let's look at an example of the fault set theory, and how it might be modified with *reachability constraints* to produce usable static propagation analysis information. The code we will consider follows with enumerated location numbers:

```
{1} read(a)
{2} if a > 5 then
    begin
{3} b := 2 * a;
{4} if b > 12 then
        begin
{5}        c := 2 * b - a
{6}        if c > 100 then
               begin
{7}            read (d)
{8}            if d = a then
                   begin
{9}                e := 22
{10}                   while e >= 1 do
{11}                       d := d * c
{12}                       i := 25
                       [COMPUTATION BLOCK]
{13}                       e := e - 1
                   endwhile
                   endif
               endif
           endif
       endif
{14} write(d);
```

What we are interested in is the impact that a "faulty" value read in for variable **a** will have on the output, **d**. We will attempt to determine this impact without ever executing the code; that is, we will try to determine statically a propagation estimate for location 1 without executing the code. First, let's find the fault sets for each location. When building a fault set, we will differentiate between whether we know for certain that a variable will be in the fault set or whether we *suspect* that a variable will be in the set. If we only suspect that a variable will be in the set, we italicize the variable name.

For location 1, the fault set is simply {**a**}, because we assumed that a faulty value was read in for **a**. For location 2, there is a chance that the program counter, *pc*, will take the wrong branch because **a** is incorrect, but there is also a chance it will take the correct branch, so the fault set for location 2 is {**a**, *pc*}. For locations 3 and 4, the fault set is {**a**, **b**, *pc*} (**b** gets added because it is a one-to-one function of **a**), and for locations 5–10, the fault set is: {**a**, **b**, **c**, *pc*} (**c** gets added because it is a function of **a** and **b**, we will assume that location 9 is correct, and we assumed that **d** has a correct value coming in). For location 11, the fault set is {**a**, **b**, **c**, **d**, *pc*}. Now suppose that in the computation block there is no further assignment to **d**. The question then is: "Do these fault sets tell us anything about whether the fault in location 1 will affect location 14?" To answer this question, we must find the earliest fault set that contains **d**. In this case, that is location 11. If we do not reach location 11, then the fault in location 1 cannot affect location 14. Also, if there had been an intervening computation affecting **d** in the computation block, that might have removed **d** from the fault set or italicized it. But in this example, we assumed no other computation directly affecting **d** other than location 11 existed. So if we execute location 11, then we know that location 1 will very likely affect the output.

After statically building the fault sets, we next statically create the reachability constraints that must be true in order to execute location 11. A *reachability constraint* for a location is a logical expression that bounds the relationships between program variables, particularly input variables, that cause the location to be executed. In this example, to reach location 3, $[a > 5]$ is the reachability constraint that must be true; and to reach location 7, $[3a > 100]$ must be true. To reach location 11, $[d = a, 3a > 100, e >= 1]$ must be true; but because we are only interested in input variables, we reduce this to $[d = a, 3a > 100]$. So we know that if our input value satisfies $[d = a, 3a > 100]$, then we will have the fault set $\{a, b, c, d, pc\}$, which virtually guarantees that propagation will occur. To get a propagation estimate from this information, all we need to know is what proportion of I with respect to D satisfies $[d = a, 3a > 100]$. (To get this proportion, we of course will need D.) Once we have this proportion, we will have determined statically the impact that a fault in location 1 will have on the output. For example, if 20% of I satisfied the constraint for reaching location 11, then the propagation estimate for location 1 is 0.2. We are not suggesting that this model that combines fault sets and reachability constraints is practical, but rather that under certain conditions where the proper information is available, it is feasible to statically estimate the propagation condition.

Let's return to the propagation analysis algorithm and look at an example. Consider the following code segment and consider that the distribution for **x** is a uniform in **[0, 9]**. **int( )** is a function that truncates any decimal places in its argument and makes the parameter into an integer.

```
read(x)
a := (x * x) + 1  {A: perturb a} {B: perturb b}
b:= int(sqrt(a));      {C: perturb x} {D: perturb a}
write(b);
```

Note that we have identified four different propagation estimates that we wish to produce: two after the assignment to **a** and two before the **write(b)** is executed. Assume that the perturbation function being used always adds one to the current value. For **B**, **C**, and **D**, the propagation estimates are immediately recognizable as 0.0, because those variables are dead at those points during the computation. This could be determined statically. The perturbation on **a** in comment **A** is the only perturbation to a live variable in this example. Interestingly enough, the propagation estimate with this perturbation function is also 0.0, because adding one to our value before the square root operator is applied only changes the decimal places, which is truncated by the **int( )** function.

The three PIE algorithms (introduced in Chapter 2) are based on the *single fault assumption*, and the results therefore are based on a single simulated fault at a location. It is known that this assumption is flawed, and a program's failure behavior can be a result of multiple faults in a program acting together. So why not try combinations of faults, and do away with the single fault assumption? The reason is simple: The combinatorics of distributed faults becomes overwhelming instantly. For a program with only three locations, we could simulate a distributed fault in the following combinations of locations: (1), (2), (3), (1,2), (1,3), (2,3), and (1,2,3).

LOCATION FAULT HIDING ABILITY AND THE ALGORITHMS

Recall the three reasons that were previously mentioned that cause a location *l* to be defined as likely to hide a fault. The three sensitivity analysis algorithms *directly* address the first of these three reasons. However, the algorithms presented also *indirectly* address the three concerns.

The second reason dealt with the failure to increase the size of the fault set when the opportunity presented itself. This is the situation of **x** := **f(a)**, where **a** is incorrect, but this computation does not cause **x** to be incorrect. Whenever a fault does not increase the size of this set, then the likelihood of propagation occurring at some location executed prior to the location *l* is reduced. So even though *l* may be the cause for a lack of infection, a location other than *l* receives a lower propagation estimate which should account for this possibility (if the hypothesis on fault set sizes is true). We say that the propagation analysis algorithm will detect this situation in an "indirect" manner, because the algorithms do not know why propagation failed to occur, but simply that it did fail to occur.

The same situation occurs with the third reason; here we are considering a data state error affecting some variable prior to location *l* that becomes clean after location *l*, masking the fault at a prior location that caused the data state error. By doing so, *l* is again decreasing the likelihood of propagation occurring for the incorrect location as well as possibly for many other locations. Thus although *l* may be unlikely to hide its own faults, *l* may be likely to hide the faults of other locations.

Information is not stored about whether a location causes the second or third reasons to be true in the PIE algorithms. With small modifications to the algorithms, such information could be revealed. For instance, once a perturbation is injected during execution, all we need to do is compare whether an additional infection occurred at each location after the perturbation was injected. This easily determines which locations do not increase the fault set when presented the chance. Similarly for the third reason, we could determine after each location whether the fault set size decreased, and, if so, we know that the location that decreased the set size is able to help hide faults.

PREDICTING MINIMUM FAULT SIZES

We have been vague about the intricacies of infection analysis, execution analysis, and propagation analysis because the details are published in Voas (1992). We now go back to the balls and urn model to address the issue of predicting the smallest nonzero failure probability (smallest nonzero length chain of black balls) from the information provided by the infection, execution, and propagation analyses.

Recall that we dismissed two possible assessments for this prediction: (1) A chain of length zero is not allowed, because that suggests a fault that could never cause failure (which by definition is not a fault), and (2) *arbitrarily* deciding a chain of length one would be the smallest and then proceeding on that assumption. Now if the algorithms predict a chain of length one, that cannot be dismissed and must be allowed to stand. We argued that the second alternative, although possible, needed better justification than to merely take such a pessimistic approach. As you will see later, the pessimistic approach is useless to testers; it provides them with no useful information, but rather a "big scare."

An actual fault's size is the number of balls that are able to execute the fault, infect, and propagate the corrupted data state created by the fault to the output space. Another way to think of this is by quantifying the probability of failure on P induced by the fault at l according to D:

$$\text{pof}_P = \Pr\{\text{executing fault}\}$$
$$\times \Pr\{\text{infection} \mid \text{execution}\}$$
$$\times \Pr\{\text{propagation} \mid \text{infection}\} \qquad (3\text{-}1)$$

At l, however, we do not know if there is a fault, so the PIE fault-based methodology performs fault simulation for a wide class of faults. Our prediction of the smallest nonzero failure probability according to D for l is simply

$$\theta_l = \text{execution estimate}$$
$$\times \mathbf{min}[\text{infection estimate}]$$
$$\times \mathbf{min}[\text{propagation estimate}] \qquad (3\text{-}2)$$

(Recall that an execution estimate is found without fault simulation during execution analysis.) $\mathbf{min}[\text{infection estimate}]$ is the smallest infection estimate for the set of mutants considered at l, and $\mathbf{min}[\text{propagation estimate}]$ is the smallest propagation estimate at l. In general, there will only be one propagation estimate, unless you decide to apply the algorithm to a variable that is different than the variable being modified at l. Equation 3-2 represents the smallest predicted impact that a fault in l could cause to O.

There are several aspects of Equation 3-2 worth noting: (1) If an infection estimate is 0.0, then we may have a semantically equivalent mutant, and we must either determine that this is true or disregard the mutant altogether, (2) if either an execution or propagation estimate is 0.0, we must replace this value with an inequality bound on the estimate and use the upper bound in Equation 3-2. We do so as follows: Suppose that the N test cases used during execution analysis did not cause l to be executed. Then the execution estimate for l becomes $< 1/N$. Similarly for propagation analysis, if the X perturbations did not propagate, then our propagation estimate is $<1/X$ and we will use this bound in Equation 3-2. And the same holds for infection analysis if we are satisfied that we do not have semantic equivalence for the Y executions of the mutant. (Note that N, X, and Y are not necessarily equal, but are all related to D.) Whenever a bound is used for one of the three parameters in Equation 3-2 instead of an actual estimate, then the resulting prediction itself becomes a bound. For example, if the execution estimate is 0.05, the infection estimate is 0.01, and the propagation estimate is <0.01, then the prediction is $<5 \times 10^{-6}$.

Also, recall that the method used by propagation analysis is *independent* of the mutants used during infection analysis. However, there is one "unsettling" situation that can arise and fool us into overpredicting testability. Suppose that the exact proportion of test cases that infect for some mutant are a proportion that would never (or at least very infrequently) propagate. So even though there would be infection occurring from a mutant, M, of some class, F, there would be no propagation occurring from M. The problem is that if we do not simulate mutant M's effect on the internal state during propagation analysis and we use the propagation results from another class F' (in our **min**[propagation estimate]), which has a higher likelihood of propagating than would M, we may overpredict that location's ability to reveal a fault. Hence the fault class represented by **min**[propagation estimate] might not be the fault class represented by **min**[infection estimate]. This may cause an overprediction of a location's testability; however, it is difficult to avoid this situation unless we perform propagation analysis with the mutants of infection analysis instead of with perturbation functions.

Even though this situation is problematic, the far greater problem which is unavoidable is the usual criticism against fault-based methodologies: They are limited by the fault classes considered. The more fault classes simulated, the better the results, but the higher the costs. The reader needs to understand that any testability prediction is only as good as the fault classes considered during infection and propagation analysis. Our prediction is not a silver bullet! It is possible that there is an actual fault in the location that has a lesser impact on O than our prediction suggests. If this occurs, then it is possible that after some amount of testing, we will be fooled into believing that no fault is hiding when in fact a fault is hiding. But of course the reverse is also true: There may be a fault in the location that was not represented by our fault simulations, but the fault there has a greater impact on O than our simulated faults did. Given practical limitations, this is the preferable situation, but it cannot be guaranteed.

Higher-Order Testabilities

We have explained how to get a testability equality or upper bound if an actual estimate cannot be found for an individual location. We now explain how to use testabilities from individual locations to find testabilities for larger blocks of code. After all, having 1,000,000 individual location testabilities for a single (but large) system is too much information! We need a way to collapse that information down to fewer pieces.

Given a testability q_l for location l, the testability for the function f, q_f, containing l is

$$q_f = \mathbf{min}_l \, [q\_l] \tag{3-3}$$

over all locations in f. Any location in f with an inequality for its testability is considered smaller than an equality for another location in f. Given two inequality locations within a function, $<X$ and $<Y$, if $X < Y$, then $\mathbf{min}[<X, <Y] = <X$.

The testability for a module m of N functions, $\{f_1, \ldots, f_N\}$, is just

$$q_m = \mathbf{min}_{\, i \in \{f_1, \ldots, f_N\}} \, [q\_f_i] \tag{3-4}$$

where the above inequality rule holds. For a program P of R modules, $\{m_1, \ldots, m_R\}$, we again take minimum as the testability for the entire program:

$$q_P = \mathbf{min}_{\, i \in \{m_1, \ldots, m_R\}} \, [qm_i] \tag{3-5}$$

Recall that if some testability value of a location, which is the lowest for a block, is considered to be "correct," then it can be removed from consideration for the block's testability, and the next lowest testability from the members of the block will be used for the testability of the block.

APPLYING THE PREDICTION TO A TESTING STOPPAGE CRITERIA

We now present a model for determining when to stop testing that is based on the predicted minimum fault size. *When* to stop testing is a question that has never been adequately answered. One answer is "test until you cannot test further," either because of time or because of monetary considerations. Others argue for 100% satisfaction of particular structural coverage criterion as their solution to this dilemma. For example, 100% branch coverage is often attempted, and once (or if) satisfied, testing is then halted. Another testing stoppage criteria is to test until it cost more to generate a test case than to actually perform the test with the input. Only exhaustive testing is truly thorough, so any stoppage criteria that is applied before exhaustive testing is satisfied must be justifiable—that is, for reasons better than "we ran out of time and money."

We recall Beizer describing nonexhaustive testing as "a shift from a deduction to a seduction." Because we cannot deduce via exhaustive testing that our program is correct, we are "seduced" into believing that the program will work correctly for inputs not selected during testing. The testing stoppage criteria selected greatly affects the confidence that we have in "the seduction." Another way of thinking about this is in terms of a hypothesis test: r is the probability of concluding that our program is correct when it is not, so a "better" testing stoppage criteria—that is, one that provides us with the less risk of "falsely being seduced"—will lower r.

Hamlet argues that reliability is not the measurable software quality that we want to determine, but rather what we really want is a confidence in the correctness of software. Hamlet's probable correctness model (Hamlet, 1987) provides this ability.

The model works as follows: Suppose that you have some probability of failure estimate (or probability of failure prediction) for your software, q, according to D. Then the probability that your software will not fail on the *next* selected input is $(1 - q)$. The probability that your software will not fail on the next N inputs selected is $(1 - q)^N$. $1 - (1 - q)^N$ is the probability of at least one failure during the next N inputs selected. If you test the program N times without failure, then you get a confidence $C = 1 - (1 - q)^N$ that the true probability of failure is less than or equal to q.

This equation for confidence C can be used to provide a testing stoppage criteria using the minimum predicted failure probability. To do so, let q be a program's testability, which recall represents the smallest-sized fault that could reside in our program given D and the fault classes that have been simulated. Now pick a C in $(0, 1)$; C should be greater than 0.9, because less than 90% confidence is generally not used by statisticians. The amount of testing needed, N, for C and q given D is

$$N = \lceil \ln (1 - C) / \ln (1 - q) \rceil \qquad (3\text{-}6)$$

This is the amount of testing needed for a confidence C that the software is correct. Why? Because we have predicted via testability analysis that our program cannot fail with a probability of failure in $(0, q]$. N is the number of test cases necessary to show that it is unlikely that the program can fail with probabilities of failure in $[q, 1]$. With confidence C, we believe that the software is correct, that is, there are no probabilities of failure for our software in $(0, 1]$.

Note that this only works when q is a probability prediction or estimate, not an upper-bound prediction. If the testability that we have is an upper-bound prediction ($<t$), the upper bound can be used for q in Equation 3-6, but *not* as a measure of probable correctness, but with N being the minimum number of test cases needed and no maximum number of test cases known. This is because an upper-bound testability prediction means that the testability assessment should be less than or equal to t, but where in $(0, t]$ is unclear. If it is later known that the testability is t, N is enough for a confidence in correctness; if the testability is later found to be less than t (call it t'), then we need $N + x$ test cases, but we need the value of t' to find x, which is the piece to the puzzle that we lack.

Table 3-1 gives the reader an idea of how different values of C, N, and q interact in Equation 3-6. The interesting thing to note here is how q dominates, and the order of magnitude increase in testing costs as q decreases an order of magnitude.

APPLYING THE PREDICTION TO RELIABILITY ASSESSMENTS: THE "SQUEEZE PLAY"

Equation 3-6 provides a means for assessing how much testing is necessary to be convinced that the true probability of failure is less than q. We now introduce a related notion termed "reliability amplification." *Reliability amplification* is the idea of predicting a reliability that is greater than that which can be measured from nonexhaustive, successful testing. This is not a formal idea but rather an informal concept at this point. To amplify reliability, we use testability predictions to increase our con-

TABLE 3-1. How Different Values of θ, N, and C Interact in Equation 3–6

θ	N	C
0.0000001	1,000	0.00
0.0000001	10,000,000	0.7
0.00001	1,000	0.01
0.00001	100,000	0.63
0.00001	1,000,000	0.999955
0.001	1,000	0.63
0.001	10,000	0.999955
0.001	20,000	0.999999998
0.1	100	0.999973
0.1	200	0.99999999929

fidence in correctness beyond what successful testing has suggested, assuming that our testability predictions are sufficiently high. Hamlet and Voas (1993) have suggested an alternative to testability for reliability amplification: the use of information concerning formal methods that were applied during development. To do this, there must be a way of quantifying how much better the code is after formal methods are applied than the code would have been had formal methods not been applied. This amounts to assessing the process that guided code development versus assessing the code directly. To date, how to quantify the value of a software development process is a mystery.

Before testing begins with the first test case (for now let's assume we are talking about system level testing), there is no information available concerning the quality of the code. The system could fail every time, produce correct results each time, fail every other time, and so on. Another way of saying it is that the probability that your code will have any particular probability of failure (pof) in [0, 1] is simply $1/\infty$, because there are an infinite number of values in [0, 1]. After you have tested once and your program produced the correct output, the probability that your software has a probability of failure equal to 1.0 is changed to 0.0. (Note that before testing began, $\Pr\{\text{pof} = 1.0\} = 1/\infty$, and after testing once successfully, $\Pr\{\text{pof} = 1.0\} = 0.0$.) If exhaustive testing occurs, $\Pr\{\text{pof} = 0.0\} = 1.0$, but before testing started, $\Pr\{\text{pof} = 0.0\} = 1/\infty$. Hence testing's ultimate goal is to move from $\Pr\{\text{pof} = 0.0\} = 1/\infty$ to $\Pr\{\text{pof} = 0.0\} = 1.0$. But going from $1/\infty$ to 1.0 via testing alone is generally infeasible.

Because going from $1/\infty$ to 1.0 is not feasible, the notion of reliability amplification has an intuitive appeal, particularly in light of the research conclusions of Butler and Finelli (1991). They argued that assessing ultrareliable levels of reliability (probabilities of failure on the order of 10^{-9}) are unrealistic for software, because of the impracticality of testing billions of times. The question then becomes: *If we cannot test to levels on the order of 10^{-9}, what orders of magnitude can we test to?* Many researchers have suggested that we are unable to assess probabilities of failure for software much below 10^{-4} or 10^{-5}, because even these seemingly lower levels of reliability can translate to hundreds of thousands of tests. This says that we are unable to demonstrate that our software is as reliable as many hardware systems, such as bridges and buildings. (Some hardware systems can be demonstrated to levels below 10^{-4} or 10^{-5}; for instance, it is rumored that the likelihood of a wing falling off an airplane is roughly 10^{-9}.) This brings up another question: *If we cannot make a software system as reliable as the hardware it operates or as reliable as the human that the software is replacing, do we really have any business doing so?* After all, we do not

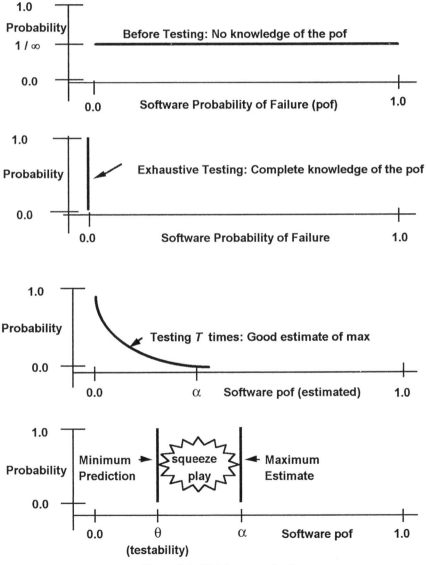

Figure 3-1. The "squeeze play."

build commercial aircraft we cannot show are reliable, nor buildings, nor other complex systems. So should software be an exception?

The ability to assess a confidence in correctness is a small step toward trying to assess greater levels of reliability than we can actually assess via testing. The "squeeze play" model is the model that we will use for showing that the actual probability of failure is 0.0 with a confidence C. Remember that we do not know what the actual probability of failure is for the code; all we have is a testability prediction and information that some amount of successful testing has occurred. A justifiable estimate of the actual value is the goal.

Note the four graphs in Figure 3-1: The x-axis represents the probability of failure of your code, and the y-axis is the probability that your code has any of the values between 0.0 and 1.0 inclusive on the x-axis. The sum of the probabilities for the values between 0.0 and 1.0 on the x-axis is of course 1.0. The first graph demonstrates the scenario where no testing has occurred, thus the equilikely (horizontal) line at $1/\infty$, because any probability of failure in [0,1] has an equal chance of being the "actual" probability of failure of the code. The second graph is the scenario where exhaustive testing has been accomplished. In short, the entire software testing process can be summarized by the attempt to go from the horizontal line in graph 1 to the vertical line in graph 2.

The third graph is the scenario where you have tested T times and observed no failures. Here, α is $1/T$, a very crude upper-bound probability of failure estimate (which is derived from the previous discussion of Laplace's rule of succession), but it does give a threshold as to which large probabilities of failure are unrealistic for the code given T successful tests; this threshold also tells which smaller probabilities of failure are still possibilities for your code. We are saying that probabilities of failure to the right of α are doubtful, and probabilities of failure to the left of α are where we believe the true probability of failure is. As T increases, α decreases. Note that the third graph is speculative. We could just as easily have drawn a horizontal line between $[0, \alpha]$ like we did in the first graph. If we had done so, this would have implied that we possessed no information about the true probability of failure in this interval. But a Bayesian perspective suggests that given previous successes, future successes are more likely, and hence we consider that it is more likely that the true probability of failure is near 0 and less likely to be near α. Regardless of what we speculate that the graph should look like in the interval $[0, \alpha]$, we have a confidence that this is where the true probability of failure lies.

In terms of fault size, as α continues to decrease, we are implying that the largest-sized fault possible in the code is getting smaller. This is because testing and not observing failure is a method for estimating what size the *largest*-sized fault could be. Continued successful testing reduces this estimate.

In the fourth graph, we see what testing and testability combine to provide: We combine the *estimate* of the largest-sized fault with the *prediction* of the smallest-sized fault. In this graph, $\alpha \neq \theta$, meaning that there are fault sizes in the interval $[q, \alpha]$ that we have not eliminated as possible fault sizes in the code.

We have confidence from testing that the fault sizes that are greater than α do not exist, and confidence from testability analysis that fault sizes less than θ do not exist.

But between these two thresholds we have no information. Technically, all that we have from testing is a confidence C that the true probability of failure is less than α. But if $\theta \cong \alpha$, do we intuitively have something better?

The goal of the "squeeze play" model is to get $\theta = \alpha$, because as we have stated, if $\Pr\{\text{pof} \geq \theta\} \cong 0.0$ and $\Pr\{\text{pof} < \theta \text{ and pof} > 0.0\} \cong 0.0$, then $\Pr\{\text{pof} = 0.0\} \cong 1.0$. This value that is approximately 1.0 is our confidence that we have tested sufficiently, and that we have tested down to the level necessary to catch the smallest predicted fault size that the code could contain. Thus the question then becomes: *What is this confidence?* Because there are two techniques whose results are being used, there are two possible sources of erroneous information that could bias this confidence. First, there is a chance that testing has failed (for whatever reason) to detect a large fault; the probability of this error occurring is $(1 - \alpha)^T$. Second, it is possible that testability analysis has used too few test cases during its analysis to assess a particular testability, particularly if that testability value is small. After all, you must use a large sample size to have any confidence in a statistic. Let u represent the error possible from using too few test cases during PIE. Because these two error spaces are independent, they can be added together.

Note another possible source of error here, and that is in the limited fault classes that were used during PIE. This, too, decreases a confidence in correctness, but because quantifying this error is not possible, what the squeeze play model will assert when a squeeze does occur is as follows: *the confidence in correctness for P with respect to the fault classes simulated during PIE and with respect to D is* $1 - [u + (1 - \alpha)^T]$. A model for quantifying u is provided in Voas, et al. (1993).

WHERE TO CONCENTRATE TESTING

The next application that we will apply the minimum predicted fault size to is *where* to concentrate validation resources. Because the low testability locations or blocks of locations are the places where testing is less powerful at detecting faults, these are the regions where other quality assessment efforts should be considered.

Admittedly, it is an unusual concept to measure the likelihood of a fault hiding in a location in a program. Normally, we would think about "fault hiding ability" at either the design, module, or program levels. But by applying this measurement at such a fine level of granularity, the information derived is expectedly more precise. This precision allows unit testers to really concentrate on those areas that have low system level testability.

We say that low testability implies high fault hiding ability, and high testability implies low fault hiding ability. A location or block of locations of low testability suggests a portion of the code that will likely hide problems during testing. A location or block of locations of high testability suggests a portion of the code that will not likely hide problems during testing. To quantify the testing needed for a particular location, function, or module, we can apply Equation 3-6 to get a rough prediction for the system level testing needed.

If the amount of testing performed at a higher level of abstraction (say at the module level) is less than that needed by some function of the module, then that module has received inadequate testing. This suggests that the module needs additional validation resources, and possibly techniques other than testing should be applied to low testability functions. These other techniques might include:

- Additional unit testing
- Manual inspections
- Formal verification at the unit level
- Redesign of the code

Because the third and fourth alternatives are very expensive and unlikely to receive consideration from management unless strongly coerced, the first two can be implemented more inexpensively and relatively easily. The British Interim Defence Standard 00-55 (1991) is an example of such coercion: in special cases, formal verification will be required.

APPLYING PROPAGATION PREDICTIONS TO DYNAMIC SOFTWARE SAFETY ASSESSMENTS

Another application area for testability, particularly propagation analysis, is software safety assessment. *Software safety* assessment is the process of showing that the system cannot produce an output that is termed "catastrophic." A *catastrophic output* is one that is capable of a loss of either life or property by putting the system that the software is controlling into a state that has been predefined by safety engineers as unacceptable. An example might be putting a commercial airliner into a hard roll. Put simply, a catastrophic output must never be produced by software controlling a critical function.

Demonstrating that a program cannot enter into a state that could lead to a catastrophic failure is difficult. Part of the difficulty lies in knowing all events that might lead up to such and being able to fully enumerate this set. Testing is not much help in safety analysis, since it is not feasible to test for safety, because of the possibly infinite and unknown size of the aforementioned set. What we need is a way to show that the program cannot get into an unsafe state; this requires knowledge about the external "environment" that the code will operate in. One way of showing safety may include applying formal methods to prove that certain output states cannot be produced; this is quite different than showing that the program is correct (Rushby, 1993). We now present a different model for *partially* demonstrating safety; the model is a refinement on the fault-based propagation analysis already presented, and thus this is a *dynamic safety assessment* technique. This technique could be used as a means for demonstrating the validity of formal analysis that has demonstrated safety.

In the propagation analysis algorithm, we defined propagation as having occurred when output states differed between what the original program output and what the perturbed version output. If an output is multidimensional, $\{v_1, v_2, \ldots, v_n\}$ (let K represent this set), only one element of K need be different for propagation to have been considered as having occurred. In general, the fewer variables that are output when compared to all variables that could be output, the less likely it will be that propagation will occur for faults in the program (remember the fault set hypothesis). This is because a fault might only affect a small portion of $\{v_1, v_2, \ldots, v_n\}$, K', where $K' \subset K$. The more variables that are output, the less likely that faults will hide. This simple principle is used every day by programmers when they insert **write( )** statements during debugging in attempts to find where a problem is originating.

Now consider a subset of K, Q ($Q \subseteq K$), where Q only contains output variables that could lead to a catastrophe if their values are incorrect; we term these *critical output variables*. Propagation is defined as having occurred with respect to K, but we can easily modify that definition to only consider Q. This provides the likelihood that if some fault exists in l, that fault would lead to a catastrophic failure (according to D), given that D represents the operational distribution. This tells us immediately that a fault in l is not only likely to cause a failure, but a catastrophic failure. We get a prediction of this likelihood by comparing the output variables in Q for the original program to the output values those variables have from the perturbed version.

A further refinement to the propagation analysis is to restrict Q to ranges on its members. For example, suppose $Q = \{v_1, v_2\}$. If we limit $v_1 < 10$ and $0 \leq v_2 \leq 5$ to classes of catastrophic output events, then we can determine the likelihood that a fault in l will propagate to v_1 *and* cause it to have a value ≤ 10 or propagate to v_2 *and* put it in the range [0,5] (according to D). For this modification, we no longer need to consider the output of the original (unperturbed) program, and we need only run the perturbed version to see if the perturbation at l outputs $v_1 < 10$ or $0 \leq v_2 \leq 5$. If so, we say that propagation occurred to some output state that we consider as catastrophic.

One additional refinement is to enumerate specific catastrophic output states, $\{O_1, O_2, \ldots, O_n\}$. For example, suppose $O_1 = \{v_1 = 9, v_2 = 4\}$. This allows for a redefinition of what constitutes a propagation to the output and allows us to determine whether we can dynamically get into some output state from the data state perturbations that we inject. Once again, we do not need to see what is output from the original program; it is the role of testing to see if the original program with any existing faults can ever get into a catastrophic state. We can determine the likelihood of a fault in l putting the program in some output state in $\{O_1, O_2, \ldots, O_n\}$ according to D via this modified propagation analysis scheme. This is the utility of the *PiSCES* Software Safety Tool™ from Reliable Software Technologies Corporation. We will return to the subject of software safety assessment in Chapters 5 and 6.

In short, the definition of what constitutes a propagation can be modified by redefining the output space in order to predict whether a fault of some class in l could ever cause that output event or class of output events to occur. This flexibility allows the propagation analysis algorithm to be applied to areas other than testability, including safety, security, and fault tolerance. Unfortunately, the criticism against fault-based techniques is still here; it is possible that we will fail to simulate some class of faults that would lead to a catastrophic output, and we could be left with a false sense that our program cannot dynamically get into that state, when indeed it could. Fault-based simulation is not capable of demonstrating a negative. But given that some risk must be accepted, the goal is to try to minimize the risk through simulating reasonable fault classes and not to associate a guarantee with the results, merely a confidence.

An example of where this technique is useful can be found in DO-178. This document sets forth the requirements for software that is installed on airborne systems in the United States. Two excerpts from this document follow:

> Testing of airborne software has two complementary objectives. One objective is to demonstrate that the software satisfies its requirements. The second objective is to demonstrate with a high degree of confidence that errors which could lead to unacceptable failure conditions, as determined by the system safety assessment process, have been removed. . . .
>
> Testing shows that functional requirements are satisfied and detects errors, and formal methods could be used to increase confidence that anomalous behavior will not occur (for inputs that are out of range or unlikely to occur).

As stated in the second excerpt, formal methods could be used to demonstrate that illegal inputs are unable to put the system into unsafe states. Our technique is empirical, and it can also be used to show whether any fault simulations were able to put the system into a catastrophic state. In combination, these techniques deliver even a greater confidence that this requirement is satisfied.

SOFTWARE TESTABILITY VERSUS SOFTWARE FAULT TOLERANCE

The term "fault tolerance" has become confused between persons in software and those in hardware. To an electrical engineer, *fault tolerance* refers to the ability of an electrical system to function correctly if corrupted input has been fed into the system. To a software engineer, the term *fault tolerance* may also include the ability of a software system to overcome programmer faults that are resident in it (as well as the ability of overcome problems with corrupted data being entered into the system). According to the IEEE (IEEE, 1991), fault tolerance is:

> (1) the ability of a system or component to continue normal operation despite the presence of hardware or software faults, (2) the number of faults a system or component can withstand before normal operation is impaired, (3) pertaining to the study of errors, faults, and failures, and of methods for enabling systems to continue normal operation in the presence of faults.

(In their definition, the IEEE also suggests that the reader review several other related definitions: error tolerance, fault secure, fail safe, fail soft, robustness, recovery, redundancy, and restart.)

We say that software has a "fault tolerance" capability if it is able to produce the correct output even if the software contains a fault or the software receives incorrect input. The idea behind software fault tolerance has roots in hardware systems that are built to contain redundancy if a subsystem fails. For example, if the primary computer fails, the secondary computer may be expected to take over almost instantly. Fault tolerance is a necessary characteristic to demonstrate for software that controls a critical function. Fault tolerance is closely related to software safety: Software is "safe" if it does not result in a catastrophic output; software is *fault tolerant* if it is able to produce the correct output even though problems arise during computation of the output. As an example, suppose that somewhere in the code we have the statement: $\mathbf{x} := \mathbf{y}/\mathbf{r}$, and suppose that $\mathbf{r}$ is read in as an input. One fault-tolerant mechanism that our system will need is a check to see that $\mathbf{r} \neq 0$; otherwise we will have a run-time (division by zero) failure.

In the 1980s, much research was done on a software fault-tolerant technique termed *N-version programming*, which is based on the conjecture that if you have multiple (and independent) programs computing a solution, then it is less likely that the group of programs will each calculate the wrong answer than would one individual program of the group (Knight and Leveson, 1986). Hence, having multiple versions executing in parallel will produce a more reliable overall system. The necessary assumption that must be true to make *N*-version programming accepted is that if programmer 1 makes a fault in version 1, and programmer 2 makes a fault in version 2, then the two faults will be different. This required situation is termed the *independence of faults assumption*. Operationally, the hope is that the versions will fail independently and that it would be unlikely for two or more versions to fail on the same input state.

In an *N*-version system, you have *N* versions and a voter; the voter collects the outputs from the versions and attempts to decide on which output is correct. Correct output is typically based on the solution that is produced by a majority or consensus of the versions, but problems arise in the situation where there are *N* different outputs or there are different outputs that each receive the same number of votes. The conjecture for *N*-version programming is that the group should be more reliable than any individual version; this conjecture seems plausible, because this same scheme has been applied successfully in hardware systems, where a back-up system exists in case the primary system fails, with possibly another back-up to the back-up. The main difficulty with *N*-version software systems, however, is in the independence of faults assumption between the versions. What do you do if all (or at least most) versions produce the same incorrect output, because all of the programmers misunderstood the specification in the same manner? Furthermore, even if the programmers understood the specification the same way, it may be the case that certain input states are just inherently hard to process. Even though the programs may come up with different approaches (i.e., different algorithms) for handling those hard input states, all the versions may tend to fail on many of those input states. In this situation, the independence of faults assumption does not hold. Also, even if there is a gain in reliability from an *N*-version system, is the reliability gain substantial enough with respect to the linear increase in cost? That is, if the same monetary resources had been applied to a single version, might it not be even more reliable than the *N*-version system? One last but important problem is termed the "consistent comparison problem." Here correct versions may arrive at completely different outputs for an application that does not apparently have multiple correct solutions (Brilliant et al., 1989). If this problem is not handled properly by the voter, an N-version system may not be able to reach a consensus even when its component versions are correct. To date, these issues have never been fully agreed upon by the scientific community at large, and N-version programming has remained as an academic research topic.

Now we propose a testability-based way of assessing fault tolerance in software. We have shown how one part of our software testability assessment technique, propagation analysis, can be used to dynamically assess safety for certain perturbations. We now highlight the difference between software testability and software fault tolerance, because even though these are both characteristics that we want critical systems to contain high levels of, they are *opposites,* and attaining both at the same time for the same piece of software is not feasible.

Software testability is a measure of the likelihood that problems that occur during execution will be revealed in the output, and fault tolerance is a measure of the likelihood that problems will not be revealed in the output. For example, if location *l* has low testability, that means that a problem in *l* is unlikely to be revealed during execution, and hence *l* is a location of high fault tolerance. The real issue here is: *When do we really want high testability for a critical system, and when don't we?*

Because the goal of testing is to reveal problems if problems exist, we certainly want high testability during the testing phase, as well as during any phase prior to software deployment. The question then is: *Do we want high testabilities after the software is released, because a high testability suggests a low fault tolerance?* Our answer is "No." When software is released and put on an aircraft or automobile, we prefer that problems that may arise are not likely to affect the output, particularly if those outputs could result in damage or a loss of life. Regions of the code that demonstrated high testability prior to deployment are candidates for receiving fault-tolerant software mechanisms to increase the system's fault tolerance.

What we are implying is that we really need two versions of the code: (1) a high testability version prior to operational usage of the code and (2) a lower testability version during operation. Is this feasible? Currently, we are not sure; it is feasible technically, but whether it is feasible economically is unknown. The benefit here is that the propagation analysis algorithm can help you dynamically assess your software's fault tolerance before deployment.

As an example of a software mechanism that enhances fault tolerance while being detrimental to testability, consider the following:

```
if (sensor_1 < lower_bound) or (sensor_1 > upper_bound)
    then sensor_1 := constant;
```

First, this statement clearly is checking to see whether a value read from a sensor is in range, and, if not, the value is put back in range. It is likely that this is an infrequently executed statement, and, if so, that is detrimental to testability for two reasons. First, it is infrequently executed. Suppose the constant sensor_1 is assigned incorrectly. If the likelihood of executing this incorrect assignment is minimal, this fault will almost certainly not be caught during testing. Also, the assignment statement immediately overwrites any problem in the sensor value, and hence that is detrimental to propagation. But in terms of fault tolerance, this mechanism is beneficial, because it attempts to keep "illegal" data from entering the state of the program.

TWISTING PIE INTO ASSESSING THE QUALITY OF INDIVIDUAL TEST CASES

We have talked at length about how propagation analysis, infection analysis, and execution analysis provide information useful to such concerns as a testing stoppage criteria, reliability, safety, and fault tolerance. There is another interesting application of these algorithms, and that is determining the likelihood of catching faults by an individual test case. Recall that structural unit testing creates sets of test cases that enable the tester to exercise particular portions of the code. And recall that mutation testing creates test suites that are able to differentiate mutated code from unmutated code.

Under various assumptions, it can easily be shown (as well as being intuitive) that coverage and fault-based test suites are better at detecting faults than test suites that are purely selected at random. One interesting question, however, might be to ask, "Given two test suites A and B that satisfy criterion C for module M, which test suite actually is more likely to reveal faults?" Of course the size of A and B may play a role in answering this question, because even though one may be better at detecting faults than the other, the better suite may contain so many test cases that it is not practical to use it. The reason that finding optimal test suites is desirable is that there are infinitely many different test suites that could be used during testing; and because testing resources are limited, a model that helps us decide between the wealth of possibilities is an attractive capability to employ.

We want a way to order the "fault revealing ability" of individual test suites that satisfy the same criteria. For now, we will simply define the fault-revealing ability of a test case or group of test cases to be the likelihood that a fault will be revealed by the tests. The greater this likelihood, the more value added during testing to ensure the quality of the code. To say that one test suite is better than the other, we need a means for quantifying the value-added by an individual test case of a test suite. With this information, we can derive a composite score for the test suite and compare the scores of different test suites.

We begin by defining the type of information that we want produced by the propagation, infection, and execution algorithms but which is currently not being produced by them: (1) the number of locations executed by some test case t during execution analysis, (2) the number of infections produced from the syntactic mutants during infection analysis at the locations that t executes, and (3) the number of perturbations at the locations that t executes that did propagate to the output. This information suggests how good t is at exposing faults, which also allows us to quantify the value that D and I are providing.

The idea here is straightforward: Certain test cases exercise more locations, cause more mutants to be distinguished, and cause more perturbed data states to propagate.

They are the test cases that *should* cause more existing faults to be revealed. For instance, suppose you have two test cases, t_1 and t_2, and t_1 only executes the first couple of statements and terminates the program, while t_2 executes all statements of the program. If you were only allowed to test the program with one of these two test cases, which would you choose? Assuming that for the locations these two inputs both exercise, they have equal fault-revealing ability, you should choose t_2, because there is syntax that t_1 fails to reach, and if you test using t_1, you will not have any information about the correctness of that syntax. t_1 has no fault-revealing ability in those sections of the code that it does not exercise. But with t_2, you will have a small piece of information about the correctness of all of the code.

Let us formalize this idea. We define a histogram H where each bin in the histogram represents a single test case t. H_t represents the fault-revealing ability of test case t. Let N_t represent the number of locations in P that t exercises. For each location j that is executed by t, there are S_j mutants used during infection analysis and there are R_j perturbations injected during propagation analysis. (R_j is probably 1 unless more than one variable was perturbed after j; also, if j is executed repeatedly by t and we decide to perturb on each iteration of j, that only counts once into R_j.) Let s_j represent the number of mutants that were exposed at j by t, and let r_j represent the perturbations that propagated from j with t. Note that if j is executed more than once for t, each time some mutant m at j is detected, s_j is incremented. We define the fault-revealing ability of t to be

$$H_t = N_t \times \left(\frac{1}{N_t} \sum_j \frac{s_j}{S_j} \right) \left(\frac{1}{N_t} \sum_j \frac{r_j}{R_j} \right) \tag{3-7}$$

Equation 3-7 produces scores in $[0, N_t]$. Note that the two summations in Equation 3-7 represent the average ability of t to cause infections and propagations to occur at the locations that it exercises. If a test case exercises many locations and causes many infection and propagations to occur, then that test case will receive a higher score from Equation 3-7.

Note a possible problem with Equation 3-7, and that is that N_t may dominate when it is multiplied by the second and third terms. For instance, t may execute few locations, but at those locations, t may have a very good ability to expose faults. With Equation 3-7, such a test case would be penalized, and might be ignored during testing if only those test cases with high scores in H were selected. To reduce the chance of this occurring, we introduce a slightly different histogram H' where each bin represents a test case and the score for an individual bin is given by

$$H_t' = \left(\frac{1}{N_t} \sum_j \frac{s_j}{S_j} \right) \left(\frac{1}{N_t} \sum_j \frac{r_j}{R_j} \right) \tag{3-8}$$

Equation 3-8 produces scores in $[0,1]$. This solely bases a test case's fault revealing ability on what occurs during infection and propagation analysis.

We now want to find a composite fault-revealing ability for a particular test suite so that we can compare test suites. We begin by assuming that the test suites are of the same size. The score for a test suite of N test cases is

$$\sum_{i=1}^{N} H_n \qquad (3\text{-}9)$$

if Equation 3-7 is applied and

$$\sum_{i=1}^{N} H_n' \qquad (3\text{-}10)$$

if Equation 3-8 is applied. If the two test suites are not of the same size, then these two equations should be weighted according to how many test cases they contain. A smaller test suite can have a higher fault-revealing ability than a test suite with more members. Hence it is not necessarily true that a greater number of test cases means better testing, but it certainly means more expensive testing.

The ability to apply the algorithms to the task of determining how good a test suite from D is at revealing faults is a significant application of the algorithms that should not be overlooked. This is one model for determining how good particular test suites are during software testing. We have previously shown how the subsumes hierarchy is a precise and formal way to rank different coverage schemes; what we have shown here is an "empirical subsumes" hierarchy that is specific to the code, the PIE algorithms, and the test suites that are applied to the code. The future pay-off in an empirical scheme such as this is that if after much experimentation common trends appear between testing criteria that cannot have the subsumes hierarchy directly applied, then we may get a clearer (and generalized) understanding of how good different techniques are at revealing faults. This will not be easy, nor easily accepted by those already biased toward certain testing techniques. For practitioners, such information could serve as a useful guide to selecting testing schemes with proven value-added benefit.

SOFTWARE FAILURE REGIONS

We have been talking about ranking test schemes. One testing scheme of little benefit would be to select test cases that *only* reveal some fault that is already known to exist—that is, selecting test cases that are associated with the same chain of black balls. We now talk about one technique that is aimed at avoiding this situation.

A *software failure region* is the portion of a program input space that is mapped by a program defect into a failure or erroneous program result. This region is bounded by inequalities deriving the combination of three sources: the reachability conditions for the code with the defect, the conditions under which the calculations in that code produces an erroneous value, and the conditions in which the value isn't masked by later processing (Shimeall et al. 1991). Note that these sources are the three conditions of the fault/failure model. The proportion of the input space in a failure region with respect to the rest of I is the fault size of the region.

The goal of software failure region analysis is to identify inputs in I that will reveal a fault that has already been identified during testing from another member of I. For instance, if the fault is of size greater than 1, and the fault has been identified but not corrected, then testing with another input that reveals the same fault is wasteful. Furthermore, if the fault has been corrected, then knowing which members of I were identified with that fault could be useful for regression testing.

The application of failure regions was introduced by Ammann and Knight in their work in data diversity, which centered on using data redundancy as a means of ensuring fault tolerance. To be successful, there must be a means for producing input values that lie outside of a failure region, provided that we know what inputs are in the failure region. The means for doing this is termed a *reexpression algorithm*, which transforms a set of inputs to a new but equivalent set of inputs. The reexpression algorithm is considered valid as long as the original information in the first set of inputs is not affected (Ammann and Knight, 1988).

Note the interesting relationship between failure region analysis and PIE. In failure regions analysis, exact knowledge of the faults and where they reside is imperative in order to find failure regions, however, PIE does not make this requirement. It should be the case that the testability of a location is less than the size of the failure region for any fault in the location. Hence the testability technique presented in this chapter provides a lower bound on the size of the failure region. If we abstract that up to the program level, then the testability of the program represents the smallest failure region for any failure region in I. The application of testability information to failure region analysis is apparent, because for certain programs, finding the expressions for bounding a region could be very difficult. If a faulty location is of low testability, this implies that almost any other input value than the one that identified the fault will likely be outside of the failure region. Although this analysis is not precise, it may provide insight into where finding failure region bounds is more practical.

PiSCES SOFTWARE ANALYSIS TOOLKIT

Reliable Software Technologies Corporation in Sterling, Virginia, has developed the PiSCES Software Analysis Toolkit™ 1.2; it is a collection of software analysis and testing tools that contains one tool, PiSCES Software Testability Analysis Tool™, that implements the PIE algorithms. The other tools in this toolkit provide safety analysis, mutation testing, and automatic coverage test case generation. The testability tool consists of three main components: (1) a browser, (2) a project viewer, and a (3) results analyzer. The browser allows the user to specify where fault simulation is desired in the source code, the project viewer allows the user to store all of the source code files, previous results, instrumentation options, and input sets or distributions into one entitiy called the *project*, and the results analyzer provides the user with a variety of different options for displaying the analysis results; this utility also provides the user with a graphical display of how much testing is needed according to the squeeze play model.

Figure 3-2 shows an example of the results of a session with this tool. In the upper left corner, we see the PiSCES Main Menu window that allows the user to select what tool (and associated options) is desired. In the lower right-hand corner, we see a project named b737.prj that contains the b737.c module under analysis, a main driver for that module, main.c, and various results, instrumentation, and input suite files. In the upper right and lower left windows, the tool shows both the results mathematically and graphically for the functions that comprise module b737.c. In this example, we see only inequalities for the functions, and no point estimates, which immediately tells that our test distribution was unable to cause one of the three conditions of the fault/failure model to occur for allocation(s) in every function. The user has the option to then determine which of these conditions did not occur, and for which locations in the code. Also, the "SQUEEZE" option on the bottom left corner of the Testability Analyzer window, when selected, allows the user to graphically see how many test cases are needed given the results in that window. The "DISABLE RESULTS" option (bottom right corner) allows the user to ignore testability scores during the squeeze play calculation if the user believes that faults are not hiding in the associated functions/modules.

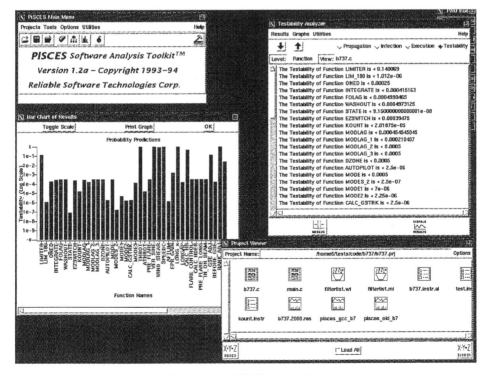

Figure 3-2. PiSCES screen shot.

SUMMARY

We have provided algorithms for predicting the smallest-sized fault in the urn. This has allowed us to find a testing stoppage criteria, assess a confidence that the code is not hiding faults, determine which regions of the code need additional validation resources, assess the safety of the system dynamically by slightly modifying the propagation analysis algorithm, and assess software fault tolerance. In short, because our fault-based method is tightly coupled to the basic model of computation, we are able to apply it to many different software assessments.

We have been forthright and have admitted the weaknesses of fault-based methodologies; they are not silver bullets, and no one should expect a silver bullet technique in software assessment. Software assessment is based on estimating characteristics that are used as parameters to predictive models: Models have limitations, and the ability to precisely measure many of the needed parameters often does not exist. The value of metrics and models, however, is evident, provided that empirical research can be found that supports the predictions that the models imply.

The ability to apply our prediction of the smallest-sized fault to other aspects of software development beyond testing shows the importance of studying this assessment further. For example, since regression testing is often applied during software maintenance, any way to use our predictions as to where to retest during that phase would be welcomed, because testing is one of the most despised activities during maintenance.

If nothing else can be said, we at least can now say that we do have software testability metrics, and we always have if you believe that hardware testability measures can be applied as software testability measures. The measure that we have explained in this section is very computational, and years of future refinements in the implementation of the algorithms and fault simulation mechanism are needed.

EXERCISES

1. What do you think the major issues are with applying the propagation analysis algorithm to software security? *Hint*: What would be the major worm and virus classes the perturbation functions would need to simulate?

2. How does fault-tree analysis differ from applying propagation analysis to safety? What are the tradeoffs?

3. Given that 1000 successful tests have been performed, and $q < 10^{-5}$ with $C = 0.99$, how many more tests must be performed in order to have tested the bare minimum according to the squeeze play model?

4. How would testabilities vary between these two different implementations:
   (a) if (a > 10) and (a <= 15) then [computation block]
   (b) if (a = 11) then [computation block]
       else if (a = 12) then [computation block]

```
else if (a = 13) then [computation block]
else if (a = 14) then [computation block]
else if (a = 15) then [computation block]
```

Look at all three conditions in your evaluation.

5. How likely do you think it is that a perturbation function will change an incorrect value into a correct value? *Hint*: Recall that the competent programmer hypothesis assumed that a typical "good" programmer writes code that, if faulty, was only a few keystrokes away from a correct version. Does it make sense then to further assume that a "good" programmer makes incorrect values that are just slightly off from the correct value?

6. *Multiple condition coverage* (MCC) is satisfied when all possible combinations of outcomes for the conditions in a decision are satisfied. For example, for the decision (a and b), we need inputs that cause (a, b) to be (TRUE, TRUE), (TRUE, FALSE), (FALSE, TRUE), (FALSE, FALSE). What minimum set of mutants are required for weak mutation testing to ensure that this decision is MCC adequate?

7. Suppose that instead of finding the minimum predicted fault size for a location we instead find an average predicted fault size. Also suppose that this average value was extremely tiny. What does this tell (if anything) about the size of any failure region that might be associated with the location? Also, can you think of any information from average execution, infection, and propagation estimates that might help find the inequalities for the three fault/failure conditions?

REFERENCES

P. Ammann and J. Knight. "Data Diversity: An Approach to Software Fault Tolerance." *IEEE Transactions on Computers*. 37(4) 418–425, April 1988.

S. S. Brilliant, J.C. Knight, and N.G. Leveson. "The Consistent Comparison Problem in *N*-Version Software," *IEEE Transactions on Software Engineering* 15(11), 1481–1485, November 1989.

R. Butler and G. Finelli. "The Infeasibility of Experimental Quantification of Life-Critical Software Reliability." In *Proceedings of SIGSOFT '91: Software for Critical Systems,* December 1991.

DO-178B: Software Considerations in Airborne Systems and Equipment Certification. Requirements and Technical Concepts for Aviation, Washington, D.C., December 1992.

R. G. Hamlet. "Probable Correctness Theory." *Information Processing Letters* 25, 17–25, 1987.

R. Hamlet and J. Voas. "Faults on Its Sleeve: Amplifying Software Reliability Testing." In: Proceedings of ISSTA93, reprinted in *ACM Software Engineering Notes* 18(3), July 1993.

IEEE. *IEEE Software Engineering Standards Collection*. Spring 1991 edition.

Interim Defence Standard 00-55. "The Procurement of Safety Critical Software in Defence Equipment," Parts 1 and 2, Ministry of Defence, April 1991.

J.C. Knight and N.G. Leveson. "An Experimental Evaluation of the Assumption of Independence in Multiversion Programming." *IEEE Transactions on Software Engineering* 12(1) 96–109, January 1986.

J. Rushby. "Formal Methods and Digital Systems Validation for Airborne Systems." NASA Contractor Report 4551, December 1993.

T. J. Shimeall, J. M. Bolchoz and R. Griffin. "Analytic Derivation of Software Failure Regions." Tech. Report NTSCS-91-003, Monterey, CA: Naval Postgraduate School, 1991.

J. M. Voas. "*PIE*: A Failure-Based Technique." *IEEE Transactions on Software Engineering* SE-18(8), August 1992.

J. M. Voas, C.C. Michael, and K.W. Miller. "Confidently Assessing a Zero Probability of Software Failure." In: *Proceedings of the 12th International Conference on Computer Safety, Reliability, and Security*, October 27–29, Poznan, Poland, 1993.

CHAPTER 4

Designing Toward the Tester's Utopia

The process of designing software is quite similar to the design processes used in any manufacturing system. In a design process, there are requirements and constraints, yet creativity can still exist. Each decision incurs tradeoffs, and the greater the number of decisions that are finalized as the design proceeds, the fewer freedoms that will remain. It is like traversing a tree; the deeper into the tree you go, the fewer branches that still remain for you to choose among. The higher in the tree you are, the more choices that exist. For example, an architect starts with a set of dimensions: cost, number of stories, square footage, type of design, type of underlying foundation, and so on. From that, many different options result, all of which fulfill the original requirements.

In software, we know that there are an infinite number of different designs and implementations that can functionally satisfy a set of requirements. Suppose that one of the testability requirements said that the software, when delivered and assessed for testability, can have a predicted minimum fault size of no less than x. This requirement reduces the amount of freedom that the development team experiences. The developers need a way to gauge what their options are during design to ensure that the resulting code satisfies this testability requirement. Ways for determining how testable a code will be *before* code is written is the focus of this chapter.

Thus the software engineers need to make "smart" decisions before the coding and testing phases begin, to ensure that the software is as unlikely to hide faults as possible. The more likely the software is to hide faults, the lower the additional value that testing will provide. If testing truly accounts for 20–50% of development costs as some statistics have shown, then testing must provide evidence that the code is not hiding faults.

We have seen the enormous values of test cases (N) when testability (θ) is low. If there is a way to design/program a system such that its testability is increased, doing so will decrease testing costs. Also, we believe that increased testability can have a positive impact during maintenance, but that is speculative. You must be wary, however, about design schemes that are solely geared toward improving testability, because as we have discussed, high testability may be detrimental to fault tolerance. Designing for higher testability may also be detrimental to other software characteristics that we desire. For instance, most development organizations use structured design principles. It may be that different design heuristics that are good for testability are bad for program structure. Or possibly good testability design heuristics are detrimental for building system components that we want to be reusable. Another problem might be that design-for-testability heuristics will make the system's performance unacceptable, by slowing it down or requiring too much memory. We mention these potential side effects to warn the reader that in software, as in life, each decision incurs a tradeoff, and designing for increased testability will be no exception. Unfortunately we cannot prove what impact design for testability will have to other software characteristics such as structured design, maintenance, readability, reusability, reliability, and so on. But we suspect that the impact might be detrimental.

In this chapter, we will provide the reader with as much *sound* design-for-testability advice as possible, and we will be careful to differentiate between what design recommendations we *know* increase testability and what we *speculate* will increase testability. The area of software design-for-testability is truly an uncharted frontier in software engineering, and this chapter is only an overview of ongoing research.

THE "STAIRCASE" DESIGN CONJECTURE

There are many different ways in which software can be defined. We begin simply, by viewing software as a mathematical function. The goal is to find a way to classify different mathematical functions and how they might fare in terms of testability before they are implemented. If successful, we can begin to create new design schemes.

Given a function to be computed, and 10 different design teams which are all given a definition of that function, the teams will likely produce 10 different designs. Now give each design to 10 different programming teams, and they will likely produce 100 versions that are "somewhat" independently designed and programmed. We say "somewhat" because the common denominator is the specification that the designs are based on and the design that the 10 versions are based on. (Recall that the independence issue was a problem for N-version programming.) Each version, although D is fixed, will likely have a unique testability according to the tradeoffs and decisions that the different design and programming teams made. Had we used 100 design teams and 100 programming teams per design for the same function, we would probably be faced with 10,000 different versions, each with a different overall testability.

The point here is that the overall testability of a program and the testabilities of its components are dependent on the design and implementation. There is an important relationship between program testabilities and the function that the programs implement. If we can successfully capture this relationship before the design and programming phases begin, then we can develop heuristics that enable software design-for-testability.

The "staircase" software design conjecture gives an interpretation for this relationship. It states: *Given (1) a particular function that we wish to compute, (2) a particular programming language, (3) design, (4) D, and (5) a program for that design, there will be a particular testability.* Because (1) and (4) are fixed, there are three degrees of freedom: the programming language, program, and design. For any combination of these three parameters, there is "probably" a theoretical upper bound on the testability that we can expect for *any* implementation of the function. This is a parallel notion to the P and NP classifications that are given to functions to give an estimate of how much time is required to complete a computation. [A function is of the class P if there is a polynomial-time decidable algorithm exists, and a function is of class NP if no polynomial-time algorithms are known, but for which polynomial-time solutions exist, if we are allowed to make guesses, but only for successful guesses leading to a solution (Gallier, 1986).] Thus no matter how we program/design function f, the testability of our implementation is less than or equal to f's theoretical upper bound.

We are suggesting that certain classes of functions may have such low theoretical testability upper bounds that there is little hope of ever being able to test these functions to any level of confidence (that they are not hiding faults). If this conjecture is true, although almost certainly unprovable, it suggests that there may be functions being programmed that we have no hope of adequately testing. Civil engineers do not build bridges unless they can demonstrate their structural integrity. Pilots are not given licenses until they can demonstrate their ability. Should we develop software to control critical tasks if we know *a priori* that we can never adequately demonstrate its integrity given testing as the main assessor of dependability? This is a question that is being asked more as software development costs and the levels of criticality increase.

As the three variable parameters in the staircase conjecture change, the testability of the resulting implementation may also change. Recall that the tester's utopia represented the maximum testability that could ever be achieved for any function. Given that these three parameters (in conjunction with D) will map to a testability that is almost certainly less than the tester's utopia, we should strive to find the proper balance among the three parameters to produce a program that has the highest possible testability for the function being implemented.

Figure 4-1 shows a pictorial representation of the staircase conjecture for the theoretical upper bound on the testability of any implementation of some function f_1. Note how the two different designs (Design$_1$ Design$_2$) and three programming languages (L_1, L_2, L_3) affect how far up the staircase we get to the predicted upper limit. In this example, Design$_1$ with L_3 is far closer to the limit than Design$_2$ with L_1.

We later speculate about different design schemes and different languages, and how we believe they fare in terms of their impact on testability. We will also talk about how different function classes (that are commonly programmed) fare in terms of testability. For example, is there any difference in the testability for a one-to-one function as compared to a Boolean function, or is it only the implementation, design, and language that impact the resulting code's testability? These are difficult questions, and very little research has been done or substantiated; however, we will suggest clues that have been shown from repeated use of the PIE model (see Chapter 2).

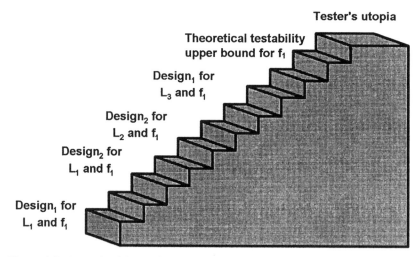

Figure 4-1. Example of the "staircase" conjecture with three languages and two designs.

TESTABILITY ANALYSIS WITHOUT THE CODE

Figure 4-2 shows a rough interpretation of the phases of the software life cycle. As we know, a lot of stopping, starting, and returning to earlier phases of the cycle occurs during development; software development is not as smooth a process as Figure 4-2 suggests. Instead there is much backtracking, particularly as mistakes from earlier phases appear in later phases or requirements are changed. Each forward arrow in Figure 4-2 can represent significant cost, and hence the further you backtrack, the more forward arrows you must re-traverse.

The previous two chapters have dealt with testability assessment *after* you have the code; their algorithms assumed that the code and D existed. This means that nearly half of the life-cycle phases (requirements, specification, design, and code) cannot have those algorithms applied directly during them, because the first four phases do not contain completed code. To have any hope of designing for increased testability, we must create different algorithms and heuristics to help make decisions as to what designs are generally better or worse for both system level testability and unit level testability. Without new heuristics, designing for increased testability before programming begins will not be possible.

Prior to having the code, even though we may have D, determining what impact D will have on S is virtually impossible. So we will search for clues in the information contained in the requirements document, specification, or design document. Realize that a specification, requirements document, and design are simply different levels of abstraction that define the mathematical function that the software will compute. A program is another representation (of definition) of a mathematical function that is formalized in a progamming language. Because there are similarities between the information provided by the code and other functional descriptors if we can find a method for *statically* analyzing code for its testability, we should be able to use this method on the requirements, specification, and design to provide testability predictor measures. Expect that without D, these predictions will be far less precise than those from PIE.

A BRIEF LOOK AT INTEGRATED CIRCUIT DESIGN-FOR-TESTABILITY

Given that hardware design-for-test is a fairly "hardened" science, we should consider the concepts they employ before we begin creating software design-for-testability heuristics. After all, hardware and software are logically equivalent. As you will quickly see, hardware can suffer from classes of failures that are not related to logic problems or problems with illegal inputs, but rather with fatigue and physical decay, which are not associated with software failures. For this reason, the hardware design-for-test models that address these failure classes are not of interest to us here.

In a digital system, information can only take on discrete values at specific times; in an analog system, analog signals occur continuously and can have any value within certain constraints. A digital integrated circuit (IC) is composed of logical gates

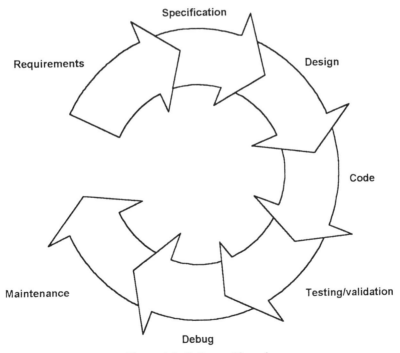

Figure 4-2. Software life cycle

and nodes, where each gate receives one or more input signals and produces one output signal, and a node is a location between gates through which digital values propagate. Each input and output signal to a gate or node is either a zero or one, hence we are only dealing with binary computations in digital integrated circuits.

Loosely speaking, the testability of a circuit refers to how easily a circuit can be "tested" to ensure that are no faults in it (Williams and Parker, 1982). Faults here take two general forms: circuit faults and node faults. Circuit fault classes that we test for in integrated circuits include the following: (1) A logical gate at some point in the circuit is the wrong gate for that point, or (2) some gate, due to fatigue, is not producing the correct output, even though it is the correct gate for that point in the circuit. An example of a node fault is a node whose value is stuck at one or stuck at zero, regardless of the stimulus (input pattern) to the circuit.

Testing for circuit and node faults is approached in two basic ways. First, a circuit can be probed to show that all connections are secure and power levels are correct at each point in the circuit. Second, randomly selected digital patterns are fed into the circuit, and the output patterns are verified; this is identical to random software testing. The manner by which digital circuits are sometimes tested is termed *controlling and observing*. *Controlling* refers to the ability to find input patterns that force some value to occur at some node within the circuit; *observing* refers to monitoring the effect that a node has on the output of the circuit, by controlling (fixing) all other nodes, to ensure that the node of interest is impacting the output correctly.

In order to "positively" show that a circuit is correct, you must feed every possible input pattern to the circuit, just like exhaustive testing in software. For a circuit with n distinct inputs, there are 2^n input patterns that must be tried. As for software, this is rarely feasible. The exhaustive testing problem led circuit designers to the concept of design-for-testability, to produce circuits that were easier to test. Circuit design-for-testability is approached in many ways, the most effective of which is termed *structured design-for-testability which uses the circuit to test itself*. This class of techniques includes exhaustive self-testing and random self-testing. Exhaustive self-testing partitions the circuit into small pieces that can be exhaustively tested; here the number of test patterns needed is reduced exponentially as the number of sections is increased. Of course the tradeoff here is the same as the difference in software system level testing and unit testing. Just because software units are thoroughly tested does not mean that there will not be problems at the system integration level. Random self-testing generates incomplete sets of test vectors to estimate an acceptably low probability of failure, much like the software probable correctness model that we described in Chapter 2.

There is one other approach in circuit design for testability that we should mention—that is, the *unstructured approach* which tries to identify potentially untestable portions of the circuit, much like the goal of the three algorithms given in Chapter 2. Testability analyzers have been developed that are used in early design stages to reduce the need for expensive testing costs after a circuit is built. As you will later see, even though there are differences between hardware and software, some of the ideas applied to circuits make excellent techniques to apply to software as well.

FUNCTION CLASSES

For completeness, we have given the reader a brief introduction to how IC designers attempt to handle the problem of exhaustive testing being infeasible through better design schemes. (Isn't it nice to know that our hardware counterparts are struggling with the same issues that we are!) It is interesting to note that although IC engineers consider testing on 2^n (for $n > 32$) input patterns as infeasible, in software, we are not that lucky. For us, $|I|$ will likely be far larger than 2^{32}. For example, for one 64-bit floating point value, $|I| = 2^{64}$, and for a program with four floating point input values, $|I| = 2^{256}$ (assuming all combinations are possible).

This chapter focuses on precoding phases; however, several of the static testability assessment techniques that you will discover in this chapter can also be applied to the code. In this section, we look at two sets of issues: how different function classes and different language classes affect the second and third conditions of the fault/failure model. Notice that we did not mention the first condition, the one most directly related to D. As it will turn out, we can only use information from the function description for the infection and propagation conditions. Whether D is available at the earlier life-cycle phases or not, you can still get a feeling for the first condition of the fault/failure model in a high-level and abstract manner by applying a static metric such as McCabe's cyclomatic complexity to the design; this will provide a rough feeling for how difficult it will be to perform coverage testing, particularly a scheme such as path testing.

We will categorize five classes of functions and their generalized testabilities; these categories are based on the ratio of the number of different input values possible to the number of different output values possible. For a specific function within a class, this will obviously depend on I, which may not be known, so determining a precise ratio may not be possible. The five classes are:

1. Many-to-one
2. One-to-one (and assuming that $|I|$ is very large)
3. Many-to-many (but not one to one)
4. Many-to-few (where few is greater than 2 but fixed)
5. Many-to-two (an example would be a Boolean function)

(Note that $|I|$ is assumed to be very large and exhaustive sampling may be infeasible.) A *many-to-one* function produces a fixed output value regardless of input value. A *one-to-one* function produces a unique output for each unique input. A *many-to-many* function produces an enormous number of different outputs (but there are at least two members of I that produce the same member of O), and a *many-to-few* function produces a fixed number of output values, where the number is greater than two. (The difference between many-to-many and many-to-few is vague, but essentially a function is many-to-few if we can statically determine the size of O, and if we cannot and the function is not one-to-one, then we label it as many-to-many.) A *many-to-two* function only has two different output values.

In general, a many-to-one function represents the tester's utopia, and an example would be an initialization statement at the top of a program like **a** := **0**. When we show that this works correctly once, we know that it always will be correct. Hence many-to-one functions are very high testability functions. (Note that for all of these function classes we have assumed that $|O| \le |I|$. Without this assumption, we would be allowing for nondeterministic functions, which we do not.)

One-to-one functions are generally the next highest testability functions, which are followed by many-to-many functions. An example of a many-to-many function would be one that takes in a 64-bit floating point value and outputs an array of 64-bit floating point values. The next highest testability class of functions is many to few, followed by many to two which are generally the worst. Let's now look at examples of each of these classes. A many-to-one function is essentially just $f(x) =$ constant. An example of a one to one function is $f(x) = x + 1$. For a many-to-many function, an example would be $f(x) = x$ div 10^6. An example of many-to-few would be $f(x)$ mod 10, and an example of many-to-two would be $f(x)$ x mod 2. Note that there are subtle differences between several of these categories, and we do not want to get bogged down in deciding exactly which class a specific function is a member of, because this determination is subjective. It is more important to note what this general ranking implies: *With the exception of the many-to-one function class, the smaller $|O|$, the worse the testability, and likewise the greater $|O|$, the better the testability.*

One question the reader might be asking at this point is: *How could so much go wrong by just adding one more output value to O—that is, many-to-one being the best for testability and many-to-two being the worst for testability?* Consider the following argument: Suppose you have a very complex program that prints either "heads" or "tails" at the end of a computation, and suppose that it produces a "heads" approximately 50% of the time and "tails" the other 50%. For a fair coin, the probability of getting heads is exactly 0.5, and tails is 0.5. Let's now start up that complicated computation on an input and see the output; but while we wait, let's take a coin and toss it and see what it produces. It is totally possible that our coin toss will result in the same output as the program. Why? Because there are only two output possibilities, and we may get lucky and get the same output as the software. In fact, over time, we should get the same output as the program about 50% of the time. So you see that having only two outputs that are equilikely can be successfully produced quite often by simply tossing a coin. Now imagine that you have a fault in the program. What do you think the chance is that you will frequently observe failure? This is hard to tell, but it could be "small," because the program could almost guess at what the output should be and it would be right at least 50% of the time.

Now suppose that your program, instead of only producing "heads" and "tails," is modified to produce one additional piece of internal information with each output: the value of some internal 64-bit real value. What do you suppose your chances are of guessing both the correct 64-bit real value and "heads" or "tails"? Pretty slim! Why? Because $|O|$ went from 2 to possibly $2^{64} + 2^{64}$, which is quite an increase. The moral to this story can be stated in the following conjecture: *The more precise the information, the harder it will be to "get lucky" and guess the correct information.* For software, this means that the more precise and detailed the output space of a program is, the harder it will be for the program to hide faults during testing. Fortunately, we can frequently determine how complex the output space is from a definition of the function to be implemented.

Given the conjecture just presented concerning precision, we now turn our attention to static methods for determining whether the second or third conditions of the fault/failure model are likely to occur. We will show the impact that increased precision has on these conditions and their probability of occurring. To begin, we introduce a software phenomenon termed "information loss" that strongly suggests the likelihood of data state error cancellation occurring. The degree to which this phenomenon occurs can be quantified by static analysis of the software, static analysis of the design, or manual inspection of the specification. This provides insight about the third condition of the fault/failure model occurring before the code is ever produced, which gives the ability to plan ahead in terms of where to allocate testing resources and to what degree. Information loss also provides some limited insight into whether the second condition will occur.

Information loss occurs when internal information computed by the program during execution is not communicated in the program's output. Information loss can be subdivided into two categories: implicit, and explicit. *Explicit information loss* occurs when variables are not validated either during execution or validated as output. The occurrence of explicit information loss can be easily observed using data flow techniques. Explicit information loss can be a result of information hiding, a design philosophy introduced by Parnas (1972). *Information hiding* is a design philosophy that does not allow information to leave modules that could be potentially misused by other modules, hence there is "good" evidence for why programmers would want to use it. The problem here is that although it is a good design principle, it is detrimental to testability, because it decreases the likelihood of the third condition occurring. As an example, if some temporary variable in a module is incorrect, and it is not able to transfer its incorrectness to any other variable leaving the module, then that problem will remain hidden from testers. We later propose a scheme where the negative effect of information hiding on testability is reduced while the design benefits of information hiding are preserved.

Another type of explicit information loss is *variable reuse*, where the value that a variable had during execution is overwritten with another value at a later time, and the original value no longer exists and hence cannot be checked. Variable reuse is commonly used both to update counters and save memory by reducing the number of statically declared variables. The classic example here is to declare a temporary variable and use it countless times throughout a program. Although variable reuse and information hiding have benefits, we are simply exposing the impact of these design decisions on testability, not judging whether these practices should be abandoned.

Implicit information loss occurs when two or more different incoming parameters are presented to a user-defined function or a built-in language operator and the same outgoing parameter is produced. An example of this is the integer division operator div x (where $x > 1$); for instance, 2 div 4 is equal to 3 div 4. After you perform such a calculation for the statement **x := x div 5** and get the result, 0, there is no way to determine what value of **x** existed before the calculation, partly because of variable reuse and partly from implicit information loss. Note that if you have a statement such as **x := x div 1**, there is explicit information loss according to our definition because there is variable reuse (however, this is a nonsense case), but div 1 is a one-to-one function, so there is no implicit information loss. Another example is $f(x) = x + 1$; there is no implicit information loss in f because it is also one-to-one.

In these two examples, the occurrence of implicit information loss can be observed by statically analyzing the code. If a specification indicates that a program is to take in 20 floating point values and produce a single Boolean output, then we also know that implicit information loss will occur in any implementation (assuming that the function is not a many-to-one function). Both program and function descriptions can provide insight to the amount of implicit information loss that will occur.

Clues suggesting some degree of the implicit information loss that may occur during execution may be visible from a program's specification via a metric termed the *domain/range ratio* (DRR). Recall that the exact degree to which implicit information loss occurs during execution will be related to D which we cannot use. The domain/range ratio is the ratio of the cardinality of the domain of the specification to the cardinality of the range of the specification. Note how closely related this metric is to the previous five classes of functions that we defined. For simplicity, we denote the cardinality of the domain as a and the cardinality of the range as b. This ratio may not always be directly visible from the specification, or there may be subranges on certain input variables that are unknown, forcing you to take the position that all values are possible. The types of functional descriptions for which we can estimate a DRR vary: unary operators, binary operators, expressions, software designs, and so on. Note also that if the program is incorrect, the cardinality of the range of the program may be different than b.

DRRs roughly predict the degree of implicit information loss that will occur. Generally as the DRR of the specification decreases, the potential for implicit information loss occurring within an implementation of that specification increases, and hence the likelihood of propagation occurring decreases, and hence the testability decreases. When $a > b$, this suggests that faults are more likely to remain undetected during testing than when $a = b$.

An interesting clue concerning whether implicit information loss will occur is whether we can invert the function and determine an input from an output. For example, for a one-to-one function, this is possible. If $f(x) = x + 1$ produces a value of 6, then **x** had a value of 5. But with $f(x) = x \bmod 2$ producing a value of 0, there are many different values that **x** may have had. Another example is $f(x) = \tan(x)$, which can have many different values of **x** that result in the same $f(x)$, but $\tan^{-1}(x)$ is not a one-to-one function. The simple rule to think about during design follows: *All functions that do not map exactly one element of the domain to one element of the range lose information that uniquely identifies the input that produced the output.* This *nondeterminism* of the inverted function should be a warning that testability will be reduced by implementations of the original (noninverted) function, and this gives the development team a rough indication of how far away they can expect to be from the tester's utopia.

Not only do DRRs suggest the likelihood of data state error cancellation occurring, but they also suggest the likelihood of infection not occurring. For example, div 5 and div 4 are frequently the same result, and this shows an example of where the function itself is incorrect but infection does not occur for incoming values such as 0, 1, 2, and 3. Implicit information loss also suggests that the second condition may also be less likely to occur during testing.

CONDITIONAL EXPRESSIONS

We now wish to explore the effect of conditional expressions on software testability. If we ignore the possibility of side effects occurring in a decision location (such as is allowed by a language such as C), then the only variable of the data state affected at a decision location is the program counter. Given that a decision either evaluates to TRUE or FALSE, then there are only two output values for the program counter. The DRR of a decision then is $|I|$:2.

To get a feeling for why decision locations are terrific places to hide faults or hide the faults of other locations, consider the following example:

```
if (a > 5) and (b > 100) then
      [Computation Block A]
else
      [Computation Block B];
```

First, you could write the decision to include faults such as **if (a >= 5)** and **(b >= 100)** or **if (a > 10)** and **(b > 101)**. Such faults will remain masked for long sequences of executions for large values of **a** and **b**, because infection will be quite unlikely. Furthermore, the original location (or any of these faults) can "partially" hide faults from other locations if incorrect values reside in **a** or **b**; this can occur by not causing the incorrect program counter value to be assigned. For instance, if **a** is 500 and **b** is 500, but their values should both be 450 before this decision location, the decision will still result in TRUE.

At this point, it may seem that many functions and constructs are so detrimental to testability that they should be avoided. Nonsense! We firmly recognize the three constructs on which all computation is based: *assignment*, *decision*, and *iteration*, and that even though decision locations may be troublesome to testability, they are a fundamental and needed capability in all programming languages. It is observations such as those just shown with decision locations that led to the conjecture that functions have an upper limit to the confidence that can be achieved via testing their implementations. For instance, there will be functions that, no matter how implemented, may require an enormous number of decision locations. If true, then specialized testing schemes such as boundary value testing or path testing might be necessary to lessen the likelihood that the decision locations are masking faults. The use of functions such as div and mod also suggest potential problems, which may be overcome through the use of particular quality assessment methods, such as inspections or formal verification.

INTEGER VERSUS FLOATING POINT OPERATORS

We have shown examples of how different operators such as mod and div can often be detrimental to testability because they can easily stop the second and third conditions from occurring. We have also shown how functions that have a smaller |O| generally have lower testabilities. We now wish to do a similar comparison between integer and floating-point operators.

We begin with an example: Suppose that **x** should have a value of 20, but has a value of 21, and this incorrect value is input to the integer function **a := x div 50**. The result will of course be 0 for **a**. Now suppose that instead we had used the statement **a := x/50**. Because 20/50 ≠ 21/50, **a** would now become infected, and an increase in the size of the fault set will have occurred, not because of a fault in the statement, but because of an incorrect value for **x** coming into the statement. This example shows that floating-point operators are better at exposing faults than are integer operators, which follows from our previous conjecture on precision and testability: The more precise, the less likely faults will hide. The tradeoff is that floating-point variables require more memory and are slower to compute; hence an increase in testability is not attained for free.

In terms of the impact of real versus integer on the third reason that a location can hide a fault, we have shown examples such as **x := x div 50**, where if **x** was incorrect coming into this statement, it may be "corrected" after the statement is executed, which stops the propagation condition (decreases the fault set size). What a statement such as **x := x div 50** strongly suggests is that, rather than being likely to hide a fault within itself, it is likely to hide a fault in the statement where **x** was last assigned. Static analysis of the code can be detect statements such as this, and static backtracking from a statement of this form will suggest where in the code a fault is likely to remain hidden because of this statement. We are not suggesting that integer calculations should be avoided and replaced with floating-point calculations, but rather that integer operators should be recognized for their increased ability to hide faults. Also, this example again shows explicit information loss *combined* with implicit information loss, which is a very difficult problem to test against.

DEAD VARIABLES

At any point during execution, the data state contains a set of (value variable) pairs. Some of these variables may no longer have any possible impact on the computation from that point forward, because their values will never again be referenced by any future computation, and hence we have referred to these variables as *dead*. (Note that this is a slightly different and enhanced definition for the term *dead* than most compiler books mean when they define dead code or dead variables.) At the point where this occurs, we have another form of explicit information loss, because even though that information may still exist in the current scope, semantically it is as if it did not exist in the scope. Hence dead variables, although they have no potential impact on the computation at the point where they "die," are an indicator of where erroneous data values will become hidden, and hence they are static indicators of where faults can hide. (Note of course that there is a difference between static deadness and dynamic deadness; it is D that truly determines deadness.)

We should point out that even though the data state may contain many variables that are infected, suggesting infection and propagation occurred often during previous computations, if these variables die without transferring their incorrectness to other variables which have remained "live," then the net gain to testability is nil. It would be prudent to run static analysis to find where during computation variables die, and insert self-tests or probes at those points to determine if those variables were infected. If you are able to determine what value or range of values a variable should have before it becomes dead, it will certainly increase your confidence during testing, but this will not always be practical.

DESIGN RECOMMENDATIONS

On the list of easily identifiable *static* software and specification characteristics that suggest lower testability we have (1) variable reuse, (2) implicit information loss, and (3) information hiding. We will now show ways of overcoming the negative effect on testability that each of these incur. As previously stated, these recommendations may be at the expense of other software characteristics.

Minimizing variable reuse is the simplest problem of the three to overcome. Simply declare more variables and quit reusing them. This means increased memory requirements and possibly reduced code readability. Another way to decrease explicit information loss without reducing information hiding is to "simulate" the effect of decreased information hiding during testing via internal self-tests or by simply outputting more internal information during testing (making local variables into out parameters). Hoffman (1989) recommends inserting assertions to check internal information dynamically. Regardless of the method used, more of the information that is produced dynamically will be checked, and that must increase the confidence that faults are not hiding. (Recall our coin tossing remedy.)

A self-test for an internal variable may either state exactly what value the variable should have for a given input, or it may provide a range of possible values. If a self-test fails, a warning is produced. This has the effect of increasing the range, and hence lowering the DRR. As you may recall from the coin flipping analogy, once we needed to also guess at that correct 64-bit value in addition to whether "heads" or "tails" came up, we were much less likely to guess at the correct output. Well the same holds true here, and by finding means of checking more internal information during validation, you automatically decrease the likelihood of faults hiding, and hence increase the testability.

Note the tradeoff here: Validating more internal information requires more precision in the specification as to what the internal computations should be, which increases the cost of the requirements and specification phases. But the benefit is that we have increased our confidence that the smallest chain of black balls is reasonably long, and there can be a big savings in that phase. Thus the unfortunate reality for us as testers may actually be the following: *Until we can specify formally more information about the internal computations that must occur during imple-*

mentation of the function we desire, testing to higher levels of reliability will not be feasible. If you stop and think about it, this conjecture is actually very reasonable. If you have evidence that the internal computations in your program are correct, then you have much more confidence that the program itself is correct.

We are not suggesting that it is easy to lessen the effects of information hiding, nor that during execution information should flow freely. We feel that during testing, however, we need better information about the internal computations of the modules and functions, and internal probes and assertions can provide us with such an ability. (An example of this is the language Eiffel.) Recall the earlier discussion concerning IC controllability and observability; this is exactly what is done in digital circuits to improve the testing of them. Not only do IC testers check the entire circuit using random input patterns, but as we described, they control various nodes in the circuit and determine what impact that node had on the output through their controlling. What we are arguing for is a similar notion in software modules, but observing the internal computations of software units. Berglund (1979) states that the principal obstacle in testing large-scale ICs is the inaccessibility of the internal signals. One method used for increasing observability in IC design is to increase the pin count of a chip (increase $|O|$), allowing the extra pins to carry out additional internal signals that can be checked during testing. These output pins increase observability by increasing the range of potential bit strings from the chip.

Freedman (1991) gives a more complex development concerning testability. Freedman bases his definitions of testability on controllability and observability. He states, "an evaluation of expression procedure $F(E)$ is controllable, if, for any state s, the domain of values of the evaluation map equals the domain of values denoted by its output specification." He also states, "F is observable if: $F(B_1, \ldots, B_n) \neq F(A_1, \ldots, A_n)$ implies $(B_1, \ldots, B_n) \neq (A_1, \ldots, A_n)$." Using our terminology, Freedman's controllability is a special term for a DRR of 1:1 and his observability characteristic formalizes the notion of a deterministic function without state memory between calls. The main difference between Freedman's approach and the DRR is that the DRR assumes observability.

Another design recommendation for improving unit testing resource allocation based on the DRR follows: Given that the DRR of the function to be computed is fixed, the overall amount of information loss is also likely to be fixed. This, however, does not suggest that you do not have tradeoffs during design at the subfunction level. It would be prudent to isolate high-DRR subfunctions away from other subfunctions when the specification is being partitioned. Why? To isolate those modules that may be problematic before coding begins. This will enable a more accurate allocation of unit testing resources to the units that are more likely to hide faults at the system level, and hence need additional unit testing or other methods applied.

To enable better partitioning of a specification into *subspecifications* (what will become modules), we define three categories of DRRs:

1. Variable-domain variable range (VDVR): many-to-many, one-to-one
2. Variable-domain fixed range (VDFR): many-to-one, many-to-few, many-to-two
3. Fixed-domain fixed range (FDFR)

An FDFR DRR is one where $|I|$ is finite and the size of this set is such that exhaustive sampling is feasible. For example, for a module that takes in five Boolean variables there are 2^5 different values to test. Another nice characteristic of FDFR DRR modules is that they are totally reusable, in that they can be shown to be correct from testing.

A VDFR DRR module is one where $|I|$ is effectively infinite, in that we could never dream of sampling all members of I, but $|O|$ is very limited, much like a Boolean function. With the exception of the "extreme" function, many-to-one, this type of module will be problematic, and even though we may not be able to avoid designing systems with this type of module, its use should be watched carefully. This class of function includes operators such as **mod 2** and integer operators such as **div x (x >1)**.

A VDVR DRR module is one where $|I|$ and $|O|$ are effectively infinite. This is the class of functions such as one-to-one. Because $|O|$ is so large, we no longer worry about the situation of simply guessing and getting the correct member of O.

A MULTIPHASE TESTABILITY METHODOLOGY

We are now ready to detail a methodology for assessing high quality in our software that is based on: (1) the algorithms of Chapter 2, (2) additional specification information (possibly beyond what the original specification directly stated), (3) injected assertions into the code (based on this additional specification-derived information) once testability analysis is performed, and (4) the "squeeze play" model. Taken together, this methodology combines testing, testability, and assertions (which are a "quasi" formal verification at a microscopic syntax level) into a development methodology for critical software. For most programs, this combination of techniques will be the only practical means for assessing high levels of reliability via the squeeze play model, because for large systems there may be many locations with very low testabilities. When there are many locations with very low testabilities, there must be a way to ignore those values because testing to their levels is not feasible. This methodology will impact the specification, coding, and testing phases of the life cycle, and hence we term it as being a "multiphase" methodology.

Hecht (1993) has indicated that rarely encountered faults may be the dominant cause of safety and mission critical failures. Rarely encountered faults can hide for long periods of time even while a system is undergoing testing and debugging that is aimed at reliability improvement. If just one rare fault has the potential to lead to a catastrophic failure, then we would have a reliable, *unsafe* system. Hence the goal of this assertion-placement model is to reduce the likelihood of *any* fault hiding in the system, by attacking the program at its "weakest" points with assertions.

This scheme has costs; those costs include (1) the decrease in performance during testing, (2) the costs of performing testability analysis, and (3) the cost of deriving assertions from the specification. Also, if the assertions are removed before the code is deployed, there will be a slight, additional cost. But for critical systems, if a value-added benefit can be demonstrated relative to cost for a scheme, the scheme cannot be automatically dismissed. By combining white-box analysis via testability analysis, black-box analysis via testing, and specification based testing via assertions, we may be able to actually assess a high confidence that faults are not hiding during the testing.

Recall from the squeeze play model that when $\theta = \alpha$ and when we test the appropriate number of times, we gain a confidence that the true probability of failure is 0.0. But when θ is very low, it is unlikely that we will be able to test to the level required to get α to θ. The question then is, "Why is θ so low?" If we could alleviate our concern about the location causing θ and be convinced that there is no problem at this location, then we could raise θ to the next most worrisome location, and so forth, in this stepwise manner until we reached a θ that we could test down to.

Assertions provide the ability to ignore low θ's, *if* we can get a correct assertion about what is supposed to occur at the location where we are observing a low testability and we are able to execute that location. (Recall that one of the problems in isolating faults stems from an inability to assert exactly what should be at a location, because of the infinite number of different correct programs for a single specification.) If the low testability is a direct result of a low execution estimate, then adding assertions is not useful, since they too will not be executed, and an assertion that is not executed adds nothing to the confidence that the location is not hiding a fault. Hence we are limited in the value of assertions, and they are only helpful in this method for locations with low infection or propagation estimates.

Our methodology is as follows: (1) Perform the PIE algorithms on the code when it is complete, and create a list, L, of the locations whose testabilities are lower than we can test down to (call this threshold e). (2) Go back to the specification phase and from the specification, find assertions for each location in L (this will be expensive and difficult). (3) Place the assertions into the program. (4) Test the program

$$N = \ln (1 - C) / \ln (1 - e)$$

times with the injected assertions in it, and do not consider a test case to have produced the correct output if either (1) the output is incorrect or (2) an assertion failed. Now with N executions and no output failures nor failed assertions, we have confidence C that our code is not hiding faults. Admittedly, N may not be nearly large enough to satisfy the θ's that are less than e, but that is a situation we cannot fix. The hope is that the assertions provide enough confidence that ignoring the low θ's is acceptable.

The idea of assertions is simply a twist on the common practice of inserting write statements in code during debugging when a program has failed. Debugging tools allow users to select particular variables and view what values they contain during an execution. Here, the programmer acts as the assertion and decides if the value that some variable has during an execution is clean or infected.

This methodology is based on the availability of correct assertions; without such the methodology will be less practical. But even if we cannot find correct assertions, there are several alternatives that are still available to us that can be used in a similar capacity. First, if the specification cannot be decomposed to the level of what should occur at some location, the programmers could be allowed to insert assertions from their understanding of the specification. The obvious problem is that if they do not understand the code well enough to write it correctly, then it is unlikely they will produce correct assertions. Second, manual inspections could be substituted for assertions, or possibly a formal walkthrough of a small section of the code could be performed. Third, a manual proof for some small section of code containing the low testability location could occur to prove that small section of the code is correct.

In short, finding assertions should not be a particularly difficult process; finding the correct assertion will be much more difficult.

LANGUAGE CLASSES

We now turn our attention to language issues, and here we shift into "speculation mode," because we are still unsure about how a particular language affects testability. Hence we only speculate on how different language classes *may* affect testability. To begin with, our observations using Reliable Software Technology Corporation's *PiSCES* 1.1 have only been on C programs, and hence we think that from that analysis we have a fairly good feeling about procedural languages. We have no empirical experience with functional programming languages, or with object-oriented languages; however, we do have enough of an understanding of several factors that are detrimental to testability, and hence our discussions will be based on those (see Figure 4–3).

From what you have seen, it should be clear that object-oriented languages, which encourage encapsulation and information hiding, will be more difficult to system level test and gain confidence that faults are not hiding. Certainly, object-orient-

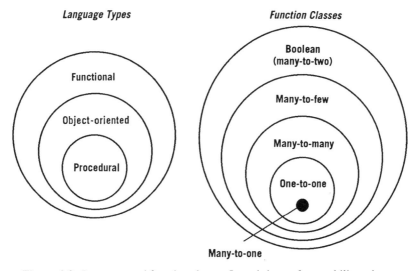

Figure 4-3. Language and function classes. Inner is better for testability, whereas outer is worse.

ed (OO) languages enable the building of small components that are beneficial to software reuse. Here is one of the design tradeoffs that we have been alluding to: reusability versus testability for OO systems.

Functional programming languages are an interesting language class. The interesting widget concerning them is their lack of memory usage; they continually return values from functions as inputs to other function calls. For example, consider the expression: **(a(b(c(d))))**. Here, **c** is called with parameter **d**, which is input to **b**, whose output is input to **a**. In this calling hierarchy, information is continually being overwritten, and our ability to get our hands on the information is quickly lost as the scope changes. This produces speculation that functional programming languages are worse that procedural languages, but of course almost any program that can be written in a functional language such as LISP can be written in the same manner in C, so this is very difficult to justify. Also, functional programming languages provide recursion; recursive programs tend to fail quickly if the recursion mechanism is improperly programmed, suggesting that fault classes that are related to the recursion mechanism should have faults members of large size. The implicit information loss associated with functional languages does suggest, however, that there are fault classes associated with the flow of information for which the propagation condition will be weakened.

EXAMPLES

We will now look at two examples of different functions and how the fault/failure model might be impacted. Note that we say "might" because we do not assume knowledge of *D*.

Consider the following segment:

```
      read(a);
      if a ≥ 5 then
          a := a + 1;
and several coding options:

                if a = 5 then
                    a := a + 1;
                if a = 6 then
                    a := a + 1;          /* Alternative
        A */
                if a = 7 then
                    a := a + 1;
                /* and so forth */
        and
                if a = 5 then
                    a := a + 1;
                else if a = 6 then
                    a := a + 1;          /* Alternative B */
                else if a = 7 then
                        a := a + 1;
                /* and so forth */
```

Several pieces of testability information about the original segment are easily identified: (1) The relational operator could be detrimental to the infection condition, (2) the one-to-one function is excellent for the infection condition, and (3) the decision may be detrimental to the execution probability of the one-to-one function; without *D* we can merely speculate. In alternative A, we expect a higher infection probability for each of the decisions (a relation where two items must be equal is harder to hide faults in than one involving an inequality); however, we will have a lower execution probability for the individual one-to-one functions than the one-to-one function in the original segment. In both alternative A and the original segment, note that each of the conditions will have a 1.0 execution probability. For alternative B, we have used **else** clauses, which will lower the execution probabilities for the decisions (once one of the decisions has been satisfied). This is interesting; it shows that the order in which the conditions are coded can impact the execution probabilities of the conditionals, and hence the testability of the code. Care should be taken when **else** clauses are applied, because of their ability to "short-circuit" execution. Given several decisions that are coded into a block of the form **if ( ) then [ ] else if ( ) then [ ] else if ( ) then else . . .** , we would prefer that the initial decisions are those that are expected to have lower infection probabilities than the others. We are not suggesting that either alternative presented here is practical, but rather how different programming options affect the likelihood of faults hiding.

Consider next the assignment statement **x := x mod 2**. One strange but correct implementation of this statement is

```
read(x);
temp := x;
while temp > 1 do
temp := temp - 2;
x:= temp;
```

We are not suggesting that any operation as simple as **x mod 2** should be implemented in this manner; we are merely emphasizing tradeoffs. In this example, it is more likely that faults would occur in the while loop body or loop termination condition. For instance, **while temp > 2** will not be caught for an input value of x = 3. The mistake, **temp := temp - 1**, would not be caught for all odd values of **x**. However, there are no inputs (x > 0) for which these two faults together will not be detected. This example suggests that even though there are language operators that are detrimental to testability, it is not necessarily advantageous to implement them ourselves; our implementations can themselves be wrought with problems that the language-supplied operators are not. The real issue in using language-supplied operators that we know enable fault hiding is whether that is the operator that we really need. If it is, then the fact that testability may be decreased is not a concern.

We have shown two small examples and their respective abilities to hide faults. From our experience and as these examples suggest, attempts to improve one condition of the fault/failure model for some block of code may damage one of the other conditions of the fault/failure model for that block. This does not mean that different implementations should not be tried, but it does lend support to the conjecture that there is a theoretical upper bound for the function to be computed that is inescapable. For example, implementation A may have a better infection profile than implementation B, but B may have a better execution profile. To properly decide between the two, it will be necessary to decide which component of the fault/failure model is more worrisome.

SUMMARY

The DRR metric allows software designers to gain immediate insights into how difficult a program will be to test, whether at the module or system level. The fact that the DRR and the second and third conditions of the fault/failure model are related is provocative; it implies that we are limited in our ability to gain confidence in the absence of faults via testing for certain functions that cannot be exhaustively tested nor proven correct. It also implies that we can have very crude approximations as to whether our resulting program will suffer from short strings of black balls in the urn, because of the relationship between the specification and how it affects ball chaining.

We have speculated about how different language classes affect testability, and we hope that in future years we will have more sound information to provide to the reader. We have also looked at different design heuristics that we feel have been demonstrated to be techniques that enhance testability. But once again, we have also speculated here and hope that research someday shows our conjectures to be true.

EXERCISES

1. Given that your assignment is to implement some function and you have the choice of using either recursion or iteration, what do you think the testability tradeoffs will be in making this decision? (*Note*: Ignore all other concerns; only consider the impact of your decision on testability.)

2. Assume that we have a simple choice between two implementations (a) and (b) of a simple function, $f(x) := a + 1$ (for $a \geq 0$):

   (a)
   ```
   read (a);
   write (a + 1)
   ```
   (b)
   ```
   read (a);
   if (a = 0) then write (a + 1)
   else if (a = 1) then write('a + 1)
   else if (a = 2) then write(a + 1)
   else if (a = 3) then write(a + 1)
   else if (a = 4) then write(a + 1)
   else if (a = 5) then write(a + 1)
           and so forth.
   ```

In implementation (b), each branch represents a partitioning of the urn with only one input in it, so each subdomain is exhaustively testable and represents the tester's utopia (FDFR); the problem, however, is that there are many subdomains. Implementation (a) represents a one-to-one function, but does not represent the tester's utopia (VDVR). For example, we could replace the correct expression with the incorrect expression **a * a + 1**, and for a = 0 we would get the correct output. Given these two extremes, no partitioning and total partitioning to subdomains of size 1, can you think of a better way to partition this problem in order to create a more realistic number of subdomains that are closer to the tester's utopia than implementation (a)?

REFERENCES

N. C. Berglund. "Level-Sensitive Scan Design Tests Chips, Boards, System." *Electronics,* 52(6), 108–110, March 15, 1979.

R. S. Freedman. "Testability of Software Components," *IEEE Transactions on Software Engineering* SE-17, 553–465, 1991.

J. H. Gallier. *Logic for Computer Science Foundations of Automatic Theorem Proving.* New York: Harper & Row, 1986.

H. Hecht. "Rare Conditions: An Important Cause of Failure." In: *Proceedings of the 8th Annual Conference on Computer Assurance.* Gaithersburg, MD: National Institute of Standards and Technology, June 1993, 81–85.

D.M. Hoffman. "Hardware Testing and Software ICs." In: *Proceedings of the Pac-ific Northwest Software Quality Conference,* 234–244, 1989.

D. L. Parnas. "On Criteria to be Used in Decomposing Systems into Modules." *Communications of the ACM* 14(1), 221–227, April 1972.

T. W. Williams and K. P. Parker. "Design for Testability—A Survey." *IEEE Transactions on Computers* C-31, 2–13, January 1982.

CHAPTER 5

Software Safety

In Chapter 3, we introduced how software testability can be employed in assessing software safety. In this chapter, we place software safety into a broader context. Software safety is a system problem, not merely a software problem. Furthermore, in any real-world scenario, the resources available for the analysis of software safety are limited. The key to successful assessment of software safety is to cut the task down to size by identifying those parts of the software that are truly safety critical and concentrate on those parts. When safety analysis starts out, it has to be assumed that all of the software is safety-critical. But after the safety hazards are identified, we can start the process of narrowing down just what parts of the design are safety critical. Because non-safety-critical ("safety independent") parts of the code can interact with safety-critical parts of the code, the software safety analyst is only entitled to ignore the safety-independent parts after he or she makes certain that the design insulates the safety-critical parts from the safety-independent parts.

This chapter puts software safety assessment into a system perspective and discusses the front end of the safety process: identification of hazards followed by backward threading to successively narrow down the safety-critical requirements. The design elements to which the safety-critical requirements are allocated become safety-critical. The firewall concept and its implementation are described for isolating and protecting safety-critical design elements from safety-independent design elements. The assessment of the safety-critical design elements themselves is described in Chapter 6.

SYSTEM SAFETY

Terminology

Risk is the possibility of something undesired occurring. Usually this refers to harm to persons, property, or the environment, but can refer to any tangible or intangible loss. Safety is relative freedom from those risks. Risk is measured by considering the likelihood (or frequency) of the undesired events and the magnitude of the attendent losses.

A *mishap* is an unintended event or series of events that results in a loss. An informal synonym would be "accident." Examples of mishaps associated with a nuclear weapon system would include accidental launch of a nuclear missile, damage requiring repair or replacement of the weapon, the unplanned destruction of a nuclear weapon, the radioactive contamination of a nuclear installation and its vicinity, and a nuclear missile boomeranging back to friendly territory. A mishap for an air traffic control system would be a collision between aircraft or between an aircraft and the terrain. For a chemical-processing plant, mishaps include intoxication and burns to personnel.

A *hazard* is a state of a system or physical situation that, when combined with certain environmental conditions, could lead to a mishap. No accident or loss has necessarily occurred. A hazard is a prerequisite to a mishap: Whenever the hazard is present, the possibility of a mishap exists. Safety is defined in terms of hazards rather than mishaps because mishaps are caused by multiple factors, and only some of those factors may be controlled by the system in question. The existence of a hazardous state does not mean that a mishap is inevitable. For example, if an air traffic system (including the human controller) allows minimum separation standards to be violated, a mishap becomes possible. If a pair of aircraft were separated by, say 1000 feet, then a collision would be impossible. Even when separation standards are violated, a mishap (collision) may still be avoided if one or both pilots are sufficiently alert and skillful. In some cases a mishap is avoided by sheer luck.

RISK ASSESSMENT

Quantitatively, risk is a composite of the probability and severity of loss. The reason that risk is quantified is to allow hazards to be ranked for prioritizing later control and mitigation.

If mishaps from different hazards are in uniform units such as dollars or deaths, then we can employ the concept of "expected loss" to compare risks with one. For instance, if we in studying accident statistics adopt "probability of death per person per year" as our unit of loss, the risk of getting killed from lightning turns out to be 5/4 the risk of succumbing to a tornado. Likewise, if the unit of loss is "one dollar," we can quantify risk as expected monetary loss. If the probability is 0.00003 of an accident that results in a financial loss of $50,000, then the risk is $(0.00003)(50,000) = 1.5$. If the probability of a different accident is 0.0015 resulting in a loss of $2000, then the risk is $(0.0015)(2000) = 3.0$, which is twice as bad.

In many cases the risks involve mixtures of monetary and nonmonetary losses, and we will not be able to express risk in terms of a common unit. In this case, risk can be expressed as an ordered pair: (*probability of mishap, severity of mishap*). Risk is not defined in terms of the probability of the hazard. However, to arrive at the probability of a mishap you might go through the steps of calculating the probability of the hazard and then the probability of the mishap occurring given that the hazardous state exists.

The severity of that worst credible mishap is often classified by categories. MIL-STD-882 (military), NHB 5300.4 (NASA), and DOE 5481 (nuclear) prescribe different categorizations. Here is a composite:

I. **Catastrophic.** Personnel: death (as a direct result). Facilities/equipment/vehicles: system loss, repair impractical, requires salvage or replacement. Severe environmental damage.

II. **Critical.** Personnel: severe injury/illness; requires admission to a health care facility (lengthy convalescence and/or permanent impairment). Facilities/equipment/vehicles: major system damage. Loss of primary mission capability. Major environmental damage.

III. **Marginal.** personnel: minor injury/illness (medical treatment but no permanent impairment). Loss of any nonprimary mission capability. Minor environmental damage.

IV. **Negligible.** personnel: superficial injury/illness (little or no first-aid treatment). Lost time is less than one day. Less than minor system or environmental damage.

Hazard or mishap probability is often categorized into several qualitative levels. Here is a composite of the levels appearing in safety standards:

A. **Frequent**—likely to occur repeatedly during the life cycle of the system
B. **Probable**—likely to occur several times in the life cycle of the system
C. **Occasional**—likely to occur sometime in the life cycle of the system
D. **Remote**—not likely to occur in the life cycle of the system, but possible
E. **Improbable**—probability of occurrence cannot be distinguished from zero; a credible mishap event cannot be established
F. **Impossible**—physically or logically impossible to occur

These frequencies would typically be derived from modeling or historical data from similar systems.

Note that risks change over time. Subtle, gradual changes within a system and in a system's environment can decrease or, more usually, increase risks.

In addition to technological means of controlling risk, risk can be managed through legal means, such as by insurance or by a contractor indemnifying a subcontractor, or by financial means, such as by setting aside a contingency fund to cover losses.

SOFTWARE SAFETY

Software by itself is harmless (unless a big listing were to fall on your foot). In isolation, it cannot do physical damage. You cannot tell whether it is safe by looking at it or by measuring it in some way; safety is not an intrinsic property of the software. You have to consider the software in the context of the system and environment in which it is embedded in space and time. For instance, a software module in a database application may not have any safety ramifications. But that same software module, when embedded in a satellite navigation system, could be safety critical.

Software safety includes the delayed impacts of nonoperational software, too. For example, a software failure in a computer-aided design (CAD) system used in the design of a bridge can lead to a structural failure when the bridge is built. In other cases, wrong business and public policy decisions can be made on the basis of information furnished by flawed software. Similarly, a failure in support software such as an assembler, compiler, linker, or math routine library can impact a vital program's later execution.

Standards are increasingly appearing on the subject of software safety.

Avionics

The RTCA (Requirements and Technical Concepts for Aviation) Committee SC-167 is responsible for the preparation and revision of standards for the certification of avionics software. They published a document DO-178 "Software Considerations in Airborne Systems and Equipment Certification" in 1982. They revised this in coordination with the European Organization for Civil Aviation Electronics (EURO-CAE), published as DO-178A in 1985. They undertook a further review and revision, which resulted in the issuance of a new document, DO-178B, in December 1992. In 1993, the Federal Aviation Administration issued an Advisory Circular stating that DO-178B can be used as the basis for submitting material required to obtain FAA approval of software.

A standard for microwave landing systems, imposing formal methods, is in draft form.

Automotive

The Motor Industry Software Reliability Association, a UK consortium of vehicle and Component Manufacturers, are producing a set of guidelines for producing safe embedded onboard software.

Department of Defense

Software safety is mandated for software that follows DOD-STD-2167A, the Defense Standard for Software Development, which states: "Safety analysis. The contractor shall perform the analysis necessary to ensure that the software requirements, design, and operating procedures minimize the potential for hazardous conditions during the operational mission. Any potentially hazardous conditions or operating procedures shall be clearly identified and documented." The standard's successor, MIL-STD-498, expands these requirements.

An attachment to MIL-STD-882B Notice 1 specifically mandates software safety activities. In 882C, software is included in the system safety program. Many more-specific standards exist—for example, AFR122-3 Air Force Nuclear Safety Certification Program, AFR122-9 Nuclear Surety Design Certification for Nuclear Weapon

System Software and Firmware, and AFR122-10 Safety Design and Evaluation Criteria for Nuclear Weapon Systems.

The United Kingdom Ministry of Defence Mod-Std-0055 imposes formal methods and limitations on software complexity. Mod-Std-0056 addresses hazard assessment.

Nuclear Power Plants

IEC-880 provides detailed software standards.

A SOFTWARE SAFETY PROGRAM

In a formal software safety program, the developer maintains a competently staffed organization specifically responsible for software safety. Management issues a policy directive and assigns responsibilities. Upper management's sincere commitment and personal involvement are crucial. The organization analyzes the safety of the software and ensures that safety is built into the design and implementation. For success, the safety organization must be granted a sufficient level of autonomy and authority, but the program manager has the ultimate responsibility for safety. It is important to keep records of the analyses and other findings to create a "paper trail."

The purpose of a system safety program—and hence software safety program—is *to eliminate hazards or reduce their associated risk to an acceptable level.* System safety engineering provides methods for identifying, tracking, evaluating and removing hazards associated with a system and ensures that safety is designed into the system in a timely, cost-effective manner, that the risk created by operator error is minimized, and that the potential effects (damage) in the event of a mishap are minimized.

What happens inside a computer's memory, processor, and so forth, is safe. Software is only capable of causing or contributing to a hazard through its output (or lack of output). This output is a flow of data or a control signal. Some other part of the system is a user (client in a broad sense) of the service that a piece of software provides. The client depends on that software and the software does not produce the required output when needed by the client. More specifically, software can cause or contribute to a hazard by:

- Not performing a function required—never executing the function or otherwise failing to produce an output (*omission*).
- Performing a function not required, including repeating a procedure or procedural step; adding unnecessary, uncalled-for steps to a sequence, or substituting an erroneous step (*commission*).
- Performing a function out-of-sequence: A known and planned function occurs but at the wrong time; failing to ensure that two operations happen at the same time or at different times or in a particular order.

- Failure to recognize a hazardous condition requiring corrective action.
- Inadequate response to a contingency.
- Wrong decision as a solution to a problem that arises.
- Poor timing, resulting in a response that is too late or too soon for an adverse situation; failure to cease an operation at the appropriate time. (Leveson, 1986)

RELIABILITY VERSUS SAFETY

Safety is a property of an executing program, just like reliability. In software reliability, every failure is taken into account: an error in the eleventh digit of a calculation is generally counted the same as a failure that results in an injury, because reliability is concerned with the frequency of failure. Each failure also has a severity associated with its consequences. Reliability looks at frequency. Safety is only concerned with those failures that result in system hazards.

While reliability concerns itself with whether the program is doing what is required, safety concerns itself with seeing to it that the software does not do undesirable things. For example, a weapon system is supposed to destroy and kill. The property that it destroys and kills the enemy is a reliability concern. The property that the software does not destroy or kill friendly forces is a safety property. Safety and reliability are not generally the same. In fact, on the surface, they often are opposites. For example, if a torpedo fails to fire, it is safe but unreliable. If a torpedo is launched and it makes a U-turn and destroys the submarine that launches it, it is reliable but not safe. In the case of an air traffic control system, reliability and safety are more aligned with each other. If software causes inaccurate safety-related information to be displayed to a controller, then the system is both unreliable and unsafe.

Testing is "to specification," but the specification can be unsafe. Ideally, all safety requirements are made explicit, so that a safety problem constitutes a system failure. Safety-related failures (those that can cause or contribute to a hazard) are then a subset of all system failures. But remember that the system's or software's specification can be wrong: A system could conform to its requirements specification and still cause a hazard. One of the safety engineer's tasks is to make sure that all safety-related failures indeed constitute a system failure.

During the 1991 Gulf War, the software controlling the Patriot missile's tracking system failed, preventing the missiles from seeking and destroying incoming Scud missiles. The failure led to the death of 28 American soldiers. The computer software was performing according to specifications. These specifications assumed that the system would be restarted often enough to avoid accumulated inaccuracies in the timekeeping mechanism. But the system was used in an unintended way, being left up too long without restart, leading to the tragic failure (Wiener, 1993).

A system is only as safe as its weakest link. When you analyze a process, you must make assumptions about the processor and the environment. The results of your analysis can be undermined if your assumptions were wrong. If you are desk-checking source code, your conclusions could be misleading if the source code will be processed by an unreliable assembler, compiler, or interpreter. If you analyze the object code, your analysis could be undone by a faulty linker or loader. When the code executes, the programming language's run-time system or the operating system could fail. The math library you linked in might have some bugs. There could be a bug in the microcode that carries out the ADD instruction under some rare conditions. The microprocessor chip or other hardware could have a subtle design flaw. The results of a machine-level operation could be altered by something in the environment such as electromagnetic interference or bombardment with alpha particles generated by trace radionuclides in ceramic chip packages, cosmic rays in spaceborne computers, and so on. If you use a software tool in the course of your analysis or testing, then if that tool has a bug, that could invalidate the results of your analysis.

Thus, analysis is important for verification, but must be performed on several levels and be accompanied by testing on the target machine, in as close to the operational environment as possible.

Sometimes there is resistance to adding software safety requirements to requirements specifications. There is a widespread belief that requirements must be stated as positives, not as negatives, because you can only test positives, not negatives. Under this theory, requirements must always be stated as a positive ("The software shall do this. . . ." as opposed to being stated as a negative ("The software shall not do this. . . .") Because most safety requirements are in the form of negatives, the safety requirements are not allowed into the software requirements specifications, or they are allowed in but in a mangled form such as "The software shall inhibit. . . ."

The belief that negative requirements are untestable comes from a misunderstanding of the nature of testing. You do not test whether a requirement is met; you run some test cases involving a few different inputs and you *infer* that the requirement has been met for *all* possible inputs. If the requirement is positive, you try the test cases and infer that the software does do what it is supposed to do. If the requirement is negative, you can just as easily test that requirement by running some test cases and inferring that the software does not do something. There are no guarantees. You are making a statistical inference. You could be wrong in the positive case if there is some input that the program fails on that you did not pick up in your testing, just as you could be wrong in the negative case. The same requirement can sometimes be expressed in a positive manner and a negative manner, but the meaning is the same in both cases. A requirement is a statement about the intended behavior of the program; whether it is phrased in a positive way (shall) or negative way (shall not) is unimportant, as long as the meaning is imparted to the software engineer and the test team.

SAFETY VERSUS SECURITY

A secure system does not permit control or information to pass to unauthorized individuals. Security is concerned with protecting authority and information. In contrast, a safe system prevents injury by devices under its control and by protecting life and property. Safety and security are not the same but are related by their negative control policies. For example, the use of access controls from security is similar to the use of lock-outs in safety. A trusted computer base, implemented as a "security kernel," can contain the most critical security measures in a small form that allows the kernel to be examined carefully for flaws and allows its correctness to be demonstrated formally. A "safety kernel" similarly can be employed to contain the safety-critical parts of the software.

OUTLINE OF SAFETY ANALYSIS

For efficiency, the bulk of the safety analysis proceeds top down. We want to start by identifying the possible hazards and narrow down what parts of the software are capable of causing/contributing to a hazard. That way, we minimize the amount of code we will have to verify in detail. The initial key steps in system and software safety analysis are discussed below.

Preliminary Hazard List

A Preliminary Hazard List (PHL) is written during the initial phases of system concept and conducted for the purpose of providing early guidance to system designers (including subcontractors) on the identification of potential hazards. Not much may be known about the design at this point. The PHL's primary use is to develop system-level safety concepts, guidelines, requirements, and criteria to be followed in the system design. The analyst consults design sketches and drawings for conceptual approaches being considered and examines functional flow diagrams of activities, functions, and operations. He or she looks at contemplated testing, manufacturing, storage, repair, and use. The analysis is used to identify, assess, and prioritize hazards early in the development process and to establish a structured framework for the other hazard analyses as well as test planning and management planning.

The analyst reviews pertinent historical safety experience. A good place to begin to find out about potential hazards is to study experiences and lessons learned on similar systems. One resource is the archives of the RISKS Digest on Internet.

When computers control systems, some typical hazards are:

1. **Release of energy**
   a. Electromagnetic energy—such as radio waves, microwaves, heat, electric currents, sound, electrostatic energy, magnetic energy, atomic energy, x-rays, light.
   b. Stored energy—geopotential energy (e.g., falling objects), mechanical kinetic energy, chemical energy, strain energy (e.g., springs). Loss of control of a vehicle. Directing vehicles to collide with one another or with objects.
2. **Release of toxins.** Harmful substances: poisons, pathogens, environmental pollutants (e.g., air, soil, water), overdose. Almost anything can be toxic in

excessive doses; for example, drinking too much water can cause potentially fatal kidney damage.

3. **Interference with life support**—asphyxia, exposure, dehydration, starvation; failure of cardiac pacemaker or other life-sustaining medical equipment.

4. **Misleading trustful humans.** A subtle way that software can cause a hazard is by providing misleading information—for example, misinforming an air traffic controller as to the whereabouts of an aircraft. Military/law-enforcement intelligence, navigation information, medical diagnostic information. All kinds of examples can be thought of. People rely on a computer to provide them with information about some situation as a basis for decision making. The information is incorrect and leads the person to take an unsafe course of action. A very simple example is a traffic light controller: Red, yellow, and green do not harm in themselves, but when drivers rely on those lights, a wrong color at the wrong time could spell disaster.

Each hazard identified in the PHL is assigned a tentative probability and severity, so that the hazards' mitigation can be prioritized by level of risk.

Hazard Analysis

As the system design evolves, one can postulate hazards that would occur in the event of malfunction. The hazard analysis identifies hazards associated with the design. Certain guide words are useful in postulating deviations from design intent: "none of"; "more of" (more of a physical property than there should be); "less of" (less of a physical property than there should be); "less of" (composition of system different than it should be); "more than" (more components present than there should be; "part of"; "other than"; "as well as"; "reverse"; "later than"; "sooner than" (Robinson, 1978).

As an example of how a hazard analysis is developed in an air traffic control systems, the hazard list is based on analysis of the interrelationships between the system services provided to the air traffic controller and the procedures the controller uses to direct air traffic. The list is developed by the safety engineering group through extensive interviews with experienced air traffic controller personnel. The specific criteria examined for each service provided to the controller are: (a) Is the information or service provided critical to providing guidance to the aircraft? (b) If the service provided is unavailable, do current air traffic control procedures provide alternate methods of obtaining the essential information required? (c) If the information/service provided to the controller is erroneous (and undetected), is misdirection of air traffic possible?

Possible mishaps are aircraft colliding with each other, crashing into the terrain, and getting thrown about in the cabin. The hazards are aircraft getting too close to each other, to the terrain, to bad weather, or to another aircraft's wake turbulence— that is, violation of separation standards. We might lump this all into one hazard: "proximity hazard." One should not be afraid of coming up with too many hazards.

Also, to some extent, the number of hazards depends on writing style and naming. Just because a hazard can be eliminated or mitigated easily does not mean it is not a hazard. If a hazard can be mitigated outside the software—for example, through training or procedures—then it is the developer's responsibility to document that the hazard mitigation relies on the specific training or procedures, because sometime in the future the customer could change the training or procedures not realizing why they were there.

The hazard analysis is not meant to eliminate or control the hazard but to recognize the implications of the hazard. The analysis provides a risk assessment in terms of a probability and a severity category for identified potential hazards and serves to gauge the safety practicability of the design concept and is useful for follow-up to ensure that all hazards recognized at the earliest stages are eliminated or are controlled as the design progresses.

The analysis also identifies potential personnel errors that could lead to system accidents avoidable by design features such as operational and environmental influences. Failure to identify hazards means no opportunity to deal with them intelligently. The hazard analysis is especially concerned with hazardous entities and hazardous situations. A hazardous entity is intrinsically hazardous. Various raw materials and semifinished/finished goods have intrinsic properties such as corrosion, combustibility, and toxicity. Examples include fuel, propellants, initiators explosive charges, charged electrical capacitors, pumps, and nuclear devices. Certain events or conditions (e.g., a spark, contamination, leakage, mechanical shock) can transform a hazardous entity into a hazardous situation. Certain conditions, undesirable events, faults, or errors can transform a hazardous situation into a mishap (Villemeur, 1992).

The developer should share the PHL and hazard analysis with the customer and gain the customer's concurrence. Technical interchange meetings (TIMs) should be periodically held on the subject of safety.

The next step is to develop a *hazard tree* to develop the hazards further. For example, an air traffic control system might start out with a single hazard, "proximity hazard," and break those down into a tree of subhazards that includes the system behavior that can lead to the proximity hazard:

1. Aircraft position symbol displays offset from correct position.
2. Aircraft data block incorrect.
3. Loss of conflict detection/resolution function without controller notification, failure to detect and correctly resolve conflicts, or false conflict alerts.
4. Mixing of simulation and live data.
5. Loss of both symbolic display (data blocks) and tabular data (electronic flight strips) for any active flight.
6. Excessive system response time.
7. Loss of, or incorrect display of, map data, heavy weather, or airways.
8. Incorrect flight data stored or displayed.

9. Loss of voice communications between controllers and pilots.
10. Loss of emergency mode capability.
11. Loss of multiple controller workstations at tower.
12. Excessive, illegible, or confusing symbology leading to controller misinterpretation.
13. Absence of proper handoffs.
14 Improper resectorization or airspace adaptation.

The hazard "trains too close to each other" might be broken down into subhazards "leading train too slow," "trailing train too fast," approaching head-on," and so on, as shown in the hazard tree of Figure 5-1. Once hazards and subhazards have been identified, the next step to is to determine all the credible ways each hazard can be caused. We need to reason "backwards," from effect to cause to effect to cause, and so on.

Causes

A cause is a set of conditions or events sufficient for a particular effect to occur. An *event* has short duration—for example, the appearance of a signal or a transition

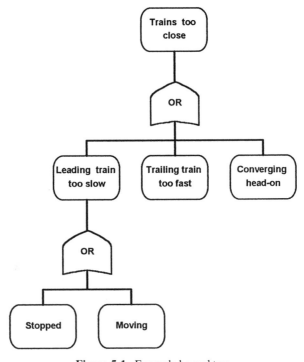

Figure 5-1. Example hazard tree.

from one state to another. A component failing is an example of an event: The component goes from a success state to a failure state. A transient or intermittent fault can cause a brief failure event. A *condition* is an existing state that a component is in; the event that caused the transition to that state has already occurred.

The most common system safety causal analysis approach is fault tree analysis (FTA).

Fault-Tree Analysis

Based on the understanding of the hazards obtained from the PHL and hazard analysis, and with the use of CSCI-specific Software Requirements Specification (SRS) and Interface Requirements Specification (IRS) documents, a system-level FTA is performed and is documented in a system-level fault tree.

FTA was developed by H. R. Watson in 1962 by Bell Telephone Laboratories at the request of the U.S. Air Force for safety and reliability studies of the Minuteman Intercontinental Ballistic Missile system. Bell Labs personnel had long used Boolean logic methods for communications equipment, and they adapted these principles to create the method. The method used to describe the flow of logic in data processing equipment could also be used for analyzing the logic that results from component failures. Engineers at Boeing such as David Haasl further developed and refined the procedures and became the method's foremost proponents as a method of performing a safety analysis of complex electromechanical systems. It is currently a widely used tool for safety analysis, especially nuclear power generation systems.

FTA is an analytical technique in which an undesired state of the system is specified, and the system is analyzed to find all credible ways that the undesired state can occur. The fault tree is a graphical model that depicts the combinations of events and circumstances that can cause the event at the root of the tree, called the "top event." The rest of the tree is a complex of gates indicating the logical interrelationships of cause and effect factors. The process begins with the events (first-level events) that could directly cause the top event. The procedure goes back step-by-step, identifying preceding combinations of events. Whenever more than one event can contribute to the same effect, a gate indicates whether the input events must all act in combination (AND relationship) or whether they may act singly (OR relationship). There are two basic types of gates: the AND-gate and the OR-gate.

AND-gate: The output event occurs if all of the input events occur. Symbolized by a shield with a straight base.

OR-gate: The output occurs if at least one of the input events occurs. Symbolized by a pointed shield with a curved base.

An event that will be further analyzed is symbolized by a rectangle, with a label (brief description of the event) inscribed inside. It is a good idea to include a unique identifier for each event. A diamond symbolizes an event that will not be developed further—for lack of information or insufficient consequences. Other gates are also used. Figure 5-2 illustrates a simple fault tree.

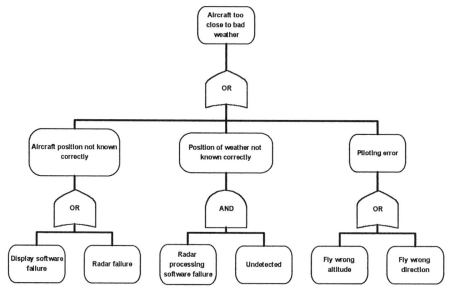

Figure 5-2. Example fault tree.

Backward Threading

The fundamental strategy of software safety engineering is to minimize the size and complexity of the design and code that has to be analyzed in detail. This allows software safety resources to be expended in the most efficient manner possible. We want to determine, through a gradual process of elimination, which parts of the software are truly *safety-critical* and which are *safety-independent.*

In some of the system-level fault trees, a software output will appear on the tree as indirectly causing or contributing to the hazard. We term such an output a *safety-critical output flow.* We say "output flow" because at this point we only have software requirements. The output flow to which we are referring will be found in some Computer Software Configuration Item's (CSCI's) dataflow diagram. The Software Requirements Specification is primarily a description of the bubbles (also called processes or transforms or, in the parlance of DOD-STD-2167A, *capabilities*).

We look at the requirements in the SRS and IRS documents to identify, first of all, which CSCI produces each output implicated in the fault tree. Backward threading from the system output is employed to identify safety-critical data flows: the chain of input and output flows that are transformed into the implicated output. Each safety-critical system output flow emanates from some CSCI. Each safety-critical system output flow is examined in turn. The CSCI from which the safety-critical system output flow emanates is designated as safety-critical. If that CSCI needs input flows from other CSCIs to produce that output, then those input flows are designated safety-critical as well. Some of those input flows may be output flows from other

CSCIs in the system, which are now identified as a safety-critical output flows. The CSCI originating such an output flow is classified as *safety-critical*. For example, CSCI A is safety-critical because it produces the implicated safety-critical output Z. Because CSCI B produces an output flow that CSCI A uses to produce Z, CSCI is critical too. The CSCIs that are not safety-critical are classified as *safety-independent.*

Not all of a safety-critical CSCI is necessarily safety-critical. The next step is to continue the backward threading, into each safety-critical CSCI, to identify those capabilities within the CSCI that are safety-critical and those that are safety-independent.

Within each CSCI, the capabilities that lie along the critical thread are identified. They are the capabilities involved in directly or indirectly producing the CSCI's safety-critical output flow. Note that a capability (or even a CSCI) is just an artifact created for the purpose of documenting the software requirements and for configuration management; a capability or CSCI does not necessarily map into a design entity. It's really the *requirements* that we want to get at: We want to identify the set of safety-critical requirements in the SRS. These are the requirements that are involved in producing the safety-critical outputs. An acid test for determining whether or not a requirement is safety-critical is, If this requirement were not met, could the safety-critical output flow become incorrect, lost, or mistimed as a result?

To summarize, in backward threading, we start with a software output implicated in the system-level fault tree as causing/contributing to a hazard. We then successively identify the CSCI(s) involved in producing that output, the capabilities within those CSCI(s), and then the specific requirements within those capabilities.

Finally, each safety-critical requirement in the SRS is *tagged*. The importance of tagging the critical requirements in the SRS is threefold: (a) The software developer needs to be alerted to the fact that software built to this requirement needs special analysis and verification, (b) software engineers involved in future changes need to know that the software is critical to ensure that previously implemented mitigation mechanisms remain intact, and (c) the tagging is the first step in providing traceability from the safety-critical requirements to the safety-critical software design elements, and from the design to the implementation.

In the course of the backward threading, we also identify safety-critical *data stores* that are involved in the production of the safety-critical outputs.

Software Requirements Hazard Analysis (SRHA)

The SRS specifies the engineering and qualification requirements for a CSCI. It is used by the contractor as the basis for the design and formal testing of the CSCI. Now that we understand what the hazards are and how the software might cause or contribute to those hazards, we need to take a good look at the SRS and see if we need to add, remove, or modify requirements to mitigate the hazards. As the system and software design take shape, we may add *mitigating requirements* to constrain the software design.

Some of the hazards and subhazards may be inverted to form software safety requirements. The safety requirements specify what the system shall *not* do, including means for eliminating and controlling hazards and for limiting damage in the case that a mishap occurs.

These additional requirements are tagged. Note that you don't eliminate a hazard simply by adding a requirement. It's not that easy. The software safety analyst has to follow through and make sure that that requirement is designed into the software, implemented, and verified.

Identifying Safety-Critical Design Elements

During the requirements analysis the safety-critical engineering requirements (input flows, output flows, capabilities, requirements, data stores) are identified because that's all there is to work with during that phase. But it is software—code—that causes or contributes to a hazard. As soon as the software design becomes available, we can start identifying the actual safety-critical software.

A module is a function or procedure—the smallest named sequence of instructions in a programming language. We shall define a safety-critical module as a module that is allocated to at least one safety-critical requirement. Now, one safety-critical requirement could be allocated to several safety-critical modules, so a module could be safety-critical if it even implements "part" of a safety-critical requirement.

In the language of DOD-STD-2167A, a computer software unit (CSU) is a set of modules that need to be tested together. That is, a CSU is the smallest individually testable software entity. The testing performed on a CSU is unit testing. The set of safety-critical modules relate to the production of one *particular* safety-critical output (or closely related set of critical outputs) and, ideally, are grouped together into a CSU, designated a *safety-critical CSU.*

So now the software is partitioned into safety critical and safety independent CSUs. Theoretically, we can concentrate our safety analysis on the safety-critical CSUs and ignore any safety-independent CSUs. But, alas, if only life were so simple. Who's to say that a failure occurring in a safety-independent CSU could not somehow propagate into a safety-critical CSU? We want to be able to ignore the safety-independent CSUs, or at least devote much less attention to them than the safety-critical CSUs, because in the real world there are limited resources. But we have no right to do this, unless we protect the safety-critical CSUs from the safety-independent CSUs. Then, and only then, can we focus our attention on the safety-critical CSUs.

The Firewall Concept

It is essential to ensure the integrity of safety-critical software. Portions of the software that are safety-independent must not have an unpredictable effect on the safety-critical portion. This integrity must be maintained under abnormal operation (i.e., when faults manifest themselves) as well as under normal operation. One approach to ensuring integrity is to analyze all possible interactions (normal and abnormal) that could exist between modules that are safety-critical and those that are safety-independent. This would in effect make all software safety-critical—clearly an undesirable and costly proposition. Another approach to protecting the safety-critical CSUs is to build a "firewall" between safety-critical CSUs and safety-independent CSUs. The firewall has two main objectives:

1. Ensure that safety-independent software does not interact with safety-critical software in an unpredictable and, therefore, possibly unsafe manner.
2. Minimize the number of data and control paths between software modules that need to be analyzed.

In order to focus the detailed safety analysis and verification procedures on only the safety-critical modules, these modules must be isolated and protected from safety-independent modules. Otherwise, a safety-independent module could, as the result of a failure, possibly interfere with a safety-critical module's data and code and invalidate the analysis and verification. Before we can justify restricting the detailed safety analysis to the safety-critical modules, we must ensure that the code and data of safety-critical modules are protected. The purpose of the firewall is to provide this protection. Each safety-critical output ideally has its own firewall, which reduces the potential for cross-interactions between modules that would require analysis (Cha, 1991).

In the firewall concept, the data flows and control flows are restricted between safety-critical and safety-independent modules. In the extreme case, the CSUs can be put on physically separate computers, but, more practically, a firewall is "constructed" using operating system or programming language features. For example, Ada packages, C++ objects, and separate address spaces are each possible ways to create a firewall.

The full C and C++ programming languages are not safe (Cullyer et al., 1990). However, subsets of those languages can be safe. Let us assume for the moment that a CSU is implemented as a set of related C/C++ functions. One way to create a firewall around a CSU in C++ or ANSI C is as follows:

1. The CSU's source code is placed in its own translation unit, that is, in a file by itself.
2. All code that is to lie behind the firewall is put in functions that are declared with the **static** keyword. That way, that code is not visible outside the current translation unit. It cannot be invoked by any function that is not defined in the same file.
3. Data that is behind the firewall and global within the CSU is declared as global variables with the **static** keyword. That way, that data is not visible outside the current translation unit. It cannot be used by any function that is not defined in the same file.
4. Each function's local data is declared within the function as **static** or automatic local variables; this data will lie behind the firewall.
5. The function(s) that are to serve as the CSU's safety ports are declared without the **static** keyword. These few functions will thus have external linkage and be visible to other translation units.

```
//
//NAME:
//  example.cc
//
//PURPOSE:
//  Implementation of firewall using ANSI C.
//

//--------------------
//          Data
//--------------------

//By declaring the variables static, they cannot be referenced
//outside of this translation unit. Therefore, these variables
//are behind the firewall. Since it is declared at
//file scope level, they are global within the translation unit,
//are accessible by the functions and procedures within the
//translation unit.

static int    data1;
static float  data2;
static char   data3;

//--------------------
//      Functions
//--------------------

//The functions foo() and unfoo(), because they are declared
//static, cannot be called from outside this translation unit.
//Thus they are behind the firewall.

static int foo ()
{
   ;
}

static void unfoo ()
{
   ;
}

//This function is visible from the other translation units, and
//so is a safety port.

int global_foo(int y, z)
{
   float x;  // this variable is behind the firewall.

//Check for satisfaction of safety preconditions (values of
//passed parameters y and z are consistent among themselves
//and with the current state).
   ;
}
```

In C++, a firewall can be created in an additional way, by using a class. This style is useful when the CSU encapsulates and manages some safety-critical data.

1. Put the CSU's source code in its own translation unit, that is, in a file by itself.
2. All code that is to lie behind the firewall is put in **private** member functions.
3. Data that is shared by the CSU's functions is declared as **private** member data; this data will be behind the firewall.
4. Each function's local data is declared within the function as **static** or automatic local variables; this data will lie behind the firewall.
5. The function(s) that are to serve as the CSU's safety ports are declared as **public** member functions.
6. The class is instantiated as an object exactly once. It should be declared outside all blocks so that it has static lifetime and external linkage.

For example:

```
// Computer Software Unit
class CSU
{
};

// Programmer creates his safety-critical CSU as a class
class my_CSU_class : public CSU
{
public:  //This procedure is the CSU's safety port
   int My_safety_port(int x, int y);
private:  // This data and procedure are completely behind the
         // firewall
   int My_Procl(int);
   float azimuth;
};

//Body of safety port procedure
int my_CSU_class::My_safety_port(int x, int y)
{
    // check for safety precondition
    assert_valid(x * y + 6 < 50);
    return My_Procl(x) + y;
}

// Instantiate an object of the class
my_CSU_class my_CSU;

main()
{
// Invoke the safety-critical CSU's safety port procedure
my_CSU.My_safety_port(3, 4);
return 0;
}
```

These schemes provide an effective firewall when memory locations in the program are referred to by name—that is, by alphanumeric identifier. The possibility exists that the firewall could be breached because code and data can be overwritten or executed not only via name but via numeric address. The variable x inside the object is actually a memory cell located at memory address, say, 1440. While software outside the object cannot get at x via name, they can nonetheless get at x by referring to x's address. Suppose that the programmer makes the following declaration: "int *iptr;" This declares *iptr* to be a pointer to type integer. The programmer intends to make the assignment "iptr = 1140" but through a typographical error types "iptr = 1440". Later in the program, the programmer makes the assignment "*iptr = 87". That assignment assigns the value 87 to the integer at which *iptr* points. That assignment is going to wipe out x's value. The firewall has been breached.

A further problem in C and C++ is that references to array elements are equivalent to using pointers. Suppose that y is declared to be an array of integers. A reference to "y[b]"—the bth element of array y—is interpreted by the compiler as "*(y+b)", which is the integer at the address of the beginning (zeroth) element of y incremented by (b times the size of an integer). Because C/C++ interprets arrays as pointers, C/C++ does not perform a check, either at compile time or run-time, on whether a subscript is out of range or not. If y was declared to contain 10 elements, and the programmer writes something to the 15th element, he or she will not be prevented from doing so. In all likelihood, the result of writing to the nonexistent 15th element will overwrite some other variable that the compiler happened to locate in memory following array y. The conclusion is that to enforce a firewall, a two-pronged strategy is necessary: First, code and data that belong behind a common firewall are encapsulated into an object. Second, use of pointers (and arrays) must be carefully controlled.

C++ can overcome the problems with arrays by allowing the subscript operator— the square brackets—to be overloaded (Murray, 1993; Smith, 1993). Whenever an element of the safe array is accessed through a subscript, the subscript is automatically checked to see if it is in range. Thus, if an array has 30 elements, the only acceptable subscript values at run time are 0 through 29. Any attempt to use a negative subscript value or one that is 30 or higher will be caught and can be recovered from.

Here is a sample C++ implementation of a "safe array." (The code is just a sample to illustrate the algorithm. You would need to thoroughly test the code on your own system before using it.)

```
//-------------------------------------------------------------
// NAME:
//    safe_array.hh - Safe array header file
//
// PURPOSE:
// Illustrates the general idea of defining a "safe array"
// class in C++. The subscript operator "[]" is overloaded to
// provide automatic subscript range checking.
//
//-------------------------------------------------------------
```

```
#ifndef _SAFE_ARRAY_HH
#define _SAFE_ARRAY_HH

#include <iostream.h>
#include <stdlib.h>

template <class type>
class Safe_array
{
  public:
    Safe_array(const int size,             // constructor
                     char* const module_name);

   ~Safe_array();                          // destructor

    Safe_array (Safe_array& array);  // copy constructor

    Safe_array& operator=
                (const Safe_array& array); // assignment operator

    type& operator[](const int) const; // Access with checking

  protected:
    void fail(const char mes[], const int i) const;
    void fail(const int i1, const int i2) const;

  private:
    type* ptr_to_array;    // Pointer to array of Types
    int   num_elems;    // Size of array
    char* name_of_module; // name of module using this class
};

//-------------------------------------------------------------------
// Template Class Member Function Definitions
//-------------------------------------------------------------------

template <class type>
Safe_array <type>::Safe_array
                 (const int size,          // size of array
                  char* const module_name) // module
                                           // containing
                                           // array
{
num_elems = size;
ptr_to array = new type[num_elems];
name_of_module = module_name;
}

//
// FUNCTION:
//    Safe_array::operator= - the assignment operator
//

template <class type>
```

```
Safe_array<type>& Safe_array<type>::operator=
                          (const Safe_array <type>& array)
{
  // verify that the arrays are of the same size
  if (this->num_elems != array.num_elems)
    fail(this->num_elems, array.num_elems);

  // test for assignment to self: array = array
  if (this == &array)
  return *this;

  // copy the contents of the array
  for (int i = 0; i < this->num_elems; ++i)
    this->ptr_to_array[i] = array.ptr_to_array[i];

  return *this;
}

//------------------------------------------------------------------
//
// FUNCTION:
//   Safe_array::Safe_array - copy constructor
//
template <class type>
Safe_array <type>::Safe_array (Safe_array <type>& array)

  // copy size of array and module name and allocate the memory
  this->num elems = array.num_elems;
  this->name of module = array.name_of_module;
  this->ptr_to_array = new type[this->num_elems];

  // copy the contents of the array
  for (int i = 0; i < this->num_elems; ++i)
    this->ptr_to_array[i] = array.ptr_to_array[i];
}

//------------------------------------------------------------------
//
// FUNCTION:
//   ~Safe_array - class destructor
//

template <class type>
Safe_array <type>::~Safe_array()
}
   cout << "DEALLOCATING AN ARRAY IN " << name_of_module << endl;
   delete ptr_to_array;
}

//
// FUNCTION:
//   operator[] - array accessing with bounds checking
//
```

```
template <class type>
type& Safe_array <type>::operator[]
                            (const int i) const // index
into array
{
  // bounds check the index - print fail message if out of bounds
  if ( i < 0 || i >= num_elems )
    fail( "Subscript error - subscript " , i );

  // index within bounds - return requested item
  return ptr_to_array[i];
}


//
// FUNCTION:
//   fail - error handler for out-of-bounds subscripts

template <class type>
void Safe_array <type>::fail
                    (const char mes[],   // error message
                     const int  i) const // subscript in error
{
  cout << endl << "Error in class : Safe array" << endl;
  cout << "Module: " << name of module << endl;
  cout << mes << " " << i << endl << endl;
  //  In field operation, revert to a safe state. In lab testing
  //  just exit.
  exit(-1);
}


//------------------------------------------------------------------//
// FUNCTION:
//    fail - error handler size mismatch in assignment
//
template <class type>
void Safe_array <type>::fail
                      (const int i1,       // size of array 1
                       const int i2) const // size of array 2
{
  cout << endl << "Error in class : Safe array" << endl;
  cout << "Module: " << name of module << endl;
  cout << "Size Mismatch: " << i1 << " != " << i2 << endl <<
          endl;
  // In field operation, revert to a safe state. In lab testing
  // just exit.

  exit(-1);
}

#endif

// Example of use of safe arrays

#include "safe_array.hh"
```

```
class example_class
{
  public:
    example_class();
    ~example_class();
    void add_item (int item);

  private:
    Safe_array <int> my_list;
};

// this is a class object that contains a safe array class object
example_class example_list_1;

// this object is a safe array class object
Safe_array <float> example_list_2 (20, "example.cc");


// NOTE: when safe arrays are used as fields in other classes,
//       the call to the safe_array constructor MUST be made
//       from the constructor function of the enclosing class.
//       The example_class constructor demonstrates:
example_class: :example_class() :
  my_list (10, "example.cc") // safe_array constructor call
{
  // do whatever else
}

example_class::~example_class()
{
    ;
}

void example_class::add_item (int item)
{
  my_list[0] = item; // just overwrite
}

// a short main program demonstrating usage of objects
// that contain/are safe arrays.
int main()
{
  example_list_1.add_item (4);
  example_list_2[0] = 0.0;
}
```

Whereas arrays are contiguous and have upper and lower subscript bounds, a general *pointer* can point to any address in memory and there is no general rule for deciding if writing to that address is "safe" or not.

Let's say you need to point to location 3450, which is a memory-mapped I/O port. The best thing to do is to declare a constant pointer to that location—for example, through a declaration like this: "char * const IOPORT3 = 3450". To write the character 'x' to the location, you would use "*IOPORT3 = 'x'". If the program-mer tries to modify the value of the pointer IOPORT3, he or she would not be allowed to.

The more error-prone situation is when pointer arithmetic is performed. If a pointer to character is declared "char * pch", an integer is declared "int j", and a character is declared "char ch" and you make the assignment "pch = &ch + j", you could be breaching a firewall, especially if *j* is uninitialized or, due to a fault, has some other unexpected wrong value. Luckily, in C++, we can overload the "new", "delete", "*", and the "–>" operators. The concept of "arenas" can be used. An arena is a contiguous area of memory. It is a miniheap that lies within a firewall. We can overload the operator "new" to allocate the dynamic memory the object needs, from the arena. Whenever a pointer to something that is supposed to be in the arena is used, the overloaded "*" or "–>" operator checks to make sure that the pointer on which it is operating lies within the arena (Murray, 1993).

```
#include <stddef.h>
class X
{
private:
void* operator new(size_t);
void operator delete(void *, size_t);
static char arena[500];
};
```

Note that these techniques do not guarantee that the subscript or pointer is correct. For example, you might reference subscript 6 when you intended to reference sub-script 5. The safe array and arena techniques just prevent subscripts and pointers from going out of bounds; you still have to verify that the code within the firewall references the intended locations within those bounds.

A frequent problem with using dynamically allocated memory is that the pro-grammer forgets to deallocate the memory when he or she is done. This memory cannot be reallocated. We have what is termed a "memory leak." If memory leakage continues and accumulates, we can run out of dynamic memory and the program will suddenly fail. Use of arenas can help prevent memory leaks because, when the object forming the firewall is deallocated, the object's destructor can delete the entire arena in one fell swoop.

Use of some other C++ features, such as friend classes and functions, and even casts have to be restricted to prevent possible breaches of the firewall.

The object associated with a firewall will have an interface to other parts of the program, the object's *safety ports*. The consists of member functions declared as **public**. In our example, the public routine is **start_code( )**. How is that routine pro-tected? The solution is that the public members each begin with assertions of the *safety preconditions* associated with the function. A safety precondition is a condi-tion that, if true immediately before a program segment is executed, then the pro-gram segment is safe; that is, the program segment cannot cause or contribute to a hazard. A module is made safe by ensuring that the design results in the preconditions always being true upon entry to the module. Mueller (1994) describes a C++ header file for writing a complex assertion that can contain quantifier operators such as ∀ ("for all") and ∃ ("there exists").

The determination of safety preconditions is performed by backward threading through the program segment and applying proof rules based on the principle of "weakest precondition." A module is "safety-independent" if the safety preconditions are tautologically TRUE. If the precondition is tautologically FALSE, then the design must be revised because the module is "inherently unsafe." The remaining modules are termed "safety critical." The design and implementation of a safety-critical module must ensure that the safety preconditions are always satisfied. We will see later in the chapter how a technique called software fault-tree analysis helps find these safety preconditions.

The "assert" macro that usually comes with C/C++ implements a debug-only assertion. Here is an example assertion macro that can be used in the released version of the program:

```
#include <iomanip.h>
#include <fstream.h>
#include <stdlib.h>

void _failed_assertion(char *strExp,char *strFile, unsigned
uLine)
{
    cout << flush;
    cerr << endl << "Assertion failed: " << strExp << ",
        file " << strFile << ", line "<< uLine << endl <<
    flush;
    abort();
}

#define assert_valid(exp) \
if (exp) NULL; \
else _failed_assertion(#exp, __FILE__, __LINE__)

void main()
{
 assert(1==1);
 assert(1==0);
}
```

(Again, you need to test this code on your own system. Note that the long underscores are actually two typed in as two successive underscores.) In the sample main program, the second invocation of "assert" will display the error message. Of course, instead of displaying an error message, the program can take recovery action at run time (Maguire, 1993).

Another type of assertion is a *trigger.* A trigger is an assertion about the environment in which the software is executing. Robust software detects and responds appropriately to violations of environmental assumptions.

The programming language Ada, with its packages and its subtypes for subscripts, is similar to C++ in allowing you to construct a solid firewall. Ada has in fact been used in a number of safety-critical systems.

Firewalls are also useful for minimizing coupling among the safety-critical CSUs.

DATA OUTSIDE A FIREWALL

Some data may have to be shared so that it is shared by several CSUs. Accessible to more than one CSU, it is a sitting duck for corruption. Also, some data may leave a firewall to travel along a communications medium before entering another firewall. Whenever safety-critical data resides or travels outside a firewall, it needs to take a "portable firewall" along with it. This is done by having an error-detecting code (EDC) or error-correcting code (ECC) accompany the data. An ECC provides protection equivalent to that of a firewall. A firewall prevents corruption of data. An ECC allows the corruption to take place but then provides a means for undoing the damage. An EDC is a little weaker than a firewall. An EDC allows the corruption to take place but provides a warning to potential users of the data that the data has been corrupted, so the software can perform some type of recovery action. Examples of EDC are parity bits, checksums, and cyclic redundancy checks (CRCs).

You are probably thinking that the hardware applies ECCs and EDC for you. While you would be right, we are talking about applying these codes at the software level, to detect software-caused corruption. It is true that some error-detection and error-correction means are built into the hardware. Hardware error detection and error correction are good for detecting hardware-caused corruption but are useless in detecting software-caused corruption, because hardware cannot tell whether a write was intended by the programmer or is the result of a software fault.

If the programmer stores a "5" but a software fault later causes the "5" to be corrupted to a "6", the hardware will accept the "6" as easily as it did the "5". The hardware EDCs/ECCs are useless in this case. But if the programmer had put a software-level error-detecting around the "5", the programmer would have detected it being corrupted to a "6" and could have taken recovery action.

Here is a simple example to point out the value of software EDCs and ECC. We will use decimal numbers. Suppose that the data to be stored is the number 32876534. As the number is stored, the hardware calculates a checksum and appends it to the 32876534. A typical checksum is calculated by dividing the data into parts, adding the parts, and taking the result modulo some number. In this example, the checksum is a digit calculated by adding up all the digits modulo 10. For 32876534, the checksum is $(3+2+8+7+6+5+3+4)$ mod $10 = 38$ mod $10 = 8$. Thus, the hardware stores the number internally as 32876534 | 8. For clarity, we show a vertical bar introducing the checksum digit. Suppose now that a fault in the software overwrites the first digit, 3, with an 8. The hardware cannot discern whether the overwriting is intentional or caused by a bug. So the hardware blithely computes a new checksum:

(8+2+8+7+6+5+3+4) mod 10 = 43 mod 10 = 3. The new internally stored number is 82876534 | 3. When the software retrieves the number, the hardware recomputes the hardware checksum: (8+2+8+7+6+5+3+4) mod 10 = 43 mod 10 = 3. Because the recomputed hardware checksum agrees with the stored hardware checksum, the software-caused corruption is not detected. The hardware strips off the checksum and hands the software the number 82876534. The software stored 32876534. Because of a software bug, that number got corrupted to 82876534, and the hardware checksum was of no use in detecting that corruption.

The hardware checksum only protects against hardware-caused data corruption. If hardware had changed the 3 to an 8, the recomputed hardware checksum would disagree with the stored checksum, and the corruption would have been detected. To detect software-caused corruption, a *software-level* checksum is necessary. Suppose in our example we start out with the number 32876534. The software computes a checksum and appends it, so as before we have 32876534 | 8. Now we store the number, including checksum. The hardware computes its own checksum on the basis of the number 328765348, since the software checksum looks like just any other digit. The hardware checksum is (3+2+8+7+6+5+3+4+8) mod 10 = 46 mod 10 = 6. The hardware appends this checksum to yield 32876534 | 8 | 6. The first vertical bar introduces the software checksum and the second vertical bar introduces the hardware checksum.

A software fault changes the first digit, 3, to an 8. Now to the hardware the number is 82876534 | 8. The new hardware checksum is (8+2+8+7+6+5+3+4) mod 10 = 43 mod 10 = 3. The number the hardware stores is 72876534 | 8 | 3. When the software reads the number it gets 72876534 | 8; the hardware strips off the hardware checksum. The hardware detects no error, because the recomputed hardware checksum is (8+2+8+7+6+5+4+4) mod 10 = 43 mod 10 = 3, which agrees with the stored hardware checksum. The software recomputes the checksum from (7+2+8+7+6 +5+3+4) mod 10 = 42 mod 10 = 2. Because the recomputed checksum, 2, disagrees with the stored checksum, 8, the software has detected the fact that software-caused corruption occurred.

DESIGN OF SAFETY-CRITICAL CSUs

With the firewall in place, attention turns to designing the safety-critical CSUs. As long as the safety-independent CSUs respect the firewall, we can concentrate on the safety-critical CSU. The software needs to be designed in such a way that hardware and software failures do not create hazards. If, due to a hardware or software fault, an erroneous state occurs, the software needs to detect that condition and treat it before it leads to a hazard. In the presence of faults, the system can still be safe, if the effects of a fault are contained through *fail-safe* techniques. Fail-operational procedures provide limited capability in the face of a failure, fail-passive procedures power down the system, fail-active procedures take action to correct the condition, and fail-soft procedures provide pre-planned degraded functional performance.

As the CSU design materializes, we may come up with (1) additional "design constraints" that will serve to mitigate the hazards such as watchdog timers, lockins, lockouts, interlocks, and timeouts to ensure that events occur in a timely fashion, (2) assertions to ensure that computation is correct, and (3) batons to ensure that steps occur in precise order. Special attention is paid to exception handling and to recovery. We must remember that technological fixes may not reduce risk because they may increase the size and/or complexity of the system. The paradox here is that if you add code to software to address a safety concern, you may add to the safety risk. If you protect a piece of "unsafe" code by adding as much or more code, it is doubtful that you will get anywhere. If you add code for safety, it has to be much shorter and simpler than the code it is protecting. It has to be more easily verifiable with the added code than without.

The goal of safety engineering in general is to keep the system at all times in a safe state. An example of putting the system in an intrinsically safe state is setting the traffic lights at an intersection all to red in the event of a system failure. A less drastic measure is to set all the traffic lights to flashing red, turning the intersection into the equivalent of a four-way stop. For a railroad, a safe state can generally be attained by simply stopping all the trains. Unfortunately, the same approach cannot be used for air traffic control systems; if something goes wrong with the system, you can't have all the aircraft in the air "stop." What constitutes a safe state is not an easy question in systems with inherent instability or great inertia or throughput. For example, in a fly-by-wire system, the safe state requires continuous control.

VERIFICATION OF SAFETY-CRITICAL SOFTWARE

We must ensure ourselves of the elimination, control, mitigation, or warning of known hazards. Verification can be accomplished by test, analysis, inspection, experience, or demonstration. Safety verification is aimed at showing that an unsafe state cannot be reached, although that state could be incorrect.

Safety verification of concurrent programs entails treating each sequential thread of execution separately and then performing a concurrency safety verification. Safety verification must take into account the run-time overhead of creating and managing the multiple tasks.

Many safety-critical systems are real-time systems. In a real-time system, processor scheduling becomes an important safety issue. In addition to showing that the program's logic is safe, you must analyze the system's deadline constraints and timing characteristics. Advances have been made in scheduling theory in recent years that simplify the analysis of scheduling. In many cases, it is possible to draw on this body of theory to prove that, even in the worst case, the real-time deadlines will be met.

A cyclic task's *period* is how often it has to run. If it has to run every 50 milliseconds, its period is 50 milliseconds. The Rate Monotonic Scheduling Algorithm (Liu and Layland, 1973; Alsys, 1992) says that you should assign higher priorities to tasks with shorter periods. For example, if you had three task periods of 10, 30, and 100 milliseconds, you should assign the first the highest priority, the second task the second-highest priority, and the third task the lowest priority. Then you determine the total processor utilization for the n tasks. The utilization of a periodic task is the amount of execution time it needs to complete its work, divided by the period. This includes any operating system overhead, such as context switching. If the total utilization is less than $U(n)$, then all deadlines will always be met. The threshold value $U(n)$ is calculated from

$$U(n) = n \cdot \sqrt[n]{2}$$

For example, $U(1) = 1.0$, $U(2) = 0.828$, and apropos to our example, $U(3) = 0.779$. As the number of tasks n goes to infinity, $U(n)$ converges to ln 2. In general, $U(n)$ is a pessimistic bound, and higher total processor utilization will be allowable. A common case is where the periods are uniformly harmonic—that is, when each task period is an exact divisor of each longer period. In this case, deadlines would still be met as long as the total processor utilization does not exceed 1.0. An example of this case would be a set of tasks with periods 10, 20, and 100 milliseconds (Shapiro et al., 1990).

The Rate Monotonic method can accommodate interaction between the tasks (Sha et al., 1988), aperiodic tasks (Sprunt et al., 1989), and burst events (Burns and Wellings, 1992).

SUMMARY

In this chapter we described an approach to software safety. To prevent having to treat all the software in a system as safety-critical, backward threading is employed to determine which parts of the software are truly safety-critical, and "firewalls" are erected to isolate and protect the safety-critical parts from the safety-independent parts. Data passed in through the firewall's "safety ports" are validated using assertions called "safety preconditions." We showed how C++ classes can be used to implement firewalls. We discussed programming-language features that should be disallowed in order to prevent firewalls from being breached. The issue of task scheduling in safety-critical real-time systems was also covered. In the next chapter, we decribe how the firewall-protected software units are verified.

EXERCISES

1. Form an initial hazard list for the following types of systems:
  (a) Cardiac pacemaker
  (b) Cruise control for a car
  (c) Electronic throttle control for a car

    (d) Braking system for a car

    (e) Train control system

2. Discuss why you think each of these situations is a hazard or a mishap:

    (a) Water in a swimming pool becomes electrified.

    (b) Room fills with carbon dioxide.

    (c) Car stops abruptly.

    (d) Long distance telephone company outage.

REFERENCES

Alsys. *The Real-Time Ada Handbook*, Burlington, MA: Alsys, Inc., 1992, Chapter 5.

A. Burns and A. J. Wellings. "Measuring, Monitoring and Enforcing CPU Execution Time Usage." University of York, UK, 1992.

S. S. Cha, *A Safety-Critical Software Design and Verification Technique*. Ph.D. Dissertation, University of California, Irvine, CA, 1991.

W. J. Cullyer, S. J. Goodenough, and B. A. Wichmann. "The Choice of Computer Languages for Use in Safety-Critical Systems," Technical Report, Department of Engineering, University of Warwick, Coventry, UK., April 1990.

N. G. Leveson. "Software Safety: What, Why, and How." *Computing Surveys* 18(2), 125–163, June 1986.

C. L. Liu and J. W. Layland. "Scheduling Algorithms for Multi-programming in a Hard Real-Time Environment." *Journal of the ACM* 20(1), 46–61, January 1973.

S. Maguire, *Writing Solid Code*, Microsoft Press. Redmond, WA, 1993.

H. M. Mueller. "Powerful Assertions for C++," *C/C++ Users Journal* 12(10), 21–37, October 1994.

R. B. Murray. *C++ Strategies and Tactics*. Reading, MA: Addison–Wesley, 1993.

B. W. Robinson. "Risk Reduction in the Chemical Industry." RSA 5/78, CEC, Joint Research Center, ISPRA, Italy, 1978.

L. Sha, R. Rajkumar, and J. Lehoczky. "Priority Inheritance Protocols: An Approach to Real-Time Synchronization." Carnegie-Mellon University Technical Report, May 1988.

R. Shapiro, V. Pinci, and R. Mameli. "Modeling a NORAD Command Post Using SADT and Colored Petri Nets." *In: Proceedings of IDEF Users Group*, May 1990.

M. A. Smith, *Object-Oriented Software in C++*, London: Chapman & Hall, 1993.

B. Sprunt, L. Sha, and J. Lehoczky. "Scheduling Sporadic and Aperiodic Events in a Hard Real-Time System." Technical Report CMU/SEI-89-TR-11, Software Engineering Institute, Pittsburgh, PA, April 1989.

A. Villemeur. *Reliability, Availability, Maintainability and Safety Assessment*, Vol. 1. Chichester, UK: John Wiley & Sons, 1992.

L. Wiener. *Digital Woes: Why We Should Not Depend on Software*. Reading, MA: Addison–Wesley, 1993.

CHAPTER 6

Assessment of Safety-Critical Software Units

In Chapter 5 we learned the up-front activities of a typical software safety program. The hazards are identified. Through backward threading, the safety-critical computer software configuration items (CSCIs), capabilities, and finally requirements are determined. The modules to which the safety-critical requirements are allocated are the safety-critical modules. Those modules involved in producing a particular safety-critical output are collected into a safety-critical computer software unit (CSU). A "firewall" is placed around each safety-critical CSU to isolate and protect it from the safety-independent CSUs, so that attention can now be focused on the safety-critical CSUs.

This chapter details the methodology for developing the safety-critical CSUs, with emphasis on assessment of that software. Here are the main steps of this methodology:

1. Modeling: Aspects of the detailed design of the CSU are modeled using Petri nets and other formal techniques to verify the design at various levels of abstraction.

2. The testability of the design (with respect to the safety-critical outputs) is maximized through the testability design principles described Chapter 4. While normally testability is applied with respect to all the output variables (that is, with respect to correctness), by restricting the output domain to just the safety-critical outputs, design for testability and testability measurement are both applicable.

3. The software is tested in the following manner:

A. The software safety engineer reviews test plans, recommends tests, and prescribes the conditions under which those tests are to be conducted. It is important that the effective specific safety design features be tested, to see that hazardous outputs are precluded. Recall that the measure of the *testability of a module* is the minimum testability of the locations in the module. Starting with the least testable part of the software, the software is verified by nontesting means. Then the location with the next higher testability is verified by nontesting means, and so on. Each location successively verified in a nontesting manner is removed from the testability measure, so that the testability measure keeps increasing. Once a threshold value of the testability measure is reached, the remaining, unverified parts are subjected to testing.

For example, imagine a very small module in which the testabilities of the locations are (6, 1, 4, 8). The overall testability of the module is thus 1. The location with testability 1 is verified by nontesting means, and the testability of the module rises to 4. Then the location with testability 4 is verified by nontesting means, and the module's testability increases to 6. The locations with testabilities 6 and 8 are verified through *testing*. Because those locations have high testability, testing is likely to uncover any faults that are present at those locations.

As we have brought out repeatedly in this book, there are great limitations to the testing. The amount of testing required to demonstrate that some event (such as a failure or hazard) does not occur is governed by the following formula: $t = -m \ln(1 - c)$, where t is the length of time the test has to run without the event (e.g., a hazard or mishap) occurring even once, m is the mean time to the event, and c is the confidence level. If zero failures have occurred in time t, there is a 95% confidence that the mean time-to-failure (MTTF) is $t/3$. If you want 95% confidence that the MTTF of your software is one year, you have to test it for three years and not see one failure. Ultrareliable software might need an MTTF of 10^8 hours. To get 95% confidence, you would need to test for 3×10^8 years. A year is 8760 hours, so the testing would take over 300,000 years. Thus naive testing is not the answer. Testability-guided testing offers the promise of less testing to achieve equivalent confidence.

B. Fault tolerance is added to the software. This includes assertions, batons, and so on. These features serve to detect erroneous internal states and prevent the erroneous state from propagating to become a software failure. Some broad-brush techniques such as *N*-version programming and recovery blocks, which people first think of when "software fault tolerance" is mentioned, have not been proven to be cost-effective, if effective at all.

C. Recall that fault tolerance, as a software quality, is in essence the opposite of testability. With the fault tolerance added in, we strive for low testability; that is, we want the software to mask the effects of faults.

D. The software is subjected to simulated hardware faults, to ensure that the software responds in a safe manner to all possible hardware failure modes.

Throughout testing, the software safety engineer reviews test results for safety-related problems and unexpected failure modes.

MODELING FOR VALIDATION

Depending on the applicable safety criteria, mathematical models that represent various aspects of the requirements, design, and coding of the software item are developed. These models are used to verify specific aspects of safety. The modeling consists of manual and automated analysis to ensure that hazards related to the logical and temporal behavior of the concept are mitigated to the extent permitted by the chosen level of abstraction. Examples of mathematical models include state machines, Petri nets, Markov processes, and mathematical proofs, among others, depending on the functionality of the software item and the criteria to be verified.

A REQUIREMENTS AND DESIGN ANALYSIS TECHNIQUE: PETRI NETS

Petri nets are used to analyze and improve the structure and dynamic behavior of systems. They are named for the German mathematician Carl Adam Petri, who in the 1960s devised a general-purpose mathematical technique for describing relations between conditions and events. Research continued at Applied Data Research, Inc., and MIT in the 1970s, and then on through the 1980s and 1990s, especially in Europe. Petri nets make it possible to model and visualize concurrency, synchronization, nondeterminism, and resource sharing. Theoretical results are plentiful, and software tools enable qualitative analysis (David and All, 1994). Petri nets are a way of applying the type of reasoning style used in formal methods but without formal proofs.

Peterson (1981) wrote the classic text on Petri nets, providing a comprehensive introduction to theory and application. Petri nets were recently successfully used to analyze the NORAD (North American Air Defense) Command and Control Center (Shapiro et al., 1990), VLSI (very-large-scale integrated circuit) chip (Shapiro, 1991), electronic funds transfer system (Jensen, 1991), and naval command and control systems (Berger and Lamontagne, 1993).

A Petri net is a graph that is composed of two different kinds of nodes: *transitions* and *places.* A Petri net has to have at least one of each. A place is represented by a circle, while a transition is represented by a bar or box. The nodes are connected by directed *arcs*—that is, by lines with arrows. A Petri net is a bipartite graph, meaning that the places and transitions alternate: An arc always connects a place to a transition, or a transition to a place.

To be useful, a Petri net has to be *marked.* This means that every place node is associated with zero or more tokens. A token is symbolized by a black dot in the place node. Figure 6-1 shows the Petri net notation. If you were to describe how many tokens are associated with each place at a particular point in time, you would be describing the *state* of the Petri net. A Petri net can be *executed.* During execution, the state of the Petri net may change many times.

A transition generally has input places and output places. A transition's input places and output places are the places it's directly connected to. If an arc extends from a place to the transition, that place is an input place. If an arc extends from the transition to a place, then that place is an output place. The net executes in this fashion: Whenever all the inputs to a transition contain at least one token, the transition is *enabled* and can *fire* (Figure 6-2). In the figure, transition T's input places are $I1, \ldots,$ In, and its output places are $O1, \ldots, Om$. When a transition fires, one token is removed from each input place, and one token is added to each output place.

Usually, the question asked is, Is a particular state or class of states *reachable* from the initial marking? For example, each state can be classified as either safe or

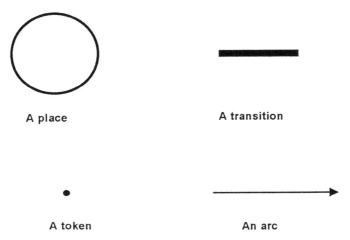

A place   **A transition**

A token   **An arc**

Figure 6-1. Petri Net Symbols.

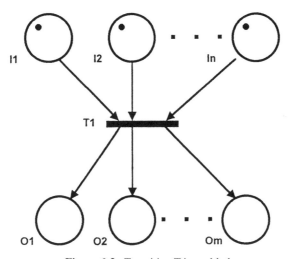

Figure 6-2. Transition T is enabled.

unsafe, and the question can be, Is an unsafe state reachable? A graph called the "reachability graph" can be constructed that shows the possible state sequences from the initial marking. Sometimes, two or more transitions are enabled, and the graph will have branches for the different possible orderings of events.

Petri nets model information flow and control flow, and they are particularly suited to the modeling of systems with parallel or concurrent activities. A condition is a predicate: It is either true or false. An event is an action that takes place in the system and has preconditions and postconditions. An event is modeled by a transition, and the preconditions and postconditions are modeled by the transition's input and output places, respectively. The fact that a condition is true is indicated by the presence of token in the place. Concurrency is modeled by the fact that more than one transition can be enabled. Nondeterminism (Figure 6-3) is modeled by the fact that when more than one transition is enabled, any one of then can fire. Conflict is modeled by the fact that the firing of one transition can disable the firing of another transition.

To determine whether a system can reach an unsafe state, the entire reachability graph can be generated, but this approach is impractical for many models. Leveson and Stolzy (1985) developed a backward analysis technique for Petri nets specifically for software safety that requires only a small part of the reachability graph to be generated in most cases. By working backwards, paths in the reachability graph are eliminated. Also, the algorithm works with partial states, because some conditions are unimportant as regards safety.

Figure 6-4 shows a sample Petri net (Leveson, 1987; Cha, 1993). A token in the place Train_Coming means that the train is on its way toward the crossing but is too far away to be detected yet. When the train reaches a certain proximity to the crossing, the system detects it and the token moves to the Approaching place node. It then enters the crossing, residing in the Within_Crossing place node until leaving the crossing. The system detects the train leaving and the token enters the Past_Crossing place node.

When the system detects the train, it employs some logic, represented by the subgraph contained in the dotted rectangle. This logic selects a Gate_Up or Gate_Down command.

The "Crossing Gate" section of the Petri net models the gate's response to the computer-generated command. When the gate is down, the Gate_Up_Cmd triggers the gate to move up. Subsequently, when the gate is up, the Gate_Down_Cmd triggers the gate to move down.

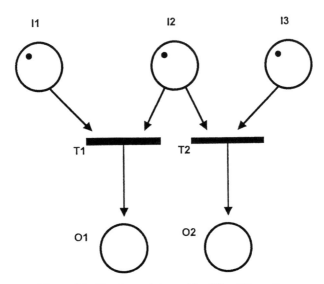

Figure 6-3. Nondeterminism: either T1 or T2 can fire.

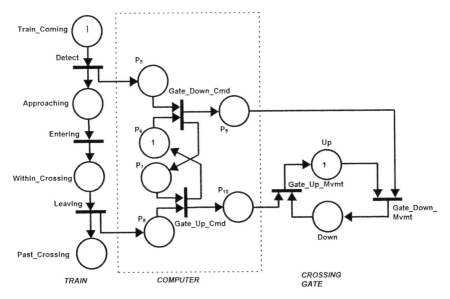

Figure 6-4. Petri net for railroad crossing.

Figure 6-5 depicts the net's reachability graph. Because of the nondeterminism in the Petri net, the reachability graph shows that you can be in a state in which the gate is up and the train is within the crossing. A possible solution is to add an interlock.

Besides the basic Petri nets we have described here, there are abbreviated and extended models. Regular Petri nets embody no notion of time, only a partial ordering of transition firings. The firing of a transition occurs instantaneously, and only one firing can occur at a time. A Petri net can be extended with timing information, such as the minimum/maximum time an enabled transition can take to fire. These "time" or "timed" Petri nets are useful in modeling real-time systems.

In a stochastic Petri net, transitions are labeled with hazard rates. Once enabled, an exponentially distributed amount of time elapses before the firing occurs. The reachability graph can be interpreted as a Markov chain (discussed in Chapter 9).

One timed Petri net variation well-suited for safety analysis is the Merlin–Farber model (Merlin and Farber, 1976). In this model, each transition is assigned minimum and maximum firing times. A transition must be continuously enabled for at least the minimum time before it can fire. However, the transition cannot remain enabled for more than the maximum time. The Software Safety Information Center at The Aerospace Corporation, a U.S. government-sponsored nonprofit organization in El Segundo, California, has developed a Petri net analysis tool set called AeSOP (Aerospace safety-oriented Petri nets). This package implements the Merlin–Farber timed Petri net model and consists of three components: a Petri net editor, a forward reachability graph analyzer, and a backward hazard analyzer. It runs on X windows systems and provides a graphical user interface.

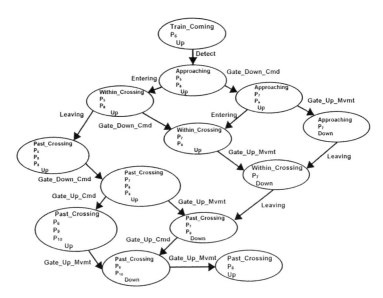

Figure 6-5. Reachability graph for railroad crossing Petri net.

The editor allows the user to draw a model consisting of places, transitions, and arc objects. The objects can be assigned attributes such as names, initial marking, and timing information. Scroll bars provide a canvas area much larger than the screen size, so that large models can be developed. As place and transition objects are dragged around the canvas, their arcs are automatically redrawn to maintain the connectivity. "Unpredictable" events, which have unknown or omitted preconditions, such as failures and operator actions can be included in the model.

The forward reachability graph analyzer starts from the initial state, specified in the editor, and creates a graph that shows all the reachable states. For large reachability graphs, the entire graph does not appear on one canvas but is presented hierarchically. It is also possible to view the progression of states in a graphical simulation. The user can intervene and inject unpredictable events for "what if" analysis.

The backward hazard analyzer lets the user start from a hazardous state and proceed backward. If the initial state is encountered, then the hazard can occur. If the system is free from causing the hazard, the backward analysis will deadlock at an intermediate state before reaching the initial state.

Here is an example of how AeSOP can be used to derive safety-related software requirements.

The Problem: The Space Shuttle Orbiter carries the Space Shuttle into orbit. What if the engine fails on the way up? During the first 40 seconds, no recovery is possible. Between 40 and 55 seconds, return to landing site (RTLS) is safe but abort once around (AOA) is not. Between 55 and 60 seconds, either RTLS or AOA is safe. After 60 seconds, only AOA is safe. Figure 6-6 illustrates the model in an AeSOP screen shot. During the period of 40–55 seconds after launch, three transitions (*phase2*, *p2_RTLS*, and *p2_AOA*) are simultaneously enabled. The transition *phase2* has minimum and maximum times of 15 seconds, whereas the other transitions have 0 seconds. These timing specifications allow the Orbiter to fire *p2_RTLS* or *p2_AOA* without delay as soon as the preconditions (detection of engine failure, initiation of recover mechanism) are fulfilled. In the absence of an engine failure, the Orbiter enters the third phase of the flight, denoted by a token present at the place *in_55–60_period*. This attribute is described in the model as having an inhibitor arc as an input condition to transitions such as *phase2* and *phase3*.

Figure 6-7 shows the forward reachability graph analyzer at the point when the RTLS or AOA recovery mechanisms (transitions from state *s5* to state *s6* or *s7*, respectively) are selected following the detection of an engine failure (from *s2* to *s5*). State transitions from *s2* to *s4* (via *s3*) illustrate normal, uneventful progress of the flight.

Figure 6-8 illustrates use of the backward reachability graph analyzer. There are three states (*s3*, *s4*, *s5*) from which the state *s2* can be reached. Firing of the *phase2* event in state *s7* causes the system to enter state *s10*. Two failure modes would ulti-

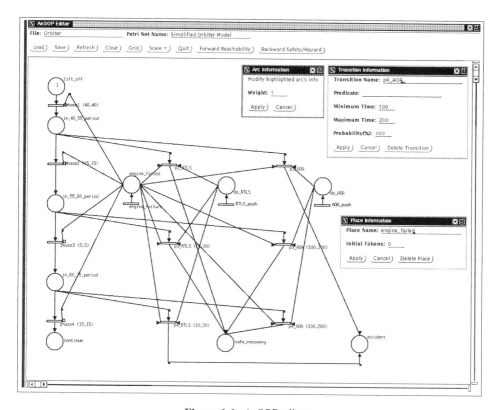

Figure 6-6. AeSOP editor.

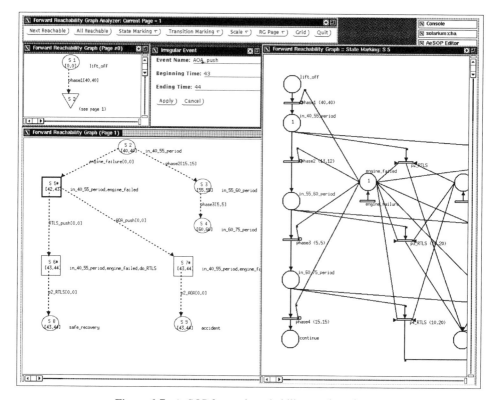

Figure 6-7. AeSOP forward reachability graph analyzer.

mately cause the system to enter the accident state (*s0*) from the (safe) state *s7*. The first failure mode is the selection of the AOA recover mechanisms following the detection of an engine failure during the 40- to 55-second window. To eliminate this hazard, the AOA recovery mechanism must be disabled until it becomes a safe option. The second failure mode is when these events occur in reverse order (i.e., intentional or accidental selection of the AOA recovery mechanism prior to engine failure), which is equally unsafe. To eliminate these hazards, inputs from astronauts initiating recovery mechanisms in the absence of an engine failure detection should be ignored. This can be added as a software requirement. The system may be designed with an override mechanism so that with positive confirmation, the astronauts could initiate any built-in recovery mechanism they wish.

Abbreviated Petri nets have the same power as basic Petri nets but are more compact, allowing large, complex systems to be represented. An example is hierarchical colored Petri nets. These Petri nets incorporate some programming language concepts. In this type of Petri net, the tokens are "colored." A color represents a set of attributes. For example, an orange token may represent (humidity: high; temperature: high; latch: opened). A place is normally restricted to hold only tokens of cer-

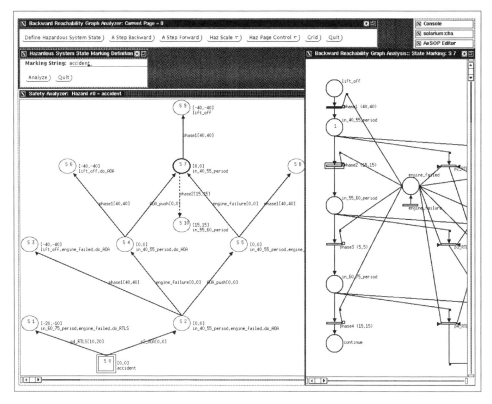

Figure 6-8. AeSOP backward reachability graph analyzer.

tain colors. Arcs are inscribed with an if-then type of expression. If the conditional part (appearing in square brackets) evaluates to true, then the remaining expression (appears after a "%") is evaluated to a set of colors. A transition can contain a *guard,* an expression that needs to be satisfied before a transition can take place (Levis et al., 1994).

As an example, suppose we have three colors of token: red (r), blue (b), and white (w). Each place is declared to be able to hold tokens of all those colors. The variable x is declared to be able to take on any one of the values $r, b,$ or w (see Figure 6-9). The transition function has a guard that says that transition cannot be enabled if x has the value w. Otherwise, the transition will fire when x has the value r, there are two blue tokens in the left input place, and at least one red token in the right input place. The effect of the transition will be for two blue tokens to be removed from the left input place, one red token to be removed from the right input place, and two red tokens to be generated in the output place. Note that the firing of the transition is only possible in the case that x has the value r. When x has the value b, the left input place does not evaluate to true, so the transition would not be enabled. When x has the value w, the guard function rules out the enabling of the transition.

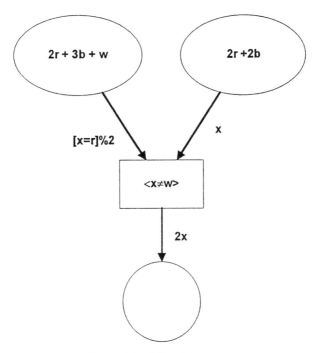

Figure 6-9. Colored Petri net.

CODING

The safety-critical software is then coded into a "safe" subset of the programming language. We have already discussed programming language features involved in constructing a firewall. It is important that coding be kept simple. "Clever" code should be eliminated. Programming features that, when used, result in code that is difficult to verify should be prohibited or greatly restricted through enforcement of a project programming standard. Real-time programming must make sure that the code execution is bounded time in time and space. For example, requests to the operating system for dynamic memory or other system resources could cause problems if the program has to wait for the resource to be freed up.

Code Analysis Technique: Software Fault Tree Analysis

Chapter 5 shows fault tree analysis (FTA) stopping at the software interfaces. On the tree appear leaf nodes that represent software output events. As we have seen, FTA is useful for helping determine which software components are safety critical. Around 1982, researchers at the University of California at Irvine showed how FTA could be *extended into the software code* as a means of verifying that the software can or cannot contribute to identified hazards (Taylor, 1982; Leveson and Harvey, 1983; Leveson et al., 1991). A software fault tree can run the gamut of formality. The analysis can be treated as an informal safety-oriented walkthrough, or more formally as an axiomatic proof of safety properties.

Proof is usually by contradiction. It is hypothesized that the software produced an unsafe control action. If a logical contradiction occurs in the software fault tree, then it can be concluded that the program segment cannot cause the top event. Otherwise, the leaves of the tree determine the *safety preconditions* of the program segment. If these conditions are met upon entry into the program segment (as checked by a run-time assertion), then the top event cannot occur. Besides assisting in coming up with run-time assertions, the tree can also assist in testing. It also helps identify critical assumptions about the environment.

Examples of where software fault tree analysis was applied are a UC Berkeley spacecraft called FIREWHEEL and the Darlington Nuclear Power Plant Shutdown software (Leveson, 1993).

Potential system hazards are determined through a hazard analysis. A traditional fault tree is built down to the software interface using standard procedures, as covered in Chapter 5. We get to the point where an event of a software output can lead to a hazard. Software fault tree analysis works backward through the program or program segment, starting from the safety-critical output and examining how the software could produce that output (or absence of output). Like the safety-oriented Petri net analysis we mentioned in the last chapter, by working backwards and focusing only on safety-related logic, we can often keep the analysis tractable.

A software fault tree's top event is a conditional expression describing the properties of the output that would make the output unsafe (as determined by the system-level fault tree). For simplicity, assume that all expressions are "pure"—that is, they are free of side effects. It is a good idea to prohibit side effects in the project's programming. The expression would typically contain the following elements: logical connectives: *and*, *or*, *not*, etc.; relational operators: $>$, $< =$, $=$, etc.; arithmetic operators: $+$, $-$, $*$, etc.; variables; functions; constants.

To build a software fault tree, use is made of predefined templates. The templates provide guidance in formal reasoning about software. There is one template associated with each programming-language statement type (construct). A template is a little software fault tree, a subtree that is grafted onto the software fault tree. The template shows how the construct can cause—or allow—an event to occur. It contains placeholders that are filled in by transferring expressions and statements from the code. The leaves of the subtree are events to which the same procedure is applied but to a truncated version of the program segment.

We start out with a program segment (a sequence of source code statements) and a top event. We work backwards to determine whether the program segment can cause the top event. The program segment can be expressed as PSP + (last statement). The PSP stands for "program segment prefix," which is simply the program segment minus the last statement in the program segment. [In an MS-DOS executable file, there is something called a "PSP," but this has nothing to do with that.] We use the "+" sign in this context to stand for concatenation. For example, suppose the program segment is

```
a := b + 2;
while (a < 7) do a := a + 1;
a := b * a * 3;
if (a > 7) then begin g := 8; a := b end
else begin g := 7; b := a - 9 end;
```

In this example, the PSP is

```
a := b + 2;
while (a < 7) do a := a + 1;
a := b * a * 3;
```

The "last statement" in this example is

```
if a > 7 then begin g:= 8; a := b end
else begin g := 7; b := a - 9 end;
```

Each template is expressed in terms of "PSP + (last statement)." We go through several Pascal-like constructs and show the associated templates.

The Assignment Statement

An assignment statement has the form $V := e$, where V is a variable and e is an expression. The assignment statement template (Figure 6-10) illustrates that "PSP + $(V := e)$" causes the template's top event when "PSP" causes the top event altered in the following way: Wherever the variable V appears in the template's top event, it is replaced by (e). The parentheses will be necessary in the case where e abuts a high-precedence operator.

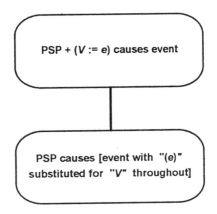

Figure 6-10. Template for assignment statement.

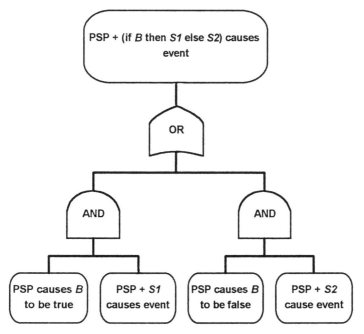

Figure 6-11. Template for if-then-else construct.

THE IF-STATEMENT

An if-statement has the form

```
if B
then S1
else S2
```

B is a conditional expression that evaluates to TRUE or FALSE. *S1* is a statement that is executed when *B* is TRUE, and *S2* is a statement that is executed when *B* is FALSE. The if-then-else statement template (Figure 6-11) shows that "PSP + (if-then-else statement)" causes the template's top event if either

PSP causes *B* to be true and (PSP + *S1*) causes the event
                            or
PSP causes *B* to be false and (PSP + *S2*) causes the event

A variation on the if-then-else construct is the if-then construct (Figure 6-12). Here there is no else clause. We have

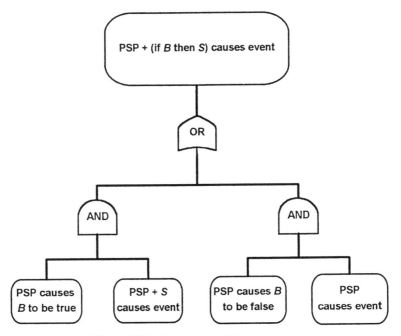

Figure 6-12. Template for if-then construct.

```
if B
then S
```

For "PSP + (if *B* then *S*)" to have caused the event, either

PSP caused *B* to be true and (PSP + *S*) caused the event
                    or
PSP caused *B* to be false and PSP itself caused the event

The While-Statement

The while-statement has the form

```
while B {assert I} do S.
```

B is a condition that is evaluated just before each iteration of the loop. If its value is FALSE, then the while-statement terminates. If its value is TRUE, then the loop repeats another time. The "assert I" is not part of the statement as compiled. It is a comment. "*I*" is a condition called the *loop invariant*. The invariant captures the essence of the dynamic processes that occur when the while-statement is executed. In general, the number of times the loop body *S* repeats is data-dependent and changes every time the while-statement is executed. The programmer chooses *I* such that if it's TRUE at the top of the loop during the *j*th iteration, it's TRUE there at the (*j*+1)st iteration. Note that *I* does not have to be true throughout the body of the loop, only at the top of the loop (Hoare, 1969).

The template (Figure 6-13) shows that there are two possible ways that "PSP + (while-statement)" can cause the template's top event:

1. The loop executes zero times. In this case the invariant is immaterial. The template's top event has to have been true prior to the while-statement. Thus, two things have to happen:

   a. PSP causes *B* to be FALSE. This makes the loop iterate zero times.

   b. PSP causes the template's top event.

2. The loop executes at least once. In this case three things have to happen:

   a. PSP causes *B* to be TRUE. This makes the loop iterate at least once.

   b. PSP causes *I* to be true.

   c. *I* AND NOT *B* implies the template's top event. The NOT *B* comes from the fact that when the loop terminates, the condition *B* will be FALSE. This implication is an exercise in logic that is performed off-line (off the tree); that's why the event is symbolized by a diamond.

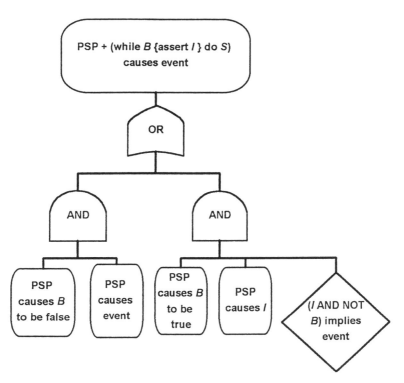

Figure 6-13. Template for while-do construct.

Note that the loop is handled by means of an inductive argument. I has the property that if it's true at one iteration, it's true at the next iteration. Step b shows that it's true at the first iteration. Therefore, it's true at every iteration. Because I is true after the final iteration and step c shows that I implies the template's top event, it can be concluded that the template's top event will occur.

The programmer may have to be consulted to find an I that meets the three requirements we have stipulated: PSP implies I, I implies the template's top event, and I is true at the top of the loop body at every iteration. If you can show that no such invariant I can exist, then this could bolster an assertion that the program segment cannot cause the top event.

Safety may be affected by whether or not the loop terminates. One way to prove that a loop terminates is to show a mapping from the state of computation to *nonnegative* integers. If you can show that each iteration causes the integer to decrease, then you can conclude that eventually the integer will get down to zero and therefore that the loop will terminate.

Consider the following sample procedure. It is in Ada but restricts itself to Pascal-like constructs.

```
with integer_io; use integer_io;
procedure example is
   x,y: integer;
begin
   if x <= 10 then
      y := 100;
   else
      y := x * x;
   end if;
— @ after_if
   put(x);
end example;
```

Assume that the postcondition that is safe is "$y \geq 100$". Figure 6-14 shows the software fault tree. From the leaves of the fault tree, the precondition is seen to be "$(x \leq 10) \vee (x > 10 \wedge x * x \geq 100)$", which is equivalent to "$(x \leq 10) \vee (x > 10 \wedge |x| \geq 10)$" or "$(x \leq 10) \vee (x > 10)$", which covers all values of x.

SOFTWARE FAULT TREE TOOLS

A tool, called Software Fault Tree Analysis Tool, was developed at UC/Irvine (Rolandelli et al., 1986); (Leveson et al., 1989). Another one, called FTE (Fault Tree Editor), was developed at the Naval Postgraduate School. In 1993, an automated tool for analyzing Pascal code was described (Friedman, 1993). Later that year, the corresponding tool for Ada code was developed (Ordonio, 1993). His Automated Code Translation Tool (ACTT) was enhanced by Reid (1994), who implemented support for concurrency and exception handling.

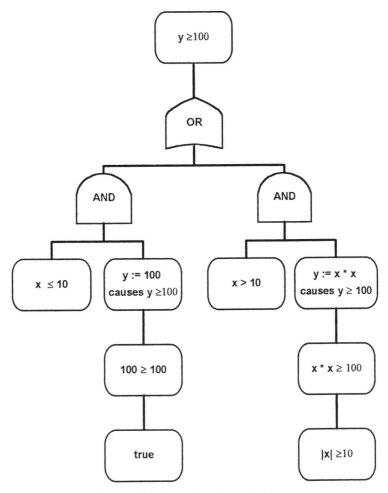

Figure 6-14. Example software fault tree.

These tools work in several steps. A program segment and a top event (expressed as a condition on program variables) are presented to the tool. The tool first performs a "lexical analysis" on the program segment. This step removes whitespace (spaces, tabs, carriage returns, linefeeds, etc.) and comments to transform the program segment into a sequence of "tokens." Each token is a keyword (such as *if*, *the*, *while*, etc.), a number, a variable, an operator (+, −, *, /, etc.), and so forth. In the second step, the list of tokens is "parsed," which means that the tool determines the syntactic structure of the program and stores it internally in a recursive data structure. An example of syntactic structure is to recognize that a certain *if*, *then*, and *else* go together and to identify what the condition, then-clause, and else-clause are. Internally (in Lisp notation) this would be stored as the list (if-then-else *condition then-*

clause else-clause). The recursion comes in that *condition, then-clause*, and *else-clause* are themselves lists.

Whenever a sequence of statements is found (***begin-end*** block), the order of the statements is reversed, because the analysis will proceed backwards through the program segment.

The whole program segment is represented in that data structure. Finally, the tool traverses the data structure. The top event becomes the root of the fault tree. As each programming-language construct is encountered, the corresponding template is formed, filled in, and grafted onto the growing fault tree. Each leaf defines an event and a shorter program segment that needs to be developed into a subtree of its own. The internal data structure corresponding to that shorter program segment is then recursively processed the same way. The tool continues until the original program segment has been fully processed. The resulting tree is then passed on to a fault tree editor tool to allow the analyst to view, manipulate, and print the software fault tree, and graft it onto a system-level fault tree.

Formal Verification of Code

A proof is a formal argument, using the rules of mathematical logic, that a formula is true. We can show consistency between levels of specification or between a specification and its implementation. In testing, a system is subjected to sample inputs and the system's behavior/results are examined. In most formal verification, mathematical reasoning is employed to determine if the system produces the specified behavior/results for every input. Such a proof says as much as exhaustive testing. While a proof of correctness may be difficult, a proof of safety is often a much more limited and tractable undertaking. In a proof of safety, we are not interested in whether the program is correct or not, only in whether the program can cause or contribute to a safety hazard. In a proof of safety, only certain output variables may be of interest. Also, note that a state could be "correct" (to spec) but unsafe; a proof of safety has to start from a specification that has been shown to be "safe."

Formal verification does not provide absolute assurance; for example, the formal specification could be wrong or the verification tool could contain a bug. The mapping between the informal requirements communicated by the customer and the formal specification, as well as the mapping between the real world and an abstract model, can be imperfect. The assumptions made about the environment can be wrong. But in conjunction with testing and other verification methods, it leads to higher levels of confidence.

The idea of using reason and mathematics for proving a property of a program is not new. Back in the 19th century, Charles Babbage wrote about "Verification of the Formulae Placed in the Cards, " referring to the operation cards of his analytic engine (Randell, 1975). Alan Turing published a correctness proof in the late 1940s. (Morris and Jones, 1984). In 1960, Lisp inventor John McCarthy devised a proof method based on functional programming (McCarthy, 1960). In 1967, Floyd devised a method of annotating flowcharts with logical assertions (Floyd, 1967). The two most prominent "textbook" methods for proving program properties are those of Hoare and Dijkstra. In 1969, Hoare (Hoare, 1969) presented an axiomatic approach in which properties of program fragments are described by sentences of the form "{PRE} P {POST}". PRE is the precondition, POST is the postcondition, and P is a program fragment. Both PRE and POST are expressed in first-order predicate calculus, which means they can include the quantifiers $\forall$ ("for all") and $\exists$ ("there exists"). The interpretation of the sentence is that if the program fragment P starts executing in a state satisfying PRE, then if P terminates, it will do so in a state satisfying POST. Each programming language construct has an associated proof rule. For example, the proof rule for the C/C++-language statement "**if** (B) S_1 **else** S_2" is

$$\frac{\{PRE \wedge B\} \; S_1 \; \{Q\}, \; \{PRE \wedge \neg B\} \; S_2 \; \{POST\}}{\{PRE\} \; \textbf{if} \; (B), S_1 \, \textbf{else} \, S_{2:} \; \{POST\}}$$

The interpretation of such a proof rule is that if the assertions in the hypothesis (the numerator, in this case "$\{P \wedge B\}S_1\{Q\}$" and "$\{P \wedge \neg B\}S_2\{Q\}$") are true, then the assertion in the conclusion (denominator) is true.

Suppose that we have the C/C++-language program fragment "**if** $(a > 0)$ $b = a$ **else** $b = (-a);$" and that to be safe the final value of the variable b has to be nonnegative. We can apply the if-then-else proof rule with P = true and $B = (a > 0)$ to

$$\{(a > 0)\} \; b = a \; \{b > 0\}$$
$$b > 0 \supset b \geq 0$$
$$\{\neg (a > 0)\} \; b = (-a) \; \{b \geq 0\}$$

to obtain the sentence "$\{true\}$ **if** $(a > 0)$ $b = a$ **else** $b = (-a);$ $\{b \geq 0\}$". Thus we are guaranteed that no matter what value a has before the if-then-else, the final value of b is nonnegative (Alagic and Arbib, 1978).

The Hoare logic led to Dijkstra's (1976) closely related "calculus of programs," based on the idea of weakest preconditions. To a great extent, the software fault-tree analysis technique described earlier is based on the notion of weakest preconditions. The weakest precondition R with respect to a program fragment P and a postcondition POST is the set of all states that, when subjected to P, will terminate and leave the state of computation in POST. The weakest precondition is written as WP(P,POST). For example, the semantics of the C/C++-language statement "**if** (B) S_1 **else** S_2;" are

$$w = WP \; (\textbf{if} \; (B) \; S_1 \; \textbf{else} \; S_2, POST;) = (B \Rightarrow \textbf{WP}(S_1, POST) \wedge \neg B \Rightarrow \textbf{WP}(S_2, POST))$$

This says that for the postcondition POST to be true after execution of the if-then-else statement, it must be the case that the condition B implies the weakest precondition of statement S_1 with respect to POST and that the complement, NOT B, implies the weakest precondition of statement S_2 with respect to POST. To prove that some precondition P will lead to the postcondition R after execution of the if-then-else, it is only necessary to show that P implies w. For instance, the fact that the weakest precondition w is, say, "$x > 27$" implies a precondition P of "$x > 20$". That is, the condition "$x > 20$" is descriptive of all those states that have the property that, after execution of P, result in the postcondition, and the condition "$x > 27$" is descriptive of a subset of those states.

Because program proving can be a tedious process, a number of support tools have emerged. The Boyer–Moore theorem prover is the most well known of these (Boyer and Moore, 1988). Another tool that has successfully proven many programs and has been used on systems where the critical software is on the order of 1000 source lines of code is the State Delta Verification System (SDVS) (Cook et al., 1991). Like AeSOP, SDVS was developed at The Aerospace Corporation. The tool helps users write and check formal proofs of correctness, safety, and security at the hardware, firmware (microcode), and software levels.

Temporal logic is a property-oriented method for specifying properties of sequential, concurrent, and distributed systems. Pnueli (1977) was the first to recognize that temporal logic could be used to reason about distributed computations. Statements involving time can be expressed in temporal languages. In addition to the usual logical operators, a temporal language commonly includes the operators *eventually* ($\Diamond$), *always* ($\Box$), and *until* (U). The *eventually* operator asserts that a statement will be true at some point in the future. The *always* operator asserts that a certain statement is true from now on. The *until* operator asserts that a statement will be true from now until a time at which another statement becomes true. The previous assertion q_1 can now be expressed as

$$q_2 \equiv \Diamond(z = x_0 + y_0 \; terminated_P)$$

The notation $tr(P)$ denotes the translation of program P into temporal logic. A proof that P is correct with respect to its specification is a proof that the formula $tr(P) \rightarrow q_2$ is a valid formula. The temporal operator of SDVS is the state delta.

The word "temporal" in temporal logic can be misleading. Note that temporal logic does not help in reasoning about real time in a quantitative sense such as seconds, minutes, and so on. It only assists in reasoning about the relative ordering of events or states and about the property of eventuality.

In SDVS, the *state delta language* is used to write formulas to be proven as well as the relevant programs and specifications. The state delta language (whose basic formulas are state deltas) is a temporal logic. A state delta is a claim of the form "if P is true now, then Q will become true in the future" (Crocker, 1977).

A proof of program correctness in SDVS is a proof that the state delta formula corresponding to the program implies the state delta corresponding to the specification. Typically, specifications of programs are of the form "if the inputs satisfy certain properties, then eventually the output satisfies certain properties." The proof that a program satisfies such a specification is done in SDVS by symbolically executing the state delta representation of the program until a state is reached in which the goal is true.

The user inputs a specification, written in terms of state deltas, and a computational object such as an Ada program, or a description expressed in a standard hardware or firmware description language. Application language translators convert the computational object into the state delta language.

SDVS provides a user interface language that allows the user to interactively construct a proof. The user expresses the proof in SDVS's proof language. During the course of a proof, there are two kinds of tasks: going from one state to the next state, and proving that certain things are true in a given state. In the proof language the user has access to axioms and automatic deduction. SDVS understands a lot about propositional and predicate logic, equality, enumeration orderings, naive set theory, bit strings, arrays, and integer arithmetic.

For a program P with variables x, y, and z, a possible execution of P generates a sequence of times $t_0, t_1, \ldots, t_i, \ldots, \ldots, t_j, \ldots$, where t_0 is the initial time. The value of the variable x at time t is denoted $x(t)$. At each point in time there is a state, which is an ordered set consisting of the time followed by the values of all program variables. For example, at time t in the execution of the program P, the state is $< t, x(y)$, $y(t), z(t) >$. A model of P is a sequence of states that represent a possible execution of P. An assertion about P is in effect an assertion about all models of P. Here is an example of an assertion:

$$q_1 \equiv \exists t (z(t) = x(t_0) + y(t_0) \wedge terminated_P(t))$$

This means that there will exist a state in which the program terminates and z equals the sum of the initial values of x and y. For example, the program starts out in state $<t_0, x(t_0), y(t_0), z(t_0), (terminated(t_0))>$, where $x(t_0) = 2$, $y(t_0) = 3$, and $z(t_0) = z_0$. At some later time t, the state is $<t, x(t), y(t), z(t), terminated_P(t)>$, where $x(t) = 2$, $y(t) = 3$, and $z(t) = 5$.

The underlying proof method that SDVS uses is symbolic execution. Symbolic execution is executing a program using symbolic values for program variables. At branch points in the program, the proof splits into subproofs of each case. Induction is employed for loops whose number of iterations is data-dependent or large.

The specification says that the program should implement a function f. The program in fact implements a function f'. We can prove that the program is correct by showing that $f = f'$. In exhaustive testing, we demonstrate correctness by showing that the specification functions f and the program function f are the same by showing that for all input states i in the input space, $f(i) = f'(i)$. Another way to demonstrate correctness is by showing that f' and f' are mathematically equivalent. We know what f is from the specification, but we do not know what the program function f' is. Symbolic execution is a way of taking a program and figuring out the function f' the program is implementing.

Consider a program

```
read(a, b, c);
y := a + b * c;
if (y > 16) write(y, a, b, c);
```

The first statement reads in the values of variables *a*, *b*, and *c*. The second statement assigns the variable *y* the symbolic value "a + b ∗ c". When symbolic execution comes to the third statement, the condition "y > 16 " is translated into the condition "a + b ∗ c > 16 ".

Here is a small proof done using SDVS. The program is the simple Ada procedure we used in the software fault-tree analysis example:

```
with integer_io; use integer_io;
procedure example is
  x,y: integer;
begin
  if x <= 10 then
    y := 100;
  else
    y := x * x;
  end if;
—@ after_if
  put(x);
end example;
```

The label after the comment is used to give the prover a breakpoint for symbolic execution.

The program's specification is a simple state data, written in Lisp notation:

```
(defsd example.sd
  "[sd pre:  (ada(example.ada))
     comod:  (all)
       mod:  (all)
      post:  (#example\\pc = at(after_if), #y ge 100)]")
```

In English, this specification says that the procedure example's program counter will eventually reach the point *after_if* and that at that point the value of *y* will be greater than or equal to 100. The notation #*y* refers to the future value of *y*.

We will now start up the theorem prover and attempt to prove the state delta.

```
<sdvs.3> prove
   state delta[]: example.sd
   proof[]:

open —[sd pre: (ada(example.ada))
       comod:  (all)
         mod:  (all)
        post:  (#example\pc = at(after_if), #y ge 100)]

Complete the proof.
```

The command *go* allows the user to symbolically execute to a particular point in the program. If, as below, we simply hit "return" at the "until[ ]" prompt, the prover will execute for as long as it can. The "applys" below are proof steps that correspond to one step of symbolic program execution.

```
<sdvs.3.1> go
  until[]:

  apply — [sd pre:  (true)
          comod: (all)
            mod: (example\pc)
           post: (<adatr procedure example is
                                   x, ... : integer
                            begin
                              if x <= 10
                                  then y := 100;
                                  else y := x * x;
                              end if;
                              ...
                            end example;>)]

  apply — [sd pre: (true)
          comod: (all)
            mod: (example\pc,example)
           post: (alldisjoint(example,.example,x,y),
                covering(#example,.example,x,y),
                declare(x,type(integer)),declare(y,type(integer)),
                <adatr x, ... : integer>)]
    go — no more declarations or statements
```

Looking at the above applys, it seems as though we have symbolically executed to directly before the "if" statement. We can verify this by seeing which state deltas are usable with the *usable* command.

```
<sdvs.3.3> usable

 u(1)  [sd pre: (~(.x le 10))
      comod: (all)
        mod: (example\pc)
       post: (<adatr if x <= 10
                            then y := 100;
                            else y := x * x;
                        end if;>)]

 u(2)  [sd pre:  (.x le 10)
      comod: (all)
        mod: (example\pc)
       post: (<adatr if x <= 10
                            then y := 100;
                            else y := x * x;
                        end if;>)]
No usable quantified formulas.
```

These state deltas correspond to the branches of the "if" statement. However, we cannot apply either of these state deltas because either of them could be true (this is why the go command did not symbolically execute beyond this point). We can verify this with the *applicable* and *whynotapply* commands.

```
<sdvs.3.3> applicable

<sdvs.3.3> whynotapply
   state delta[ highest usable]: u
                        number: 2
 Because the following is not known to be true — .x le 10
```

The notation .x is used to refer to the current value of x. The usual way of handling this is to consider the branches as two separate cases in the proof. We can do this with the *cases* command.

```
<sdvs.3.3> cases
   case predicate: .x le 100

   cases — .x le 100

     open — [sd pre: (.x le 100)
           comod: (all)
             mod: (all)
            post: (#example\pc = at(after_if),#y ge 100)]
```

We will now attempt to go until after the *if* statement (now we will make more interesting use of the "until[ ]" prompt).

```
<sdvs.3.3.1.1> go
   until[]: #example\pc = at(after_if)

      go— no more declarations or statements
```

But for some reason, it seems that the state delta corresponding to the branch of the "if" statement we want to symbolically execute through cannot be applied! What went wrong?

```
<sdvs.3.3.1.1> applicable

<sdvs.3.3.1.1> whynotapply
   state delta[ highest usable]: u
                        number: 2

Because the following is not known to be true — .x le 10
```

To get more information, we look at the proof state with the *ps* command.

```
<sdvs.3.3.1.1> ps
<< initial state >>
adatr ~/demo/example.ada <6>
read ~/demo/example.spec <5>
proof in progress of example.sd <4>
   go <3>
   go <2>
```

```
case analysis in progress on: .x le 100 or ~(.x le 100) <1>
   1st case: in progress
      you are here <—
```

We see that we have mistakenly done a case split on *.x le* 100, rather than *.x le* 10. We can remedy this by going back to where we made the case split with the *pop* command.

```
<sdvs.3.3.1.1> pop
   number of levels[1]:

 One level popped.

<sdvs.3.3> ps

  << initial state >>
  adatr ~/demo/example.ada <5>
  read ~/demo/example.spec <4>
  proof in progress of example.sd <3>
    go <2>
    go <1>
      you are here <—
```

We now make the correct case split.

```
<sdvs.3.3> cases
   case predicate: .x le 10

   cases — .x le 10

     open — [sd pre: (.x le 10)
           comod: (all)
            mod: (all)
            post: (#example\pc = at(after_if),#y ge 100)]
```

The *applicable* command now tells us that the state delta for the branch we want to go down is indeed applicable.

```
<sdvs.3.3.1.1> applicable

u(2) [sd pre: (.x le 10)
     comod: (all)
       mod: (example\pc)
      post: (<adatr if x <= 10
                        then y := 100;
                        else y := x * x;
                        end if;>)]
```

For further assurance, we use the *simp* command to simplify the expression *.x le 10,* which should be true.

```
<sdvs.3.3.1.1> simp
   expression: .x le 10

 true
```

Everything seems in order, so we attempt to execute to the point after the "if" statement again.

```
<sdvs.3.3.1.1> go
   until[]: #example\pc = at(after_if)

       apply — [sd pre: (.x le 10)
             comod: (all)
               mod: (example\pc)
               post: (<adatr if x <= 10
                                       then y := 100;
                                       else y := x * x;
                                   end if;>)]

       apply — [sd pre: (true)
             comod: (all)
               mod: (example\pc,y)
               post: (#y = 100,
                   <adatr y := 100;>)]

   close — 2 steps/applications

   open — [sd pre: (~(.x le 10))
             comod: (all)
               mod: (all)
               post: (#example\pc = at(after_if),#y ge 100)]
Complete the proof.
```

The "close" above tells us that the prover was able to automatically solve the goals when it reached the point after the "if" statement, and that now the proof for the other branch has been "opened." We can verify this by the *ps* command.

```
<sdvs.3.3.2.1> ps

  << initial state >>
  adatr ~/demo/example.ada <6>
  read ~/demo/example.spec <5>
  proof in progress of example.sd <4>
    go <3>
    go <2>
    case analysis in progress on: .x le 10 or ~(.x le 10) <1>
      1st case: complete
      2nd case: in progress
        you are here <—
```

We will now attempt to prove the specification for the second branch. We begin as we did for the first branch.

```
<sdvs.3.3.2.1> go
   until[]: #example\pc = at(after_if)

        apply — [sd pre: (~(.x le 10))
                   comod: (all)
                     mod: (example\pc)
                    post: (<adatr if x <= 10
                                           then y := 100;
                                           else y := x * x;
                                         end if;>)]

        apply — [sd pre: (true)
                   comod: (all)
                     mod: (example\pc,y)
                    post: (#y = .x * .x,
                         <adatr y := x * x;>)]

        go — breakpoint reached
```

However, this time the proof for the other case did not close. Let's attempt to find out why with the *whynotgoal* command.

```
<sdvs.3.3.2.3> whynotgoal
   simplify?[no]:

 g(2) #y ge 100
```

Apparently, the prover is not able to automatically deduce that the current value of *y* is greater than 100. Note the "g(2)" in front of expression #y = 100. This means that it is the second goal (the first is that the current value of the program counter is at(after_if), which is true by virtue of the fact that we get the "breakpoint reached" message from the *go* command. We now try to find out what the problem is by simplifying various expressions.

```
<sdvs.3.3.2.3> simp
   expression: .x gt 10

 true

<sdvs.3.3.2.3> simp
   expression: .y = .x * .x

 true

<sdvs.3.3.2.3> simp
   expression: .x * .x gt 100

 x\30 * x\30 gt 100
```

Taken together, these simplifications tell us that although the prover knows that .x gt 10, it does not know that this implies that .x * .x gt 100. One way to remedy this is to simply create a lemma to this effect.

```
<sdvs.3.3.2.3> createlemma
                name: example.lemma
             pattern: z gt 10 z * z gt 100
    free variables[]: z
  constant symbols[]:
  function symbols[]:
 predicate symbols[]:

 Lemma 'example.lemma' created.
```

We can now use this lemma to prove the remaining goal.

```
<sdvs.3.3.2.3> provebylemma
   formula to prove: .x * .x gt 100
      lemma name[]:

      provebylemma example.lemma — .x * .x gt 100

   close — 3 steps/applications

 join — [sd pre: (true)
       comod: (all)
         mod: (all)
        post: (#example\pc = at(after_if),#y ge 100)]

close — 3 steps/applications
```

Now we have proved the state delta. We can see this by looking at the proof state.

```
<sdvs.4> ps

  << initial state >>
  adatr ~/demo/example.ada <3>
  read ~/demo/example.spec <2>
  proved example.sd <1>
   you are here <—
```

For further assurance, we can simplify the state delta itself.

```
<sdvs.4> simp
   expression: formula(example.sd)

 true
```

We now quit out of this session.

```
<sdvs.4> quit

 Proof session closed using unproved lemmas: (example.lemma)
 The proof for this session is in 'sdvsproof'.
```

It is important to note that the prover keeps track of any proof obligations one might have incurred in the course of doing a proof (Bouler, 1994). For example, above we see a message reminding us that we never actually proved the lemma *example.lemma.*

Software Failure Modes And Effects Analysis

Fault-tree analysis is a deductive form of fault analysis. Another, complementary approach that is used to identify hazards is a bottom-up technique called a software Failure Modes and Effects Analysis (software FMEA) (Goddard, 1993). It is an inductive method of analysis, generally performed after the initial design is completed. The analyst starts with a software unit, identifies all its possible failure modes, and assesses the effect of those failures on other software and hardware components and the system as a whole. In addition, each potential failure mode is classified according to its severity. The analysis identifies all the ways that software failure can affect the system. The immediate effect of software failure is the loss of a service or incorrect, missing, or superfluous output. For example, a Boolean value can exhibit the failure mode of being true when it should be false, or false when it should be true. A routine that calculates a value can have failure modes of "calculates value high" and "calculates value low." As the effect propagates through the system to affect system behavior, safety hazards can be identified.

To be effective, the FMEA must be iterative so that it corresponds to the design process. Configuration management is very important here, so that the analyst knows what and where the current design is.

The drawback to FMEA is that it generally only looks at single-point failures.

Error Analysis

In practical circumstances, we have a physical situation. Some simplifying assumptions are made to allow a mathematical representation to develop. Some error is inherent in this modeling.

Mathematics uses the continuum of real and complex numbers for quantitative statements, for relations between numbers, and for objects such as vectors and matrices. Every arbitrarily small interval on the real axis contains infinitely many values. Often software is called upon to implement a mathematical formula.

On a computer you have only finite many numbers to work with, each with only a limited number of digits of precision. You only have a small implementation-defined subset of the real numbers to work with. This gives rise to *roundoff error.* The initial data of the problem and the intermediate results of every step are falsified. This roundoff error can accumulate and propagate. To top it off, numbers in a computer are represented in the binary system. Some numbers that can be exactly represented in decimal turn out to require an infinite number of digits to represent in binary and vice versa. You can also encounter underflow and overflow conditions, if the result of an arithmetic operation is too small or too great to represent.

Approximation error arises from summing up only to a finite number of terms of an infinite series. Every transcendental operation must be replaced by a finite chain of realizable operations such as addition, subtraction, multiplication, and so on. Transcendental operations include exponentials, logarithms, and trigonometric equations. In other cases, discretizing is performed: Definite integrals are replaced by finite sums, differential quotients by difference quotients, and so on.

EXERCISES

1. Create a software fault-tree template for
   (a) The C/C++ **switch** statement
   (b) The Pascal **repeat**-**until** statement
   (c) The C/C++ condition expression statement (C ? Z : Y)

2. Describe cirumstances under which the following C++ features might allow a firewall to be breached:
   (a) friend class
   (b) friend function
   (c) operator .*
   (d) operator –>*
   (e) cast of a pointer
   (f) returning the address of a member function

3. Form an initial hazard list for the following types of systems:
   (a) Cardiac pacemaker
   (b) Cruise control for a car
   (c) Electronic throttle control for a car
   (d) Braking system for a car
   (e) Train control system

4. Create a Petri net model of the following system: red/yellow/green traffic lights at an intersection. Just include a single north–south traffic light and a single east–west traffic light.

5. Do you think that, in general, automation increases or decreases safety?

6. One problem that may be encountered with software fault-tree analysis is excessive fan-out; that is, the tree widening as we go down the page until it becomes unwieldly. Suppose the tree structure was liberalized to allow one node to have multiple parents. This structure is called a *directed acyclic graph* (DAG). Describe the templates you would then use for if-then-else and while statements.

REFERENCES

S. Alagic and M. A. Arbib. *The Design of Well-Structured and Correct Programs.* New York: Springer-Verlag, 1978.

J. Berger and L. Lamontagne. "A Colored Petri Net Model for a Naval Command and Control System." In: *Application and Theory of Petri Nets.* New York: Springer-Verlag, 1993, pp. 532–541.

M. Bouler. SDVS demo handout, The Aerospace Corp., 1994.

R. S. Boyer and J. S. Moore. *A Computational Logic Handbook.* New York: Academic Press, 1988.

S. S. Cha. "Petri Net-Based Software Safety Tool Demonstration." Tutorial handout, Software Safety Information Center, The Aerospace Corp., September 26, 1993.

J. Cook, I. Filippenko, B. Levy, L. Marcus, and T. Menas. "Formal Verification in the State Delta Verification System (SDVS)." *AIAA Computing in Aerospace VIII,* Baltimore, October 21–24, 1991, AIAA-91-3715.

S. D. Crocker. *State Deltas: A Formalism for Representing Segments of Computation.* Ph.D. thesis, University of California, Los Angeles, 1977.

R. David and H. All. "Petri Nets for the Modeling of Dynamic Systems—A Survey." *Automaica* 30(2), pp. 175–202, 1994.

E. W., Dijkstra. *A Discipline of Programming.* Englewood Cliffs, NJ: Prentice–Hall, 1976.

R. W., Floyd. "Assigning Meanings to Programs." *Proceedings Symposium in Applied Mathematics* 10, American Mathematical Society, 1967, pp. 19–32.

M. A. Friedman. "Automated Software Fault Tree Analysis of Pascal Programs." In: *Proceedings, Annual Reliability and Maintainability Symposium,* Atlanta, 1993, pp. 458–461.

P. L. Goddard, "Validating the Safety of Embedded Real-Time Control Systems using FMEA, *Proceedings of the Annual Reliability and Maintainability Symposium,* 227–230, Atlanta, 1993.

C. A. R. Hoare. "An Axiomatic Basis of Computer Programming." *Communications of the ACM* 12(10), 576–580, October 1969.

N. G. Leveson. "Building Safe Software." In: B. Littlewood (Ed.), *Software Reliability: Achievement and Assessments,* pp. 1–18, Oxford Blackwell Scientific Publications, 1987.

N. G. Leveson. "An Introduction to Software System Safety." Handout, course in High Assurance Software, April 1993.

N. G. Leveson and H. R. Harvey. "Analyzing Software Safety." *IEEE Transactions on Software Engineering.* SE-9(5), 569–579, September 1983.

N. G. Leveson and J. L. Stolzy. "Analyzing Safety and Fault Tolerance Using Time Petri Nets," In: H. Ehrig et al. (Eds.), *Proceedings International Joint Conference on Theory and Practice of Fault Development* (TAPSOFT), 2. Lecture Notes in Computer Science, Vol. 186, pp. 339–355. New York: Springer, 1985.

N. G. Leveson, S. Cha, and T. J. Shimeall. "Safety Verification of Ada Programs Using Software Fault Trees." *IEEE Software* SE-17, 48–59, July 1991.

A. H. Levis, N. Moray, and B. Hu. "Task Decomposition and Allocation Problems and Discrete Event Systems." *Automatica* 30(2), 203–216, 1994.

J. McCarthy. "Recursive Functions of Symbolic Expressions and Their Computation by Machine." *Communications of the ACM* 3(4), 184–195, 1960.

P. Merlin and D. Farber. "Recoverability of Communication Protocol—Implications of a Theoretical Study." *IEEE Transactions on Communications* Com-24, 1036–1043, 1976.

F. L. Morris and C. B. Jones. "An Early Program Proof by Alan Turing." *Annals of the History of Computing* 6, 139–143, 1984.

R. R. Ordonio. "An Automated Tool to facilitate Code Translation for Software Fault Tree Analysis." Master's thesis, Naval Postgraduate School, Monterey, CA, September 1993.

J. Peterson. *Petri Net Theory and the Modeling of Systems.* Englewood Cliffs, NJ: Prentice–Hall, 1981.

A. Pnueli, "The Temporal Logic of Programs." In: *Proceedings of the 18th Symposium on the Foundations of Computer Science*, Providence, RI, November 1977.

B. Randell (Ed). *The Origins of Digital Computers: Selected Papers,* 2nd edition. New York: Springer-Verlag, 1975.

W. S. Reid, Jr., "Software Fault Tree Analysis of Concurrent Ada Processes." Master's thesis, Naval Postgraduate School, Monterey, CA, September 1994.

C. Rolandelli, T. J. Shimeall, C. Genung, and N. Leveson. "Software Fault Tree Analysis Tool User's Manual." Technical Report No. 86-06, Information and Computer Science Department, University of California, Irvine, 1986.

R. Shapiro. Validation of a VLSI Chip using Hierarchical Colored Petri Nets, *Journal of Microelectronics and Reliability,* 1991.

R. Shapiro, V. Pinci, and R. Mameli. Modeling a NORAD Command Post Using SADT and Colored Petri Nets. In: *Proceedings of IDEF Users Group,* May 1990.

J. R Taylor. *Fault Tree and Cause Consequence Analyses for Control Software Validation.* Risø National Laboratory, DK-400 Doskilde, Denmark, pp. 5–17, January 1982.

CHAPTER 7

Software Reliability Modeling

Software testability concerns itself with the extent to which a piece of software would reveal faults, *if* it had faults. Testability says nothing about how many faults the piece of software contains, nor how often those faults cause the piece of software to fail. Software reliability is concerned with how often a piece of software fails during use as the result of the faults it does contain.

SOFTWARE RELIABILITY ENGINEERING

Software reliability engineering involves the tasks of software reliability requirements analysis, prediction, combination, allocation, combination, growth modeling /testing, and demonstration testing, as well as building reliability into the design and implementation. Figure 7-1 shows a classical software development life-cycle model. We will relate the software reliability engineering activities to phases in this model, while acknowledging that variations and alternative models exist.

Software reliability *requirements analysis* entails analyzing the customer/end-user's needs for software reliability in light of the tradeoffs among reliability, safety,

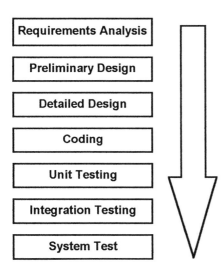

Figure 7-1. Software development life cycle—waterfall model.

171

other quality needs, cost, and schedule. The needs are then translated into objective engineering requirements. Failures differ in the severity of their consequences. A customer will have more tolerance for cosmetic and minor failures than for major and catastrophic failures. A separate failure rate requirement can be set for each severity class. Negotiations between the developer and the customer determine the customer's tolerance for rates of failures of various severity classes. This activity takes place during the requirements analysis phase of the software life cycle.

Software reliability *allocation* concerns apportioning an overall software failure rate requirement to lower-level software elements. For example, a subsystem may consist of three executing programs. Allocation addresses what quantitative reliability requirements should be flowed down to each program in light of their respective criticality, complexity, and utilization. Allocation of reliability objectives to lower-tier elements allows each part of the design team to target a specific reliability goal for their part of the system design so that the design of lower-tier elements can proceed without continual reference to system-level requirements. Additionally, the allocated reliability for an individual software element provides the design team with a means of assessing the acceptability of their design and serves as a figure of merit to assess the need for corrective action within the design process. Because this activity requires knowledge of the software reliability requirements, it takes place after the requirements analysis stage, generally during the preliminary design phase.

Software reliability *prediction* is an early forecast of a program's reliability based on measurable characteristics of the software development process and the intermediate work products of that process, before the software can be integrated and tested in an environment representative of operational usage. A prediction methodology provides a uniform, reproducible basis for evaluating potential reliability during the early stages of a project. Predictions assist in evaluating the feasibility of proposed reliability requirements and provide a rational basis for design and allocation decisions. Predictions that fall short of requirements at any level signal the need for both management and technical attention. Software reliability prediction is performed at each phase of the software development process. Product/process metrics are collected and used to predict the reliability that the software will exhibit at the beginning of system test as well as the software reliability growth model parameters. The growth curve is then used to estimate the amount of time the software will need to have its reliability grow through system test in order to achieve the allocated software reliability at release. If the allocated software reliability is achievable within planned schedule and resource constraints, no action is necessary. If achieving the allocated reliability will result in an unplanned impact to program schedule and resources, one of three decisions is possible: reassignment of needed resources if the impact is tolerably small, reallocation of software reliability objectives if other elements of the system are achieving beyond their allocated requirements by a sufficient margin, or design corrective action. Design corrective actions may include structural changes in the system interrelationships as shown in the reliability modeling. Design changes that result in a more robust design may allow reallocation of the system reliability requirements into lower-tier software reliability objectives that are more achievable. The prediction activity begins in the proposal/precontractual stage of the software. The predictions are updated as more information becomes available during the requirements analysis, preliminary design, detailed design, coding, unit testing, and integration testing phases of software development.

Software reliability *combination* involves creation of a system reliability model for the purpose of aggregating software reliability figures for individual software elements into an overall software reliability figure, as well as combining hardware and software reliability figures into an overall system reliability figure. This activity is performed during the preliminary design phase, when the static and dynamic structure of the software is determined.

Software reliability *growth modeling* allows testing progress to be tracked and completion to be determined. Software evolves as failures during testing uncover faults and those faults are removed. Growth testing is employed to measure the software's current reliability and where the software is on its software reliability "growth curve." Growth testing provides management-by-objectives information on current status and expected time to reach the objective. The information can alert management when reliability growth is deviating from plan. Besides present failure rate, the growth model provides a forecast of what the failure rate will be at any future time and the number of failures that will occur in any future time interval. Reliability growth for software is the positive improvement of software reliability over time, accomplished through the systematic removal of software faults. The rate at which the reliability grows depends on how fast faults can be uncovered and corrected. A software reliability growth model allows project management to track the progress of the software's reliability through statistical inference and to make projections to future milestones. A software reliability growth model provides a family of growth curves. A number of software reliability growth models have been proposed. A growth model specifies the general form of the dependence of failure process on fault introduction and removal. The history of the program's failure times during growth testing is used to statistically estimate the values of the growth model parameters, thereby singling out one growth curve (within a confidence band). This growth curve can be employed to forecast the reliability the software can be expected to exhibit after specific additional amounts of growth testing. Throughout growth testing, constant operating conditions are maintained.

Growth testing provides valuable information on software quality from a user perspective. It furnishes a customer-oriented view of software quality by focusing on failures as opposed to faults. It is true that counting the number of faults found can be important for studying and improving an organization's software development process. But end-users do not experience faults; instead they experience failures. A computer program could be riddled with faults, but the customer could use the software in such a way that its failure rate is acceptable. Conversely, a program could have just a few faults, but the end-user uses the software in such a way as to encounter those faults over and over, resulting in an unacceptably high failure rate. Thus software failure rate fits in with world-class customer-oriented quality movements such as TQM (total quality management). The software reliability growth testing activity is performed during the system test phase of the development cycle, when the software components have been integrated and are executing in an environment representative of field usage.

Software reliability *demonstration testing* determines whether software is ready to be used—that is, whether, to a stated degree of statistical confidence, the software meets its reliability requirements. It is an objective test designed on statistical principles to quantify and limit the risks the developer and customer bear because of chance variation producing a misleading test outcome. This activity is performed toward the end of the system testing phase.

Yes, software reliability engineering activities cost money, but they can also save the developer and the customer significant costs. When looking at the cost of a system over its entire life cycle, both reliability and unreliability have a cost. The cost to unreliability in the field is the cost of fixing failures (maintenance) and the costs incurred by the consequences of operational failures.

Often, system reliability and safety programs are mandated through contractual requirements. In recent years, attention to software reliability and safety are increasingly being called out specifically. Yet, software reliability and safety are often given short shrift, because of the perception that these areas are immature and academic and that the techniques only work on "toy" programs found in research papers. Project managers are sometimes unsure of the payback from these techniques. The money that may have to be paid out to settle a liability claim years in the future comes from a different, distant pot of money than do the development funds, and thus it is less palpable. The truth is that proper specialty engineering activities like software reliability and software safety build qualities into the system design and implementation that save money during development as well as down the road. This book shows how the advances in the areas of software reliability and safety that have emerged in recent years can be employed on a practical level on small and large projects.

HARDWARE VERSUS SOFTWARE RELIABILITY

Until surprisingly recently, it was customary for reliability engineers to assume in calculating system reliability that the failure rate of software was zero. But hardware reliability has improved greatly while the size and complexity of the software elements of the system have increased. With a system containing both hardware and software elements, it does not matter much to the end-user whether the system failure he or she has experienced was caused by hardware or software. An instruction doesn't break or corrode; it doesn't experience fatigue, but a software failure can cause system failure just as easily as a hardware failure can. The proportion of system failures attributable to software has grown to the point where software has become the critical, pivotal element in achieving system reliability goals.

The principal sources of hardware failures are as follows: manufacturing defects from poor quality of materials and fabrication; overload; adverse effects of environmental phenomena such as atomic particles or electromagnetic fields; physical deterioration due to wearout, fatigue or old age; and design errors. For software, the source of failures is the presence of software faults—logical defects. When a fault is encountered, under the right circumstances, a failure occurs. When the fault is removed, that particular failure will not recur. The manufacturing process for software is the copying of media and is not a significant source of problems. The mixing-up of software modules due to configuration-control problems could be considered an analogue of poor fabrication. Software does not wear out, although a medium on which it resides can.

Software faults correspond most closely to hardware design errors. Both hardware and software design errors are systematic, in that they cause the system to fail every time particular inputs or environmental conditions are encountered. As the manufacturing defect and wearout characteristics of hardware become less of a factor in hardware reliability, and as the complexity of integrated-circuit chips becomes higher and higher—in, for example, hermetically sealed very-large-scale integrated circuit (VLSI) chips—design errors are becoming a significant failure mechanism in hardware. Software reliability concepts—both engineering and measurement—are applicable to hardware design errors. The fields of hardware and software reliability are converging.

One could argue that because software does not physically fail, its reliability is binary: either 0 or 1. Either the software is correct with respect to its specification or it is incorrect. Certainly, one can talk about the correctness or incorrectness of a program. But when we talk about reliability, we are not talking about a property of a program in the sense of a static piece of code; we are talking about a property of an executing program. The same program will have different "reliabilities" depending on the environment, the operational conditions under which the program executes. This environment is a stochastic environment in that the values and timing of inputs cannot generally be predicted in advance. The reliability is really the probability that the program, executing in a particular environment, encounters an input sequence that causes it to fail.

Hardware repair generally restores a hardware system to its previous, pre-failure state, but correction of a software fault changes the software to a new state. Hardware failures are often heralded by degradation, but software failures occur without advance warning. Hardware can usually be made more reliable by using redundancy or using higher-quality parts. For software, simply executing identical copies is of no benefit because all copies will fail under the exact same circumstances. (Software reliability might be improved by executing different versions that are developed from the same specification. We discuss multiversion programming in a later chapter.) Off-the-shelf "parts" are not widely available for software. (Object-oriented programming offers the promise of off-the-shelf software parts in the future.)

Occasionally, software failures are caused by hardware failures. For example, a program adds 2 plus 2. A power glitch or an alpha particle causes the result to come out as 5. There was no software fault, but if later the result 5 is output, then a software failure has occurred (because the external results of program operation are wrong), although the failure should be counted against the hardware, not the software.

Regardless of the differences between the phenomenon of hardware failure and the phenomenon of software failure, at some level of abstraction the two phenomena are amenable to the same treatment: They can both be modeled as random processes in time. "Random" means that the failure times cannot be predicted with certainty. The results of hardware and software reliability measurements and forecasts can be combined into an overall system reliability figure, and hardware and software reliability can be managed as an integrated system attribute. In software reliability modeling, we create a quantitative description of the phenomenon of software failure. We employ a mathematical model to answer questions such as:

- How often does this piece of software fail?
- What is the probability that it will fail if I execute it for 10,000 hours?
- Does this piece of software meet its specified reliability requirement?

There are two major classes of mathematical models: deterministic and stochastic. A deterministic model predicts a single outcome from a set of circumstances. For example, Newton's second law of motion utilizes the deterministic model $F = ma$. In contrast, a stochastic model predicts a set of possible outcomes and a description of how likely each of those outcomes is. The vast majority of phenomena are not inherently deterministic or stochastic; the use of a deterministic model or stochastic model is a choice. But there are many phenomena—such as the toss of a coin or the throw of a die—whose causes are so complex that it is futile to attempt to put together a deterministic model. In many cases, the relevant laws of nature are not sufficiently well known. Even the laws of nature that we do know are often complicated and are strictly valid only for idealized phenomena. Another difficulty in formulating a deterministic model is that we might not know the initial state, and a tiny variation in the initial state can cause a large variation in the final state. For example, small variations in the initial rotational velocity of a roulette wheel can greatly affect the number into which the ball rests. The initial state may be so complicated that it's practically impossible to determine it accurately enough. For example, to even begin to predict the roll of a die, we would need to know the precise initial position of the coin in the hand, atmospheric conditions, torque, velocity, geometric form, mass, moments of inertia, elastic properties of the die and the table. For some phenomena, uncertainty principles may come into play: Measurement may produce an uncontrollable change in the phenomenon being investigated.

The occurrence of software failures over time is modeled stochastically, for two reasons:

1. We generally don't know the locations of the faults in the program. Presumably, any faults whose whereabouts are known have already been removed.
2. We generally don't know what inputs the program will be presented with, and when. The inputs determine what path the processor will take through the program and, hence, which faults will be encountered.

We can't answer yes or no to the question, Will this piece of software fail when executed for a particular length of time in a particular environment? At best, we can give a probability of failure occurring. Software reliability is in fact defined as the *probability* that the software will execute without failure over a specified amount of usage or time period, in a specified environment. We assume that the reader is acquainted with the elementary concepts of probability and statistics.

RANDOM VARIABLES

When looking at the result of an experiment or observation, often we are not interested in the outcome itself but in some particular numerical characteristic of the outcome. In probability and statistics, such numerical characteristics are called *random variables*. A random variable is a function that assigns numerical values to the outcomes of a trial. The random variable thus takes on a value determined by the outcome. Suppose we toss a pair of dice. One conceivable random variable is the sum of dots on the faces. For example, if one die comes up 2 and the other comes up 4, the value of the random variable is 6. If one die comes up 3 and the other comes up 2, the value of the random variable is 5. Another example of a random variable is as follows: Pick a word at random from a dictionary and count the number of letters in the word. If the word is "peppermint," the value of the random variable is 10; if the word is "karate," the value is 6.

A *discrete* random variable is one that can take on a countable number of values—for example, a set of integers. An example: Roll two dice and form the product of the number of dots on the faces that come up. If one die shows 5 and the other shows 6, the value of the random variable is 30. A continuous random variable can take on a continuum of possible values in an interval. For example, if an electric current can have any value between 5 amperes and 15 amperes but no others, it is a continuous random variable. One possible value is 7.88765 amperes.

One random variable customarily used in reliability is an item's time-to-failure, which we denote T. The "item" could be a piece of hardware or it could be an executing computer program. T is a continuous random variable, because it can take on any value in its range. The lower end of its range is zero, because time is nonnegative, and the upper end of its range is infinity. In the case of software, a perfect program (no faults) will exhibit a time-to-failure of infinity. The experiment or observation is to run the program, starting from a random input state, until it fails. The value of T is then the recorded time at which the program failed.

The whole idea of a random variable is that you can't predict the value it will take on. However, if you repeat a trial many times, some values or ranges of values may tend to occur more frequently than others. Consider rolling two dice and taking their sum as the random variable. It turns out that it's three times as likely that the random variable will take on the value 7 than the value 4. Over the long run, one would expect the value 7 to come up approximately three times as often as the value 4. We will denote a random variable by an uppercase letter—for example, X—and a particular realization of that random variable by the corresponding lowercase letter, x in this case.

How do we mathematically express this long-term tendency for a random variable to assume certain values or ranges of values over other ranges or values? Just as the probability of the sample space is 1, the total probability of all the various possible values of a random variable is 1. The random variable's *probability distribution* says how that total probability of 1 is allocated to the various possible values.

One of several ways to characterize a random variable's probability distribution is by its cumulative distribution function (Cdf). All random variables—whether discrete or continuous—have Cdf's. In particular, the Cdf of X is a function that gives the probability of the realization of X being less than or equal to the value x, for any value of x you are interested in:

$$\text{Cdf}\{x\} \equiv \Pr\{X \le x\}$$

The Cdf starts out at 0 at negative infinity ($-\infty$) and eventually becomes 1, and stays at 1 until positive infinity (∞). With the curly braces, we are adopting the notation recommendations of the *IEEE Transactions on Reliability*. For a discrete random variable, the Cdf is a step function.

For time-to-failure, T, the cumulative distribution function $\text{Cdf}\{t\}$ can be thought of as the unreliability of the item: the probability that it fails by time t. When t is 0, the Cdf is 0. This makes sense, because when you start up the item—software or hardware—it's operating. The Cdf is a nondecreasing function of t.

It is possible that, once started, the item will never fail. A fault-free computer program will never fail due to software. Even a computer program with faults will never fail if it's exercised only with inputs that do not trigger those faults. For example, if a program can add 2+2 properly but a fault prevents it from adding 3+3 properly, but you only exercise the program with 2+2, it will not fail. For now, we will assume that all items eventually fail; that is, the Cdf eventually becomes 1 and stays at 1 until infinity.

The reliability of an item is the probability that it survives past time t. It is described by the reliability function $R(t)$:

$$R(t) \equiv \Pr\{T > t\} = 1 - \Pr\{T \le t\} = 1 - \text{Cdf}\{t\}$$

The Cdf and the reliability function are complements: For any value of t, $\text{Cdf}\{t\} + R(t) = 1$. The reliability function is a nonincreasing function of time. It starts out at $R(0)=1$ and eventually declines to 0, staying there until infinity. Thus, $R(\infty) = 0$.

Bear in mind that reliability and unreliability only have meaning with respect to a specified environment. For hardware that environment includes temperature, humidity, vibration, and so on, and for software the environment consists of the types of inputs the software is being subjected to.

For hardware, the reliability function has a simple relative frequency interpretation. Suppose we place N_0 identical components under test. Let $N_s(t)$ be the number of components surviving after t hours of testing. The estimated value of the reliability function is

$$R(t) = \frac{N_s(t)}{N_0}$$

In addition to Cdf{ }, a random variable can also be described by two more functions: a probability mass function (pmf)—in the case of a discrete random variable—or a probability density function (pdf)—in the case of a continuous random variable. The terms "mass" and "density" are physics terms, because an analogy exists between distributing a probability of 1 onto the real number line and distributing a unit mass onto the real number line.

In either case—pmf or pdf—a probability distribution is created by taking a total probability of 1 and distributing it along the real number line. The analogy is taking 1 unit of mass and distributing it along that line.

When the 1 unit of mass is distributed, it can be done in at least two ways: Clumps of mass can be assigned to specific points or the mass can be spread out (smeared) onto the line.

As an example of assigning clumps, suppose that a discrete random variable can take on exactly the three values 6.789, 90, and 100.4. We can assign 1/3 to point 6.789, 1/3 to point 90, and 1/3 to point 100.4. Then the probability mass function is pmf{6.789} = 1/3, pmf{90} = 1/3, and pmf{100.4} = 1/3. The value of the pmf for all other arguments is 0. Example: pmf{12.3} = 0.

As another example of a discrete random variable, suppose that the random variable X is the number of dots that show up when a fair die is thrown. The resulting probability distribution can be created by assigning the number 1 a mass of 1/6 gram, the number 2 a mass of 1/6 gram, the number 3 a mass of 1/6 gram, the number 4 a mass of 1/6 gram, the number 5 a mass of 1/6 gram, and the number 6 a mass of 1/6 gram. The points outside and in between those numbers are assigned zero mass. This assignment can be described by the probability mass function pmf$\{x\}$:

$$\text{pmf}\{x\} \equiv \Pr\{X = x\} = \frac{1}{6}, \qquad x = 1, 2, \ldots, 6$$

Unlike for a continuous random variable, for a discrete random variable it makes sense to ask what the probability of a single value is. The probability that N takes on the value n is denoted

$$\text{pmf}\{n\} \equiv \Pr\{N = n\}$$

The pmf appears as a bar histogram. Because N must take on one of the values, it follows that the area of the bars in the histogram total to 1:

$$\sum_{n=-\infty}^{\infty} \text{pmf}\{n\} = 1$$

In reliability theory, whenever we have a random variable that gives the cumulative number of failures in a time interval, we are dealing with a discrete random variable. However, whenever we are dealing with time-to-failure or other times, we generally represent that time as a continuous random variable.

A continuous random variable can take on any value over its range. In this case, the one-unit probability mass is spread out over an interval of the real number line.

In calculus notation, the probability density function is the time derivative of the Cdf:

$$\text{pdf}\{t\} \equiv \frac{d}{dt}\text{Cdf}\{t\}$$

Recall that a derivative of a function at a point is the instantaneous rate of change. By "instantaneous" we don't mean "prompt" or "immediate"; instead we mean "at an instant of time." Geometrically, the derivative is the slope of a line tangent to the curve at the point in question. For example, for a car, the derivative of the distance traveled at a certain point in time is the car's velocity at that point. Likewise, the derivative of the velocity is the acceleration.

Because T is a continuous random variable, the probability is accumulated continuously: The probability that any specific value occurs at any specific time is zero. There is no mass at an individual point on the real number line; all that an individual point can possess is density. The function $\text{pdf}\{x\}$ just defines the rate at which the mass (probability) is accumulating. Only an interval has a mass associated with it. For an individual point x the value of the pdf function is always 0. Symbolically, $\text{pdf}\{x\} = 0$, $-\infty \le x \le \infty$. Only an interval has mass (probability). The probability is obtained by integrating—that is, finding the area underneath the pdf curve of the interval of interest. Consider the random variable X. The probability of X realizing a value falling between x_1 and x_2 is given by the area under the pdf curve between those two points:

$$\Pr\{x_1 < X \le x_2\} = \int_{x_1}^{x_2} \text{pdf}\{x\}dx$$

For example, suppose that the total probability is spread over the interval from 6.0 to 7.0. If the one unit is spread out *evenly* between 6.0 and 7.0, then we can conclude that one-half of the probability lies between 6.0 and 6.5, and one-half lies between 6.5 and 7.0. Then we know that $\text{pdf}\{x\} = 1$ when $6.0 < x \le 7.0$, but is 0 otherwise. Geometrically, we have a square area 1 unit by 1 unit, so the area equals 1, so all the mass, all the probability is accounted for.

Suppose instead that it is three times as likely for the value realized by X to be in the interval from 6.0 to 6.5 as in the interval 6.5 to 7.0. Then we have $\text{pdf}\{x\} = 1.5$ when $6.0 < x \le 6.5$, $\text{pdf}\{x\} = 0.5$ when $6.5 < x \le 7.0$, and 0 otherwise. Here, the area is one rectangle that is 0.5 width and 1.5 height, and another rectangle that is 0.5 width and 0.5 height. All the probability is accounted for, because $(0.5)(1.5)+(0.5)(0.5) = (0.5)(2.0) = 1$.

For a continuous random variable X, the Cdf is related to the pdf as follows:

$$\text{Cdf}\{x\} = \int_{-\infty}^{x} \text{pdf}\{u\}du$$

Because time cannot be negative, the lower limit can be replaced with zero in the case of the time-to-failure random variable.

For a discrete random variable, the Cdf is a summation:

$$\text{Cdf}\{x\} = \sum_{u=-\infty}^{x} \text{pmf}\{u\}$$

Certain probability distributions occur over and over again in stochastic models. They have names like the Poisson distribution, the binomial distribution, the normal, exponential distribution, and the gamma distribution, to name a few. We will define them as we come across them.

While the Cdf and pdf completely characterize a continuous random variable's distribution, we will sometimes want to summarize key features of the distribution. A physicist would find that if a mass of one unit was distributed over the real number line, most important mechanical properties could be described by the center of mass and the moment of inertia. The center of mass is that point that, if you put a fulcrum under the number line, it would just balance. (Just as there is a point you can put the fulcrum under a seesaw that will cause it to balance.) In probability, the measure analogous to "center of mass" is the *mean* of the distribution, often called s-expected value. In accordance with the recommendations of the *IEEE Transactions on Relia-bility,* we will prefix words that are meant in their statistical meaning by "s-", in order to distinguish that usage from the ordinary English meaning of words like "expectation," "expected value," "independent," "independence," and so on.

For a discrete random variable, the s-expected value is calculated by

$$E\{X\} = \sum_{x=-\infty}^{\infty} x \bullet \text{pmf}\{x\}$$

For a continuous random variable, the summation is replaced by an integral:

$$E\{X\} = \int_{u=-\infty}^{\infty} x \bullet \text{pdf}\{x\}dx$$

In particular, $E\{t\}$ of the time-to-failure distribution is called the *mean time-to-fail-ure* (MTTF). It is defined as follows:

$$\text{MTTF} = E\{t\} = \int_{o}^{\infty} t\,\text{pdf}\{t\}dt$$

The MTTF is a popular measure in hardware reliability. Although we have used MTTF in previous chapters, the MTTF needs to be used cautiously in talking about software reliability. If there exists even the remotest possibility that the software is perfect (contains no faults), then the MTTF does not exist, because no matter how improbable the infinite time-to-failure is, it will swamp the calculation. In this case, the median time-to-failure is a preferable statistic. The *median* of a distribution is that value of the random variable for which the Cdf equals 1/2. Also, for some probability distributions used in software reliability modeling, no mean exists. But the median will always exist.

The summary measure that corresponds to the physicist's moment of inertia is the distribution's *variance*. The variance is defined by the following formula:

$$\text{Var}\{X\} = E\{(X - E\{X\})^2\}$$

The variance is a measure of dispersion about the mean. A shortcut formula for variance is

$$\text{Var}\{X\} = E\{X^2\} - (E\{X\})^2$$

The *standard deviation* is the positive square root of the variance.

Repairable Items

Some items, such as a lightbulb, have a finite lifetime. For such nonrenewable items, the reliability is often expressed by the item's *hazard rate*. This is the failure probability per unit time at time t, given that the item has not yet failed by time t. The hazard rate is defined by

$$\text{hr}\{t\} \equiv \frac{\text{pdf}\{t\}}{R(t)}$$

Many systems are repairable. When an item inside the system fails, the system can be repaired by replacing or fixing the failed item. For example, a hardware item such as a lamp can be repaired by replacing the lightbulb, and a computer program can often simply be restarted. In the context of software reliability, a software fault is considered to have a hazard rate. A fault's hazard rate is the amount the fault contributes to the overall program failure rate. Ideally, all faults have a finite lifetime: As soon as the fault causes a software failure, debugging activity removes the fault and, in the next release of the software, that particular fault cannot again cause a failure. To paraphrase Shakespeare, the software fault struts and frets its hour upon the stage and then is heard from no more.

In the literature of reliability, the terms "hazard rate" and "failure rate" are sometimes perverted or used interchangeably, so be careful.

STOCHASTIC PROCESSES

In terms of probability concepts, the next step beyond the concept of random variable is that of *stochastic process*. A stochastic process is simply a sequence of random variables. Each of the random variables in the sequence has an index number. In our case, the index number is a point in time t, the cumulative time spent in system test. Because time is a continuum, t can take on an infinite number of values, so there are an infinite number of random variables in the sequence, one per "moment" of time. A stochastic process is denoted by curly braces. For example, the failure counting process is denoted $\{N(t)\}$. It is a set of random variables, one for each value of t. For a specific value of t, the random variable $N(t)$ gives the cumulative number of failures experienced by time t. Suppose t is in units of seconds. Then $N(4)$ is a random variable denoting the cumulative number of failures experienced up until 4 seconds of system operation.

Counting is initialized to zero at time zero, so $N(0) \equiv 0$. The s-expected value of the random variable $N(t)$ is symbolized $m(t) = E\{N(t)\}$ and is called the *mean value function*. Thus, $m(t)$ is the s-expected cumulative number of failures by time t. While $N(t)$ can only take on integer values, such as 3 or 16, the mean value function m(t) is not so constrained: It is a smooth, continuous curve that can take on values such as 4.56.

The time derivative of the mean value function is the instantaneous failure rate, which we will call the *failure intensity* $\lambda(t)$:

$$\lambda(t) = \frac{d}{dt}\,\mu(t)$$

Conversely, if we know the failure intensity function, we can obtain the mean value function:

$$\mu\{t\} = \int_0^t \lambda(x)\,dx$$

Let's distinguish among similar concepts. The expression "hr$\{t\}$ dt" is the conditional probability that an item survives to time $t + dt$, given that it has survived to time t. The expression "pdf$\{t\}$ dt" is the probability that the system survives the interval from time t to time $t + dt$. The expression "$\lambda(t)$ dt" is the expected number of failures in the time from t to $t + dt$.

The failure intensity $\lambda(t)$ is the rate of failures per unit time, at one, infinitesimally small moment. The time that a program runs can be measured in at least two ways: *execution time* and *system operating time*. Execution time is often expressed as CPU seconds. A program cannot fail when it is not executing; thus, reliability growth is usually modeled as a function of cumulative execution time. Some programs are CPU-intensive—for example, number-crunching programs. Other programs often have to block themselves to wait for input/output to complete. A failure intensity expressed with respect to execution time is linearly proportional to the processor speed: If the program is moved to a CPU that is twice as fast, then the execution-time failure intensity doubles. This phenomenon occurs whether or not the input stream "keeps up." You may find the fact that software failure rate is affected by processor speed to be counterintuitive. But remember that we are talking about failure rate in terms of execution time. If the speed of the input stream remains the same when the program is moved to a faster processor, the result will be that the program will be idle, waiting for input, more of the time. The software gets its work done faster, so it "hurries up and waits." But idle time is not counted as execution time. *During the time the program is executing,* its failure intensity will be higher on the faster machine. Failure rate is failures over time. For a given amount of work, the software running on the faster machine will have the same number of failures as on the slower machine, but the amount of execution time expended is less. Because time is in the denominator, the shorter the execution time required to do the work, the higher the failure rate.

When multiple hardware and software components are operating over a period of time, it is helpful to express all the component failure rates in a common time frame. The failure rates can all be expressed in terms of system operating time. System operating time advances whenever the system operates. A hardware or software component has a certain duty cycle or *utilization.* A program's utilization is the ratio of its execution time to system operating time. If the program executes continuously during the period, then its utilization is 100%. A program's utilization can exceed 100% if more than one process is executing the same program on different input streams. Software has a zero failure intensity during periods when it is not executing. An execution-time failure intensity can be converted to a system-operating-time (average) failure rate by multiplying by the utilization. For instance, if the execution-time failure intensity is 0.0004 failures per CPU second, and the utilization is 50%, the system-operating-time failure rate will be 0.0002 failures per second.

CASE STUDY—UTILIZATION

This case study shows the utilization figures that were predicted for an air traffic control system. The predictions were made through performance modeling using SIMSCRIPT. SIMSCRIPT is a popular modeling and simulation language. The performance model employed was particularly elaborate and was based on queueing theory.

An automated air traffic system is a computer-based system that automatically acquires, processes, distributes, and displays flight data, as well as related aeronautical information concerning aircraft which are under the jurisdiction of an air traffic controller. The system consists of several subsystems, one of which is flight data processing. The major computer software configuration items (CSCIs, a DOD-STD-2167A term) that comprise the subsystem are:

Maintain Airspace Model (MAM). Manage adaptation data. Sectorization consolidation/deconsolidation. Organize track generation/distribution. Restricted airspace definition activation/deactivation.

Communications Services (COM). Provides the interface between open systems that are external to the air traffic control system and open applications within an air traffic control segment.

Flight Plan Processing (FPP). Flight plan processing, route processing, clearance coordination, hold coordination, hand-off coordination, alert processing, flight data distribution

Flight Path Assurance (FPA). Detect airspace-to-airspace conflict. Detect track-to-airspace conflict. Detect track-to-terrain conflict (minimum safe altitude [MSA]). Detect track-to-track conflict. Generate conflict resolutions.

Flow Management (FLM). Manage airspace capacity data. Monitor airspace demand. Determine traffic overload. Flow metering.

Environmental Processing (ENV). Acquire/validate meteorological data. Acquire/validate Notices to Airmen (NOTAM) data. Classify meteorological data. Generate critical weather alerts. Manage winds aloft model. Manage MET data store. Manage NOTAM data store. Distribute data.

Altitude Reservation Processing (ARP). Coordinate approval requests. Detect conflicts. Distribute altitude reservation data.

Simulation/Training/Playback (SIM). Exercise generation. Exercise control. Data playback.

System Monitoring and Control (SMC). Monitor system performance. Manage configuration. Manage faults. Access modules. FDP application. Communication application. Physical devices. Application agents. System control. Recording.

Database Services (DBS). Database access service. Database distribution services. Communication database services. Initialize database. Monitor lock timeout. Notify tasks.

The first column of Table 7-1 lists the CSCI. The second (MIPS) is the processor speed in units of million instructions per second. The third column (UTIL) is utilization, expressed as a percentage of total CPU time. The fourth column (MIPS Used) is the product of MIPS and UTIL and represents the amount of object instructions executed per system-operating second on behalf of the CSCI. Note that MIPS Used will remain constant if the program is moved to a faster machine of the same architecture (for example, from one VAX to another VAX). Moving to a different architecture would require that the software be recompiled, and the number of object instructions needed to accomplish the same work could vary, especially if the move is from a CISC (complex instruction set) architecture to a RISC (reduced instruction set) architecture. The last column (KSLOCs) gives the size of the CSCI, expressed in thousands of lines of executable source code. Note that executable source code excludes comments and data declarations.

TABLE 7-1. Air Traffic Control CSCIs

CSCI	MIPS	UTIL	MIPS Used	KSLOCs
ARP	95	0.00000411	0.00039045	26
SIM	95	0.0476761	4.5292295	50
FPA	95	0.00078948	0.0750006	50
FPP	95	0.0126658	1.203251	100
DBS	95	0.02707	2.57165	20
FLM	95	0.00238872	0.2269284	72
MAM	95	0.0394509	3.7478355	85
ENV	95	0.00142326	0.1352097	24
SMC	95	0.00152	0.1444	35
COM	95	0.150358	14.28401	5

The total utilization of the host computer can be found by adding up the utilizations of the CSCIs. The remaining utilization out of 100% includes time spent waiting for I/O operations to complete or wait for other resources to become available, as well as "cushion," an allowance for inaccurate prediction and for future capacity growth.

UTILIZATION—DISCUSSION

A CSCI can consist of several concurrently executing tasks. The utilization of the CSCI is simply the sum of the utilizations of each task. It does not matter how the executions of the tasks are interleaved.

A hardware or software component's utilization can vary according to mission phase and mission mode. A mission consists of a sequence of several phases of operation. An example of the phases of a satellite's mission is boost, orbit, reentry, and recovery. A particular system can be utilized for several different missions. For example, a military aircraft could be used for a reconnaissance mission, a bombing mission, an intercept mission, or a strafing mission. Orthogonal to the idea of phases, the system can be in one of several selectable modes of operation. For example, a radar system can be in a searching mode of operation and a tracking mode of operation. During each possible conjunction of a mission phase and a mode of operation, a computer program will have a certain utilization.

Note that by our definitions, if a machine contains several CPUs, a program or CSCI's utilization is expressed in terms of a single one of those CPUs. If a program fully utilizes two CPUs, then its utilization is 200%. If we knew the execution-time failure of a program, and we knew that two copies were running continuously at the same time on two different CPUs, then it makes sense that the system-operating time failure rate is twice the execution-time failure rate. If a machine has five CPUs altogether, then its total capacity is 500%, and that program would be utilizing two-thirds of that capacity.

An alternative to using system operating time for expressing failure rates is to use wall-clock time. Wall-clock time is the familiar, ever-advancing passage of time. For a continuously operating system, system operating time and wall-clock time will be identical. When the system goes through alternating periods of operation and nonoperation, then wall-clock time and system operating time will differ.

FAILURE INTENSITY AND OPERATIONAL PROFILE

As we have discussed, a conventional computer program, regardless of how many faults it may contain, implements a deterministic function mapping inputs into outputs. Software failure, however, is a random phenomenon, because you cannot generally predict in advance what inputs the user will subject the software to and when. A program's input space is the set of all possible input states. An input state consists of an assignment of values to all of the program's input variables. An input variable exists external to the program and is used by the program. A program's output space is the set of all possible output states. An output state consists of an assignment of values to all of a program's output variables. An output variable exists external to the program and is set by the program. An output variable can be a control signal, an item on a display screen, a command, an item on a printout, an item of data transmitted over a network, and so on. A run is a subdivision of program execution with a well-defined input state. An operational profile associates each of the program's possible input states with a probability of selection. The use of an operational profile allows field usage to be emulated and helps provide a high cost/benefit ratio during testing. Let there be n input states. Denote the probability of selection of the ith input state by $p(i)$. It must be the case that

$$\sum_{i=1}^{n} p(i) = 1$$

The set of possible outcomes of a run—the sample space—is {success, failure}. The event that we are interested in is the event of failure.

To express the probability of failure, based on a frequency interpretation of probability we see that a run is an experiment that can be repeated as often as we desire under the same set of relevant experimental conditions. The relevant experiment conditions include the operational profile. If the experiment is repeated n times, the relative frequency of failure is computed as the ratio of the number of runs ending in failure over the total number of runs: The frequency interpretation of probability of failure defines the probability of failure to be

$$\text{pof} = \sum_{i=1}^{n} p(i)e(i)$$

For a run starting from any particular input state, the program reliably and deterministically either succeeds or fails. Theoretically, we could run every input state in the input space and record whether the program succeeds or fails. Imagine that there exists a binary function $e(i)$ that evaluates to 0 if a run starting from input i would result in success, and evaluates to 1 if the run would result in failure. In most practical situations, we would not know whether $e(i)$ is 0 or 1 for many or all of the input states. For our purposes here, that knowledge is unimportant.

OBJECTIONS TO THIS MODEL

The main objection people have brought up regarding this model is they believe that the assumption of independent runs is not justified. They believe that a "successful" run could still end up corrupting the data state, with the consequence that later runs are more likely to fail. This objection does not make sense. If we accept the basic model of Chapter 1 that a program is a function mapping an input state to an output state, then a run can only corrupt another run's input state, not any of the other run's intermediate states. Why? Because any data that is not set by a run but affects that run has to be considered part of that run's input state. All of a run's intermediate states are determined by the input states.

So if a run starting from input state i_1 corrupts the next input state and makes that input state into input state i_2, all that has happened is that the frequency of input state i_2 is higher than it otherwise might have been. This higher frequency is—or should be—reflected in $p(i_2)$.

ESTIMATION

The value of pof is estimated by the proportion of observed runs that result in failure. For instance, if you run the software 200 times and three of those runs result in failure, then pof is $3/200 = 0.015$.

The accuracy of the estimate for pof is provided by the confidence level. A confidence level is in the form $100(1 - \alpha)\%$. The confidence level gives the fraction of time that the true value of pof is less than or equal to the estimated value. The following relationship holds (Thayer et al., 1978):

$$1 - (1 - \text{pof})^N \le \alpha$$

By solving for N, we can determine the number of runs required to demonstrate a failure probability pof with confidence $1 - \alpha$:

$$N = \frac{\ln \alpha}{\ln (1 - \text{pof})}$$

Note that a tradeoff is available: The same number of runs can provide a high confidence of a low failure probability or a low confidence of a high failure probability. This formula is useful for illustrating the limitations inherent in demonstrating the failure probability of an ultra-reliable computer program without additional information (Butler and Finelli, 1993). We presented a similar formula in Chapter 6 in terms of time rather than number of runs.

The reliability of the software, expressed as the probability of surviving m runs without failure, is

$$R(m) = (1 - \text{pof})^m$$

The way this equation is obtained is by reasoning as follows: The probability of surviving a single run is $(1 - \text{pof})$. Runs are assumed to be s-independent. By the multiplication law for probabilities, that probability is multiplied by itself m times to get the probability of surviving all m runs. In fact, one of the early software reliability models—the Nelson model (Nelson, 1973)—is based on this approach.

Let the number of failed runs out of m runs be denoted by the random variable X. The probability of x *particular* runs failing and the remaining $m - x$ failing is $\text{pof}^x(1 - \text{pof})^{m-x}$. The number of distinct ways x successes out of m runs can occur is simply the number of combinations of m things taken x at a time, which is

$$\binom{m}{x} = \frac{m!}{x!(m - x)!}$$

The exclamation point stands for factorial: $n! = n(n - 1)(n - 2)\cdots 1$. Thus, the pmf is

$$\text{pmf}\,\{x\} = \binom{m}{x}\text{pof}^x\,(1 - \text{pof})^{m-x}$$

This probability distribution is called the *binomial distribution.*

In some cases, such as operating systems, it is not quite apparent what constitutes a run. For that reason, and for compatibility with hardware reliability models, the unit of exposure is best expressed as time. Most software reliability models are *time-domain* models: The failure rate is expressed with respect to time. If there are an average of k runs per unit time, the failure rate is

$$\lambda_{\text{ave}} = \text{pof} \cdot k$$

The reliability function is

$$R(t) = (1 - \text{pof})^{kt}$$

[In all the equations in this book that involve time, the unit (seconds, hours, days, etc.) is omitted. Any time unit in a formula is permissible as long as it is consistent throughout the equation.]

Time-domain software reliability models go a step further than just expressing average failure rate: They assume the average failure rate to be an instantaneous failure intensity $\lambda = \lambda_{\text{ave}}$ To get from an average failure rate to an instantaneous failure intensity, those models invoke the so-called Law of Rare Events, which describes how the binomial distribution behaves in limiting situations. Recall that in the binomial distribution the probability of failure per run is pof and the number of runs is n. To create the time-domain software reliability model, we divide a run into sub-runs. We let m now represent the number of sub-runs. One or more failures can occur per sub-run. We divide a run into sub-runs and keep subdividing those sub-runs into shorter and shorter sub-runs, letting m tend to infinity. Meanwhile, the sub-runs become shorter and shorter as pof tends to 0. All the while, we maintain the relationship $m \cdot \text{pof} = \lambda$. Finally, the duration of a sub-run becomes so short that only one failure can occur during that sub-run. In calculus notation, such a small interval is denoted dt. It is assumed that dt is sufficiently small that the probability of more than one failure occurring in that infinitesimal interval is zero. The probability of a failure occurring in an interval of length dt is $\lambda \, dt$; that is,

$$\Pr\{N\{t + dt\} - N(t) = 1\} = \lambda \, dt$$

Recall that $N(t)$ is a random variable that gives the cumulative number of failures experienced by time t. It can be shown that the case of constant failure intensity results in the number of failures in a fixed interval of time following a Poisson distribution. The probability of exactly n failures in the interval $(0, t]$—or any interval of length t for that matter—is given by the Poisson pmf:

$$\text{pmf}\{n;t\} = \frac{(\lambda t)^n \exp[-\lambda t]}{n!}$$

The notation exp[ ] stands for the mathematical constant e (which is approximately 2.71838) raised to the power in the square brackets. The Poisson model (sometimes called the Law of Small Numbers or the Law of Rare Events) we employed here is widely applied by statisticians for modeling random variables distributed over time or space. The Poisson probability law is applicable when the probability that an event occurs is proportional to the length of the time interval (or volume or area of space).

In a Poisson process, each failure interarrival time is identically distributed; each is governed by the same random variable, the time-to-failure random variable T'. The failure interarrival time T' follows an exponential distribution. The cumulative distribution function, reliability function, probability density function, and s-expected value of the exponential distribution are, respectively:

$$\text{Cdf}\{t'\} = 1 - \exp[-\lambda t']$$
$$R(t') = \exp[-\lambda t']$$
$$\text{pdf}\{t'\} = \lambda \exp[-\lambda t']$$
$$E\{t'\} = 1/\lambda$$

Almost all software reliability growth models assume explicitly or implicitly that when the software code is "frozen," the phenomenon of software failures over time is modeled by a (homogeneous) Poisson process. Frozen code is a version of the software that is actually or hypothetically released. No changes are made to the code until the next version is released. A Poisson process has a constant failure intensity λ. The interfailure times are exponentially distributed with mean $1/\lambda$. A constant failure intensity does not mean that the software is equally likely to fail at all points in time. For example, at the machine code level, when the executing software is between instructions, it cannot fail: momentarily its failure rate, in some sense, is zero.

(We will see in the next chapter that most software reliability growth models are based on a generalization of the Poisson process, called the nonhomogeneous Poisson process [NHPP]. At any moment in time, the software is behaving like a Poisson process, but the failure intensity is allowed to vary as a function of time).

The constant failure intensity model is appropriate for software that is restarted periodically. Restart clears out accumulated "bad state." The problem is that as faults are encountered, their execution can infect the state of computation. A common example is "memory leaks," which occur when the software neglects to properly deallocate memory. The longer the bad state is allowed to build up, the higher the likelihood of failure, with the result that the failure intensity trends upward, a sort of creeping paralysis.

Figure 7-2 illustrates the pdf of the exponential distribution. In a repairable system, the reciprocal of a constant system failure rate is called the MTBF (mean time between failures). The time between failures includes the time-to-repair and the time-to-failure. Thus MTBF = MTTF + MTTR. The estimate for the failure rate is

$$\hat{\lambda} = \frac{r}{t}$$

where r is the number of failures and t is the length of the observation period. There is $100(1 - \alpha)\%$ confidence that the true failure rate is less than or equal to

$$\lambda' = \frac{\chi^2_{\alpha,2r+2}}{2t}$$

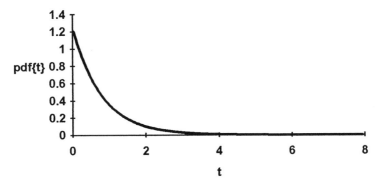

Figure 7-2. Exponential Cdf.

where $\chi^2_{\alpha, 2r+2}$ is found from a table of the chi-square distribution, found in almost any statistics textbook.

A two-sided $100(1-\alpha)\%$ confidence interval for λ is

$$\frac{\hat{\lambda}\chi^2_{2n, 1-\alpha/2}}{2n} < \lambda < \frac{\hat{\lambda}\chi^2_{2n, \alpha/2}}{2n}$$

This means that for $100(1-\alpha)\%$ of the occasions on which you construct such an interval, that interval will contain the true value of λ. Unfortunately, you will not know which occasions those are.

SUMMARY

This chapter discussed the reliability model for a computer program. It is assumed that the code is "frozen"; that is, no changes are made to the software during the period of interest. Furthermore, it is assumed that the software is being subjected to a stationary operational profile. The resulting model is that of a constant failure rate and exponentially distributed times-to-failure.

EXERCISES

1. A piece of software completes a run of 8340 hours with 8 failures. Estimate the failure intensity, a one-sided 90% confidence interval for the failure intensity, and a two-sided 95% confidence interval for the failure intensity.

2. If you doubled the size of a program, would its failure intensity double? Why or why not?

3. If you wrote a program and the answer was off by 0.004%, would that constitute a failure?

REFERENCES

R. W. Butler and G. B. Finelli. "The Infeasibility of Quantifying the Reliability of Life-Critical Real-Time Software." *IEEE Transactions on Software Engineering* 19(1), 3ff, January 1993.

E. C. Nelson. "A Statistical Basis for Software Reliability Assessment," TRW-SS-73-03, March 1973.

R. Thayer, M. Lipow, and E. Nelson. *Software Reliability*. Amsterdam: North-Holland, 1978.

CHAPTER 8

Software Reliability Growth Modeling

A software reliability growth model provides a family of growth curves that depict the decline of the failure intensity, denoted $\lambda(\tau)$, as faults are uncovered and removed during the *system test* phase. The quantity τ is the cumulative execution time spent in system test. A growth model can answer questions such as:

- What is the current failure intensity of the software? This information is important for considering the adequacy of the software for a particular task and for determining whether the software is mature enough to be released.
- What will the failure intensity be if I carry on testing? A model provides a reliability growth curve (failure intensity decline curve) that can be projected into the future to forecast the failure intensity at any future point during system test.
- How much more testing has to be performed to reach a particular failure intensity objective? This information is important for project scheduling, costing, and resource management.
- How many faults are left in the software? This information is important for software maintenance and software development process improvement.

Time. When we use t we are speaking generically of time. When we want to emphasize that the time involved is execution time, we will use the Greek letter tau (τ). Figure 8-1 illustrates the notation we will be using for time. We distinguish between two measurements of time: time epoch and time interval. A time epoch is the cumulative time counted from an origin. For example, cumulative execution time is denoted τ. Usually the point of origin is the start of system test. The cumulative execution time τ is associated with the maturity of the software: how much time it has been subjected to system test.

During system test or a demonstration test, the time at which the first software failure occurs is denoted by appending a subscript of 1: τ_1. The time of the second failure is indicated by τ_2.

The other type of time is time between failures. We indicate this time by appending a prime. The execution time between the first and second failure is denoted τ_2'.

The time τ', without a subscript, denotes the time-to-failure. This time is reset to zero whenever the software is restarted. The more reliable the software is, the larger this number will tend to be on average.

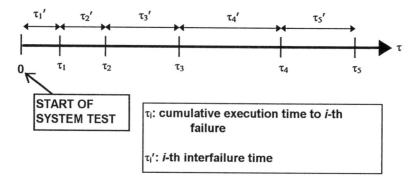

Figure 8-1. Execution time line.

System test is the period between the time the software is fully integrated and the time it is released to the customer. A model contains a small number of parameters that fit the model to your particular project. Point estimation provides a value for each parameter to single out one growth curve from the family of curves a model provides. Confidence intervals provide an interval of plausible values for a parameter. The degree of plausibility is specified by the confidence level—for example, 95% or 99%.

A large number of growth models have been proposed. From a data-analytic point of view, the objective of the research into modeling is to find a model that explains failure data well enough to forecast the future. For credibility, the model should have natural, meaningful parameters. Each model mathematically summarizes a set of assumptions the researcher has made about the phenomenon of software failure and debugging. The models may give fairly accurate results even though all of the assumptions are not satisfied. The selection of a model needs to be justified by the realism of the model's assumptions and the model's "predictive validity."

The practitioner has several choices:

1. One model can be chosen a priori, and then that model is the only one used.
2. One model can be chosen a priori, but a recalibration technique is later applied to adapt the model to the project.
3. Several models can be employed. A goodness-of-fit test is applied to determine the model that is fitting best.
4. Several models can be employed. The results can be combined into a weighted average. The weighted average with the best goodness-of-fit is used.

It is important not to use too many models in approaches 3 and 4, because two models might fit the failure data well but disagree on how to extrapolate to the future. There is a Yiddish proverb, "The man who owns one watch always knows what time it is; the man who owns two watches is never quite sure."

At the start of system test—time $\tau = 0$—the software contains ω_0 faults. For simplicity we assume that each fault contributes equally to the overall program failure intensity. Thus, the failure intensity at any time is proportional to the current fault content. Let ϕ denote the per-fault hazard rate, the contribution any one fault makes to the overall program failure rate. If the further assumption is made that the occurrence of a failure always results in the instant removal of exactly one fault, then the program hazard rate between the occurrence of the ith and $(i+1)$st failure occurrence is

$$\lambda_i = \phi(\omega_0 - i), \quad i = 0, 1, \ldots$$

This model was developed independently by the team of Jelinski and Moranda (1973) and by Shooman (1977). Musa (1975) published and popularized a similar model that made further refinements and emphasized that the failure-inducing stress on software is execution time as opposed to calendar time. The mere passage of time does not result in software reliability growth; only time spent testing the software in a test-analyze-and-fix activity counts. (Walkthroughs, reviews, and other nontest ways of finding faults generally are performed during unit test, not during system test.)

   In reality, debugging is imperfect. Sometimes the causative fault behind a failure is found, sometimes not. Sometimes a whole class of related faults is discovered and removed. Other times, new faults are inadvertently introduced into the code. Musa introduced the *fault reduction factor B* to represent the average net number of faults removed per failure. Once your organization uses the growth model on a project, you can obtain B from historical data; otherwise, a default value of $B = 0.955$ is sometimes suggested. Now the decrement in program hazard rate per failure is not ϕ but instead

$$\beta = B\phi$$

The initial failure rate, as before, is

$$\lambda_0 = \phi\omega_0$$

The (s-expected) total number of failures that must occur for all faults to be uncovered and removed is

$$\nu_0 = \frac{\omega_0}{B}$$

Thus the failure intensity after the ith failure has occurred is

$$\lambda_i = \beta(\nu_0 - i) = \lambda_0 - \beta i$$

NONHOMOGENEOUS POISSON PROCESS

In the Jelinski–Moranda model, the Shooman model, the original Musa basic execution time model, and some other models, if you looked at the failure intensity as a function of time, you would observe that the failure intensity is piecewise constant and drops discontinuously, like a staircase. At the moment of fault removal, the failure intensity ratchets down a notch. This is mathematically ugly. We would like the failure intensity to be a smooth, continuous function of cumulative execution time spent in system test, τ. The justification for smoothing the failure intensity curve out is that we are dealing with a statistical model. Faults are not removed "instantly" upon the occurrence of a failure, as we have been assuming; there is variability in the exact point in time at which the number of faults declines and hence when the failure intensity declines.

While you can express the failure rate of a stable program (frozen code) with respect to cumulative execution time, system operating time, or wall-clock time, the preferred way to express growth time is cumulative execution time τ. The mere passage of time does not cause the reliability of software to grow; only execution time uncovers faults. (Walkthroughs, reviews, and so on, come before system test.) When the failure intensity varies through time, the failure intensity will be a function of time $\lambda(\tau)$. As faults are discovered and repair activity is undertaken, the failure intensity will change. At time any time τ, the failure rate is $\lambda(\tau)$.

A nonhomogeneous Poisson process (NHPP) is a type of stochastic process $\{N(\tau)\}$. Recall that a stochastic process is a sequence of random variables indexed by time. In this case, each random variable $N(\tau)$ represents the cumulative number of failures experienced by time τ. In the case of an NHPP, the probability of failure in the interval between cumulative execution time τ and cumulative execution time $(\tau + d\tau)$ is

$$\Pr\{N(\tau + d\tau) - N(\tau) = 1\} = \lambda(\tau)\, d\tau$$

In an NHPP, the failure intensity is a function of time but at any one moment behaves as if it were a Poisson process with a constant failure intensity of $\lambda = \lambda(\tau)$. If you actually or hypothetically release the software (freeze its code) at time τ, it would exhibit that failure intensity λ. Goel and Okumoto (1979) published a paper describing a simple NHPP software reliability growth model.

An NHPP is completely described by either its mean value function $\mu(\tau)$ or its failure intensity function $\lambda(\tau)$. The number of failures in the interval $(0, \tau)$ follows a nonhomogeneous Poisson distribution:

$$\text{pmf}\{n;\tau\} = \frac{[\mu(\tau)]^n \exp[-\mu(\tau)]}{n!}$$

Because the point in system testing you call the "start" of system test ($\tau = 0$) is arbitrary, this formula applies to any interval during system test. Note that a regular, run-of-the-mill Poisson process, introduced earlier, is simply a special case of NHPP in which $\mu(\tau) = \lambda\tau$. Around 1987, Musa (Musa et al., 1987) redescribed his basic execution time model as an NHPP.

The mean value function of the basic execution time model is

$$\mu(\tau) = v_0[1 - \exp(-\beta\tau)]$$

The failure intensity is found as the time derivative of the mean value function:

$$\lambda(\tau) = \frac{d}{d\tau}\,\mu(\tau) = \nu_0\beta \exp(-\beta\tau) = \lambda_0 \exp(-\beta\tau)$$

Figure 8-2 illustrates a typical failure intensity curve in this model. Note that the failure intensity curve approaches the τ-axis asymptotically.

The basic execution time model growth curve can be used to answer a number of questions. The *s*-expected additional number of failures $\Delta\mu$ that will be experienced from a present failure intensity λ to reach a future failure intensity objective λ_F is found from

$$\Delta\mu = \frac{\lambda - \lambda_F}{\beta}$$

where, as before, β is the failure-rate-decrement-per-failure parameter. The additional execution time $\Delta\tau$ required to reach the failure intensity objective is found from

$$\Delta\tau = \frac{\ln(\lambda - \lambda_F)}{\beta}$$

As already noted, when the program is installed in the field after τ cumulative units of execution time, its failure rate is deemed to be $\lambda = \lambda(\tau)$. Each time the software is restarted, the execution time that advances is symbolized τ'. This is execution time projected into the future. Whenever the software is restarted, τ' is reset to zero. The mean time-to-failure (MTTF) is $1/\lambda$. The reliability function is

$$R(\tau') = \exp[-\lambda\tau']$$

The probability that the software executes for, say, 10,000 time units without software failure would be denoted $R(10000)$. Suppose that the failure intensity is 0.0003. Then $R(10000) = \exp[-(0.0003)(10000)] = 0.0498$.

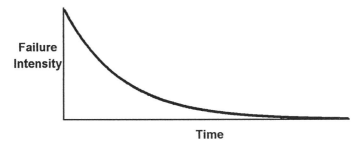

Figure 8-2. Basic execution time model.

The main critique of the basic execution time model is that every fault is assumed to contribute equally to the overall program failure rate. One can argue that the faults have different failure rates and that the faults that are uncovered first tend to be the faults with the highest failure rates. Musa and Okumoto (1984) described their logarithmic Poisson execution time model. The logarithmic Poisson model is also an NHPP-type model. In the basic execution time model, the failure intensity expressed as a function of failures experienced is

$$\lambda(\mu) = \lambda \left(1 - \frac{\mu}{v_0} \right)$$

The change in failure rate per failure experienced is

$$\frac{d\lambda}{d\mu} = \frac{\lambda_0}{v_0} = -\beta$$

In the logarithmic Poisson model, the change instead is

$$\frac{d\lambda}{d\mu} = -\varphi\lambda$$

The idea behind the logarithmic Poisson model is that each fault's hazard rate—what the fault contributes to the overall program failure rate—is different. Each fault that is successively found has a lower failure rate. The earlier a fault is uncovered, the higher its failure rate presumably was.

The parameter φ is a positive quantity called the *failure intensity decay parameter.* Expressed as a function of cumulative execution time, the failure intensity is

$$\lambda(\tau) = \frac{\lambda_0}{\lambda_0\varphi\tau + 1}$$

The mean value function is

$$\mu(\tau) = \frac{1}{\varphi} \ln(\lambda_0\varphi\tau + 1)$$

In the logarithmic Poisson model, the additional failures and test time required to meet a failure intensity objective are, respectively,

$$\Delta\mu = \frac{1}{\varphi} \ln \left(\frac{\lambda}{\lambda_F} \right)$$

and

$$\Delta\tau = \frac{1}{\varphi} \left(\frac{1}{\lambda_F} - \frac{1}{\lambda} \right)$$

PARAMETER ESTIMATION

Every software reliability model and software reliability growth model contains unknown parameters. To make use of a model, the values of those parameters have to be determined. The process for estimating the values of the parameters from observations is called *statistical inference*.

An *estimator* is a formula or procedure used to infer the value of a model parameter from observed data. When we calculate a specific value of a statistic based on observed values, that value is called an *estimate*. Two types of estimates are in common usage:

- Point estimate—a single number that serves as an educated guess at the true value of the parameter.
- Interval estimate—specifies a range that includes or captures the true but unknown parameter.

For large samples, there is generally no better estimator than that obtained through the *method of maximum likelihood*. This method was introduced in the 1920s by R. A. Fisher, who was a geneticist and statistician. The maximum likelihood estimator has several important properties:

1. *Unbiasedness.* The *s*-expected value of the estimate agrees with the actual value of the parameter.
2. *Consistency.* As the sample size (observation period) increases, the estimate approaches the true value.
3. *Effectiveness.* The variance of the estimate is small compared with other candidate estimators.
4. *Sufficiency.* The estimate makes use of all the statistical information available in the data.
5. *Invariance.* The estimator of a function of a parameter is that same function applied to the estimator of the parameter. For instance, the estimator of X^2 is the estimator of X, squared.

The principle of the method of maximum likelihood consists in choosing the estimate in such a way that the *likelihood function* is maximized. Let Θ be the parameter that is to be estimated.

The likelihood function tells how likely the observed sample is as a function of the possible parameter values. Let $x_1, x_2, \ldots, x_n$ be the observed sample values. The likelihood function is then

$$L = \mathrm{pdf}\{\theta | x_1, x_2, \ldots, x_n\}$$

$$= \prod_{i=1}^{n} \mathrm{pdf}\{x_i | \theta\}$$

The parameter estimate $\hat{\theta}$ is determined as the estimate of Θ for which the likelihood function L assumes a maximum. The standard calculus approach for maximizing a function is to take the derivative with respect to the unknown parameter and set it equal to zero:

$$\frac{dL}{d\theta} = 0$$

For example, let's calculate the maximum likelihood estimator for the constant failure rate λ when the times-to-failure t_i' are exponentially distributed. The likelihood function in this case is

$$L = \prod_{i=1}^{n} \lambda \exp[-\lambda t_i'] = \lambda^n \exp\left[-\lambda \sum_{i=1}^{n} t_i'\right]$$

The maximum likelihood estimator (MLE) is found by setting

$$\frac{dL}{d\lambda} = 0$$

and solving for λ. The result is

$$\hat{\lambda} = \frac{n}{\sum\limits_{i=1}^{n} t_i'}$$

which agrees with the intuitive idea that the best estimator of failure rate is failures over time. A clever trick is to work not with the likelihood function directly but with the "log-likelihood" function. Maximizing the logarithm of the likelihood function is equivalent to maximizing the likelihood function itself. But taking the logarithm often changes a product to a sum, which is easier to work with. In the case of exponential time-to-failure, the log-likelihood is

$$\ln L(\theta | x_1, x_2, \ldots, x_n) = n \ln \lambda - \lambda \sum x_i$$

When we take $(d \ln L)/d\lambda$ and set it to zero, we get

$$\frac{n}{\lambda} - \Sigma x_i = 0$$

or

$$\lambda = \frac{n}{\Sigma x_i}$$

the same result we got before.

Let's turn now to parameter estimation for software reliability growth models. The basic execution time model has two parameters, β and v_0. Recall that β can be interpreted as the (s-expected) decrement in failure intensity per failure experienced and v_0 can be interpreted as (s-expected) total failures. This is not the only way to parameterize the model. For example, for the purposes of prediction, we will use a different pair of quantities, λ_0 and β, as parameters.

Using the method of maximum likelihood, Musa et al. (1987) show that the parameter β is estimated by solving the following equation for β:

$$\frac{n}{\beta} - \frac{n\tau_e}{\exp[\beta\tau_e] - 1} - \sum_{i=1}^{n} \tau_i = 0$$

Here τ_i is the time of the ith failure and τ_e is the cumulative execution time expended during system test. Note that τ_e doesn't necessarily coincide with a failure.

It's impractical to solve this equation by hand. You need the help of a computer or programmable calculator. If you can't find a canned program that does the job, any numerical analysis text will provide many algorithms for solving an equation $f(x) = 0$. Examples of such algorithms include

Bisection method
Fixed-point iteration
Newton–Raphson (also called Newton's) method
Secant method
Method of false position

Once you obtain the estimate for β, you determine the estimate of the parameter v_0 from the equation

$$\hat{v}_0 = \frac{n}{1 - \exp[-\hat{\beta}\tau_e]}$$

where n is the number of failures observed and τ_e is the test duration.

A point estimate is a single number. An estimate can rarely be expected to be exactly equal to a parameter's value. Reporting only this estimate is often unsatisfactory; some measure of how close the point estimate is likely to be to the true parameter is required. An interval estimate describes a range of values within which we can reasonably be sure that the true value of the parameter lies. *Confidence intervals* provide a way of stating how close the estimate is likely to be to the parameter's value, as well as the chance of it being that close. The probability that we associate with an interval estimate is called the confidence level. Different observations yield different intervals; if the confidence level is $100(1 - \alpha)\%$, then $100(1 - \alpha)\%$ of the intervals so constructed will contain the true value of the parameter. Figure 8-3 shows an 80% confidence interval. In four of the five intervals (80% of the intervals), the true value of β lies in the interval. The true value does not lie in one of the five intervals (20% of the intervals).

For the case of exponentially distributed interfailure times (the model for frozen code described in Chapter 7), the limits of the confidence interval of λ are given by the chi-square distribution. A table of values can be found in almost any statistics textbook. We will consider the most common case, in which the test does not necessarily end at a failure occurrence; the test ends after a predetermined amount of time τ_e. The upper limit of the confidence interval is

$$\frac{\chi^2_{2(r+1),\,\alpha/2}}{2\tau_e}$$

and the lower limit is

$$\frac{\chi^2_{2r,\,1-\alpha/2}}{2\tau_e}$$

where r is the number of observed failures. The first subscript of χ^2 is the number of degrees of freedom, and the second subscript is the area in the right tail of the chi-square distribution.

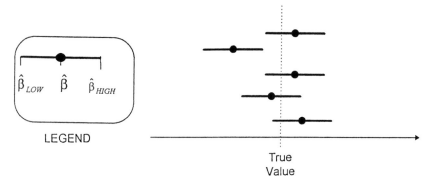

LEGEND

Figure 8-3. Illustration of 80% confidence interval.

You must exercise care in the interpretation of the confidence interval. It would appear that a 95% confidence interval implies that the probability is 95% that the true value of the parameter falls into the interval. That interpretation is a common misconception and is not correct. The parameter has a definite constant value even though this value is unknown. Thus, the parameter value either is in the interval or is not. The interval is the random variable, not the parameter value. If thousands of such intervals were calculated on different observed failure times, then in the long run about 95% of those intervals would include or capture the true value of the parameter.

Now let's see how maximum likelihood estimation is applied to software reliability growth models. A maximum likelihood estimator $\hat{\theta}$ is asymptotically normally distributed with mean equal to θ and variance

$$\frac{1}{I(\theta)}$$

Figure 8-4 illustrates the familiar bell-shaped normal curve. Figure 8-5 illustrates how the maximum likelihood estimate of β and its lower and upper confidence limits relate to a normal curve. The quantity $I(\theta)$ is called the *Fisher information.* For the basic execution time model, the upper $100(1 - \alpha)\%$ confidence limit for the parameter β is

$$\beta_{high} = \hat{\beta} + \frac{z_{1-\alpha/2}}{\sqrt{I(\hat{\beta})}}$$

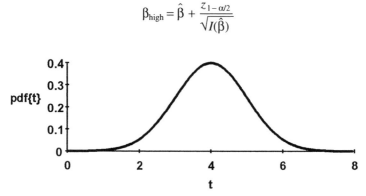

Figure 8-4. Normal pdf.

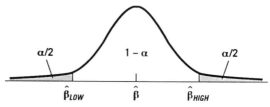

Figure 8-5. Confidence bounds for $\hat{\beta}$.

and the lower limit is

$$\beta_{\text{low}} = \hat{\beta} - \frac{z_{1-\alpha/2}}{\sqrt{I(\hat{\beta})}}$$

The quantity $z_{1-\alpha/2}$ is the standard normal deviate, a table of which can be found in almost any statistics textbook. On average, four out of five constructed intervals $(\beta_{\text{low}}, \beta_{\text{high}})$ will contain the true value of β.

The Fisher information for the basic execution time model is

$$I(\beta) = \frac{1}{\beta^2} - \frac{\tau_e^2 \exp[-\beta_{\text{low}}\tau_e]}{(\exp[\beta\tau_e] - 1)^2}$$

Because of the invariance property of maximum likelihood estimators, the corresponding confidence intervals for v_0 can be established by successively substituting β_{low} and β_{high} into the estimation equation for v_0:

$$(v_0)_{\text{low}} = \frac{n}{1 - \exp[-\beta_{\text{low}}\tau_e]}$$

$$(v_0)_{\text{high}} = \frac{n}{1 - \exp[-\beta_{\text{high}}\tau_e]}$$

To find the confidence bounds for the failure rate $\lambda = \lambda(\tau_e)$ that the software would exhibit if it were released at this point, we first define a function

$$f(\beta) = \beta \exp[-\beta t]$$

Then the confidence bounds for the failure rate are

$$(v_0)_{\text{low}} f(\beta_{\text{high}}) \le \lambda \le (v_0)_{\text{high}} f(\beta_{\text{low}})$$

GOODNESS OF FIT

A model is an abstraction of reality. All the relevant factors in the real-world situation cannot be taken into account, because doing so would make the model too complex and difficult to solve. Because of the many software reliability models that are available, it is helpful to apply a goodness-of-fit measure to determine how well a particular model is performing on your specific project. If several growth models are used with the same failure data, comparing the goodness-of-fit measures from each model will allow you to see which model is working best. One model may have its parameters estimated by several different methods, each producing different para-

meter values. Thus the goodness-of-fit measure really applies to a model/estimation combination, not a model per se.

Prequential Likelihood

A popular objective goodness-of-fit measure that enables comparisons to be made between models is called the *prequential likelihood*. Suppose the observed interfailure times are $\tau_1', \tau_2', \tau_3', \ldots$.

Let $\widetilde{\text{pdf}}_i \{\tau_i\}$ be the estimated time-to-failure probability density function of the ith interfailure time obtained from a particular model/estimation combination based on the preceding i-1 interfailure times. The prequential likelihood statistic is the product of the past n such pdf's, the ith pdf being evaluated at the actual ith interfailure time τ'_i. Let m be the current failure number. The prequential likelihood is defined by

$$\text{PL}_n = \prod_{i=m-n}^{m-1} \widetilde{\text{pdf}}_i \{\tau'_i\}$$

An alternative to choosing the one model/estimation combination that has the highest prequential likelihood is to form several weighted averages of two or more model/estimation combinations and choose the weighted average that provides the highest PL_n.

To form a weighted average of pdf's, let there be k modeling/estimation combinations. Let w_j be the weight for the jth modeling/estimation combination, and let $\text{pdf}(j)$ be its pdf. The weighted-average pdf (Lyu and Nikora, 1992) is

$$\sum_{j=1}^{k} \text{pdf}(j)\{\tau'\} w_j$$

CURVE FITTING

The weighted-average approach is a bit strange because it forgets assumptions behind the models. You can no longer say that you are working with a probabilistic model. You are actually doing curve fitting.

Another curve-fitting approach is to take a single software reliability growth model and then fit the observed failure data to the curve the failure intensity function defines. You strip the probabilistic aspects out of the model and just deal with the model as a curve. When you fit a family of curves to a set of data points, you want to find the curve that fits "the best." The most popular criterion for determining the best fit is *least squares*. You compute the vertical distances from the points to the curve. If the point is above the curve, this distance is a positive number; if the point is below the curve, it's a negative number. The distances are each squared, and those squares are added up. The curve parameters that minimize the sum are pronounced to be the best fitting. Least squares estimation can be better than maximum likelihood for small or medium sample sizes (number of failures experienced).

u-PLOT

A u-plot (Littlewood, 1987) is a visual method of determining a software reliability growth model/statistical inference technique's goodness of fit to a particular project. The plot can be hand-drawn. You could also write a little computer program that will draw the u-plot on a computer monitor. The u-plot is constructed according to the following scheme. During growth testing, the user employs a statistical inference procedure, such as maximum likelihood, to estimate the parameters of the basic execution time model.

The estimated cumulative distribution function (Cdf) after i failures have occurred is given by

$$\hat{F}_i(\tau') = 1 - \exp[-\lambda(\tau_i)\tau']$$

where τ_m is the cumulative execution time, $\lambda(\tau_m)$ is the failure intensity at that time, and τ' is execution time measured from the present. You would obtain the failure intensity from the basic execution time model or some other software reliability growth model. When the interfailure time τ'_i is later observed, the probability integral transform

$$u_i = \hat{F}_i(\tau_i)$$

is recorded. Each failure results in another u_i. Each u_i is a number between 0 and 1. The probability integral transform implies that the u_i's should look like a random sample from a uniform distribution over the interval $(0,1)$, if the sequence of predictions was good. The accuracy of the model with respect to the particular program can be gauged by drawing a u-plot. We are using the word "prediction" because even an assessment of current reliability is a prediction: We are predicting the time-to-failure distribution. In a u-plot the sample cumulative distribution function of the u_i's is compared with the cumulative distribution function of the uniform distribution over $(0,1)$, visually or through use of numerical goodness-of-fit measures such as the Kolmogorov distance. The specific points plotted to form the cumulative distribution function are

$$(u_{(1)}, 1/(r+1))$$

$$(u_{(2)}, 2/(r+2))$$

$$...$$

$$(u_{(r)}, r/(r+1))$$

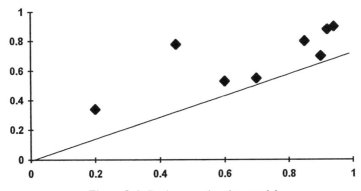

Figure 8-6. Basic execution time model.

where $u_{(1)}, u_{(2)}, \ldots, u_{(r)}$ are the u_i's rearranged in ascending order. You would plot these points. Figure 8-6 illustrates a u-plot. If the prediction is very good, then the points would follow very closely a line segment extending from the point (0,0) to the point (1,1). If the points oscillate above and below the line segment, then you would say that the model is noisy. If the plotted points lie fairly consistently above the line segment, then you would conclude that the model is giving optimistic predictions. If the points lie fairly consistently below the line segment, you would say that the model is giving pessimistic predictions.

RECALIBRATION

The u-plot can be employed to perform a kind of "adaptive modeling." The u-plot shows how well the model is fitting the failure data. The information in the u-plot can be used as a feedback mechanism to modify and improve the model, to "recalibrate" it (Brocklehurst et al., 1990). The recalibrated model corrects for systematic bias or noisiness that the model is experiencing when being used on a particular program. The recalibration takes place by applying a function $G^*(\cdot)$ to the estimated Cdf. The function $G^*(\cdot)$ is expressed as

$$G_i^*[\hat{F}_i(t)] = \frac{\hat{F}_i(t) + j(u_{(j+1)} + u_{(j)})}{(r+1)(u_{(j+1)} + u_{(j)})}, \quad u_{(j)} \le t \le u_{(j+1)}$$

where $u_{(j)}$ is the jth value when the u_i's are put in ascending order of magnitude, and r is the number of u_i's, with $u_{(0)} \equiv 0$ and $u_{(r+1)} \equiv 1$ (Rome Laboratory, 1992).

To perform the recalibration the user applies the transformation

$$\hat{F}_i^*(\tau) = G_i^*[\hat{F}_i(\tau)]$$

The accuracy of recalibrated models has been shown (Brocklehurst et al.,1990) to be generally better than that of the original model.

ADDITIONAL SOFTWARE RELIABILITY GROWTH MODELS

A curve is usable as a software reliability model if

$$\frac{d\lambda(\tau)}{d\tau} < 0$$

over $\tau > T_0$ if not over all $\tau > 0$ (Knafl, 1992). That is, the failure intensity is decreasing to 0 after time T_0. Software reliability models can be divided into two broad categories: finite failure models and infinite failure models. Consider s-expected number of failures as cumulative test time approaches infinity:

$$\mu(\infty) = \lim_{\tau \to \infty} \mu(\tau)$$

In finite failure models, $\mu(\infty) < \infty$. In infinite failure models, $\mu(\infty) = \infty$. Most important software reliability models are NHPP models, whose failure intensity functions and mean value function $\mu(\tau)$ are characterized by two positive parameters that we will denote α and β.

In finite failure models, α is the scale parameter, indicating the overall vertical positioning of the failure intensity curve, and is defined by

$$\alpha = \lim_{\tau \to \infty} \mu(\tau)$$

Because α is merely a scale parameter, the illustrated plots of the models in this chapter use $\alpha = 1$.

Goel–Okumoto NHPP Model

The Goel–Okumoto NHPP model is a finite failure model. It assumes an exponentially decaying failure intensity function. In this model the failure intensity is

$$\lambda(\tau) = \alpha\beta \, \exp[-\beta\tau]$$

The basic execution time model is in fact the Goel–Okumoto model with

$$v_0 = \alpha, \quad \lambda_0 = \alpha\beta$$

Figure 8-7 illustrates the basic execution time model with $\lambda_0 = 5$. The mean value function of the Goel–Okumoto NHPP model is

$$\mu(\tau) = \alpha(1 - \exp[-\beta\tau])$$

which for the basic execution time model is

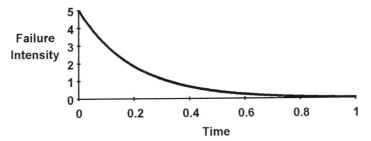

Figure 8-7. Basic execution time model.

$$\mu(\tau) = v_0(1 - \exp[-\beta\tau])$$

The logarithmic model is an infinite failure model. Faults repaired early reduce the failure intensity more than those removed later. The failure intensity decreases exponentially with the expected failures experienced. As a consequence, the expected number of failures is a logarithmic function of time. The failure intensity is

$$\lambda(\tau) = \frac{\alpha\beta}{(1 + \beta\tau)}$$

The mean value function is

$$\mu(\tau) = \alpha \ln(1 + \beta\tau)$$

The logarithmic Poisson model is the logarithmic model with

$$\alpha = \frac{1}{\varphi}, \quad \beta = \lambda_0\varphi$$

where λ_0 is the initial failure intensity and φ is called the *failure intensity decay parameter.* Thus, the failure intensity of the logarithmic Poisson model is

$$\lambda(\tau) = \frac{\lambda_0}{1 + \lambda_0\varphi\tau}$$

Figure 8-8 illlustrates the logarithmic model. The mean value function is

$$\mu(\tau) = \frac{\ln(1 + \lambda_0\varphi\tau)}{\varphi}$$

The power model [also called the Duane model, the Crow model (Crow, 1972; Duane, 1964), the AMSAA model, and the Weibull process model] is an infinite fail-

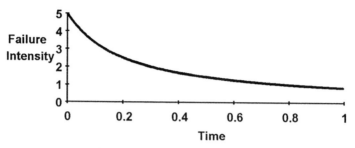

Figure 8-8. Logarithmic model.

ure model. In the hardware reliability growth realm, Duane plotted $\mu(\tau)/\tau$ on ln–ln paper and obtained a straight line. Crow made that observation the basis of an NHPP in which the failure intensity is a power function of time. The failure intensity is

$$\lambda(\tau) = \alpha\beta\tau^{\beta-1}$$

Figure 8-9 illustrates the power model. The mean value function is

$$\mu(\tau) = \alpha\tau^{\beta}$$

The delayed S-shaped model (Yamada et al., 1984) is a finite failure model. The assumptions are that the initial fault content is a random variable, failure occurrences are independent and random, and the time between failures ($i-1$) and i depends on the time-to-failure ($i-1$). The time-to-failure of an individual fault follows a gamma distribution with a shape parameter of 2. The failure intensity is

$$\lambda(\tau) = \alpha\beta^{2}\,\tau\exp[-\beta\tau]$$

Figure 8-10 illustrates the delayed-S-shaped model. The mean value function is the S-shaped curve:

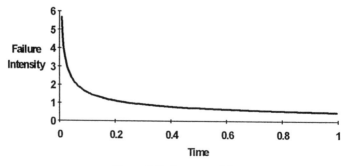

Figure 8-9. Power model.

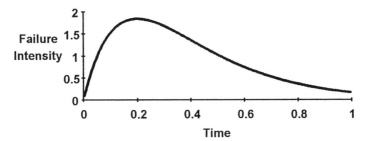

Figure 8-10. Delayed S-shaped model.

$$\mu(\tau) = \alpha\{1-(1+\beta\tau)\exp[-\beta\tau]\}$$

The inverse linear model (also called the Littlewood–Verrall model) (Littlewood and Verrall, 1973) is an infinite failure model. The failure intensity is

$$\lambda(\tau) = \frac{\alpha\beta}{2\sqrt{1+\beta\tau}}$$

Figure 8-11 illustrates the inverse linear model. The mean value function is

$$\mu(\tau) = \alpha(1 - \sqrt{1+\beta\tau} - 1)$$

The log power model (Zhao and Xie, 1992) has a failure intensity of

$$\lambda(\tau) = \frac{\alpha\beta[\ln(1+\tau)]^{\beta-1}}{1+t}$$

Its mean value function is

$$\mu(\tau) = \alpha[\ln(1+\tau)]^{\beta}$$

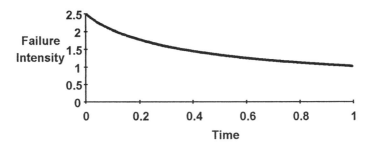

Figure 8-11. Inverse linear model.

The inflection S-shaped model (Ohba, 1984) is a finite failure model. The failure intensity is

$$\lambda(\tau) = \frac{\alpha\beta(1 + \gamma)\exp[-\beta\tau]}{1 + \gamma\exp[-\beta\tau]}$$

Binomial Models

The Jelinski–Moranda model assumes that the failure intensity is proportional to the current fault content. The fault that causes a failure is assumed to be instantaneously removed. The failure intensity remains constant throughout the interval between failure occurrences. The per-fault hazard rate of every fault is the same. Faults cause failures independently. The failure intensity in the ith interfailure interval is

$$\lambda_i = [v_0 - (i - 1)]\phi$$

The Schick–Wolverton model (Schick and Wolverton, 1973) is a modification to the Jelinski–Moranda model. The Schick–Wolverton model assumes that the failure rate is proportional not only to the number of faults present but also to the time spent in debugging. The failure intensity is

$$\lambda_i = [v_0 - (i - 1)]\phi(t_{i-1} + s)$$

In the Schneidewind model (Schneidewind, 1975) the mean number of detected failures decreases from one equal-sized interval to the next. The mean number of detected failures decreases from one equal-sized interval to the next. The failure intensity in the ith interval is

$$\lambda_i = \alpha\exp[-\beta i]$$

The mean value function for that interval is

$$\mu_i = \frac{\alpha}{\beta}(1 - \exp[-\beta i])$$

BAYESIAN SOFTWARE RELIABILITY MODELS

Knowing ignorance is strength,
Ignoring knowledge is sickness.

—Lao-tzu

Thomas Bayes, an 18th-century English minister, combined the definition of conditional probability, the multiplication rule, and the law of total probability into a very powerful result known as Bayes' rule: Let A and B be mutually exclusive and exhaustive events with nonzero probabilities. Then

$$\Pr\{A|B\} = \frac{\Pr\{A \text{ and } B\}}{\Pr\{B\}} = \frac{\Pr\{B|A\} \Pr\{A\}}{\Pr\{E\}}$$

where

$$\Pr\{B\} = \Pr\{B|A\} \Pr\{A\} + \Pr\{B|A\} \Pr\{A\}$$

You can see that the fraction is from the definition of conditional probability, the numerator is from the multiplication rule, and the denominator is from the law of total probability. Here, the meaning of the symbol "$|A$" is "given that I know A."

The usefulness of Bayes' rule is that it lets us update probabilities in light of new evidence. The old probability of an event is called its *prior probability*. The new probability of the event is called its *posterior probability*.

Different people may assign different subjective probabilities to the event of failure. This can occur even if they have access to the same information. The process of assigning a numerical value to a subjective probability is called "scoring."

Getting the person to quantify his subjective probability can be done by relating the probability to betting odds. He is asked to consider the following gamble:

1. You pay an ante of p units to play.
2. You receive 1 unit if failure occurs and nothing if success occurs.

The gamble offers odds of $1 - p$ to p on the occurrence of failure. For the person to regard the gamble as "fair," he must be indifferent as to which side of the gamble he's on; he would just as soon be the person relinquishing p units as the person who relinquishes either 0 or 1 unit. If there is a value of p between 0 and 1 for which the person regards the gamble as fair, then the person's subjective probability for failure is $\Pr\{\text{failure}\} = p$. Thus, $\Pr\{\text{failure}\}$ is defined as the fraction of a whole unit value that the person feels is fair to exchange for the promise that he would receive a whole unit value if failure occurs and zero units if success occurs. A person can assign any probability he wants to an event, but he needs to be "coherent" because otherwise you can come up with a bet that he is sure to lose. Failure and success are mutually exclusive events, so the person had better assign subjective probabilities that add up to 1. Suppose that the probability he assigns to failure is 0.4 and the probability he assigns to success is 0.65. Then you could make what is termed a "dutch book" against him: A combination of bets is possible in which he will lose no matter what the outcome is. Make two bets with him on a single run, a bet on success and a bet for failure. He would give you 1.05 units to play the two bets, and regardless of whether the outcome is success or failure, he will win exactly 1 unit. Thus he is certain to lose 0.05 units. Thus while the person can assign any probability he wants to an event, if we make him "put his money where his mouth is," his assignment should result in the probability of the sample space equaling 1.

A person may even have an opinion, belief, or judgment about the probability of failure before the experimentation. This is known as a *prior probability*. After some experimentation is performed, the person may have a new opinion about the probability, known as a *posterior probability*. A probability theorem based on Bayes' rule, called Bayes' theorem, provides a formal mechanism—an algorithm—for revising subjective probabilities in the light of experimental evidence (hard data). The theorem states that the posterior distribution is proportional to the prior distribution times the likelihood function:

$$\text{posterior} \propto \text{prior} \times \text{likelihood}$$

In the Bayesian approach, an attempt is made to use all available information to reduce the amount of uncertainty present in a statistical inference problem. In classical statistics, p is considered fixed (though unknown). In Bayesian statistics, the quantity p is considered to be a random variable. Before testing begins, the information is summarized by a prior distribution. A person's beliefs about the distribution of P are captured by fitting them to a prior distribution such as a beta distribution with parameters a_0 and b_0. A beta distribution covers the range 0 to 1 and has mean

$$\mu_0 = \frac{a_0}{a_0 + b_0}$$

The beta distribution is the natural conjugate of the binomial distribution, which means that the posterior distribution will also be beta. When $a_0 = b_0$, it becomes a uniform distribution. After N runs yielding x failures, the posterior distribution is also beta, with parameters

$$a_1 = x + a_0$$
$$b_1 = n - x + b_0$$

The mean of the posterior distribution is

$$\mu_1 = \frac{a_1}{b_1} = \frac{x + a_0}{n - x + b_0}$$

Bayesian Growth Models

In the basic execution time model and the logarithmic Poisson model, the failure intensity of a stable program (frozen code) subjected to input states randomly selected from a stationary operational profile is considered constant. In classical models, the growth parameters are considered to be fixed but unknown quantities. In the Bayesian approach to software reliability, software reliability is viewed as a measure of the strength of belief that the parameters are considered to be random variables. The distributions of the random variables are chosen for flexibility and mathematical tractability. For example, the per-fault hazard rate ϕ is often assigned a gamma distribution, and the initial number of faults ω_0 is often assigned a Poisson distribution. The Bayesian approach allows the incorporation of experiences from similar software and previous information about the software development. This information is then combined with failure data in a systematic manner. The uncertainty in the failure rate in each interfailure interval arises from two sources: the randomness of the testing and ignorance of the location of the faults. Fixes are not certain to reduce the failure rate and, even if the fix does reduce the failure rate, there is uncertainty about the magnitude of the reduction. To model growth, the sequence of failure rates can be treated as a sequence of stochastically decreasing random variables by having one of the parameters vary with the number of failures experienced.

Littlewood and Verrall (1973) introduced just such a model. It uses the Jelinski–Moranda model as a point of departure. Recall that the Jelinski–Moranda model assumes that the failure intensity is piecewise constant between successive failure occurrences. Thus, between the start of system test and the first failure time is λ_0. Between the first and second failure, the failure rate is λ_1, and so on. The pdf of the ith failure intensity is gamma-distributed. Let $j = i + 1$. Then

$$\text{pdf}\{\lambda_j\} = \frac{[\psi(j)]^\alpha \lambda_j^{\alpha-1} \exp[-\psi(j)\lambda_j]}{\Gamma(\alpha)}$$

The function $\psi(j)$ determines the reliability growth. It needs to be increasing in j, and the failure intensities form a stochastically decreasing sequence. Littlewood and Verrall suggested and inverse linear family

$$\psi(j) = \beta_0 + \beta_1 i$$

and an inverse second-degree polynomial

$$\psi(j) = \beta_0 + \beta_1 i^2$$

Musa suggested the rational function

$$\psi(j) = \frac{v_0 \alpha}{\lambda_0(v_0 - i)}$$

so that the parameter is inversely related to the number of failures remaining.

SUMMARY

This chapter discussed the theory behind software reliability growth modeling and surveyed some of the existing models. Each model mathematically summarizes a set of assumptions a researcher has made about the phenomenon of software failure and about the debugging process. A classical model contains unknown parameters whose values are estimated via statistical inference procedures such as the method of maximum likelihood.

You can determine how well a model/estimation procedure combination is working on your project by performing a goodness-of-fit test. "Recalibration" is a technique that lets you adapt a model to your project in light of the goodness-of-fit information.

In Bayesian software reliability models and software reliability growth models, the parameters are considered to be random variables, and prior information, even subjective information, can be incorporated into the modeling

EXERCISES

1. Suppose the observed interfailure times (in CPU seconds) are 12, 13, 16, 19, 20, 18, 19, 22, 30, 30, 30, 29, 40, 45, 50, 51, 52, 66. Estimate the parameters of the basic execution time model.

2. Create a u-plot for the results in exercise 1.

3. Recalibrate the basic execution model based on the results in exercise 2.

REFERENCES

S. Brocklehurst, P. Y. Chan, B. Littlewood, and J. Snell, "Recalibrating Software Reliability Models." *IEEE Transactions on Software Engineering* SE-16(4), 458–470, 1990.

L. H. Crow. "Reliability Growth Modeling." Army Materiel Systems Analysis Activity Technical Report, No. 55, Aberdeen Proven Ground, Maryland, 1972.

J. T. Duane. "Learning Curve Approach to Reliability Monitoring." *IEEE Transactions on Aerospace* 2, 563–566, 1964.

A. L. Goel and K. Okumoto. "Time-Dependent Error-Detection Rate Model for Software Reliability and Other Performance Measures." *IEEE Transactions on Reliability* R-28(3), 206–211, 1979.

Z. Jelinski and P. B. Moranda. "Applications of a Probability-Based Model to a Code Reading Experiment." In: *Proceedings, IEEE Symposium on Computer Software Reliability,* April 30–May 2, 1973, p. 78.

G. Knafl. "Overview of Software Reliability Models, Estimation Procedures, and Predictive Performance Measures." Tutorial, Third International Symposium on Software Reliability Engineering, Raleigh, NC, October 1992.

B. Littlewood. "How Good are Software Reliability Predictions?" In: B. Littlewood (Ed.), *Software Reliability: Achievement and Assessment.* Blackwell Scientific Publications, Oxford: 1987, pp. 145–166.

B. Littlewood and J. L. Verrall. "A Bayesian Reliability Growth Model for Computer Software." *Applied Statistics* 22, 32–346, 1973.

M.R. Lyu and A. Nikora, "Applyng Reliability Models More Effectively." *IEEE Software* 9(4), pp. 43–52, July 1992.

J.D. Musa. "A Theory of Software Reliability and Its Application, *"IEEE Transactions on Software Engineering.* SE-1(3), pp. 312–327, September 1975.

J. D. Musa and K. Okumoto. "A Logarithmic Poisson Execution Time Model for Software Reliability Measurement." In: *Proceedings of the International Conference on Software Engineering*, pp. 230–238, March 1984.

J. D. Musa, A. Iannino, and K. Okumoto. *Software Reliability: Measurement, Prediction, Application.* New York: McGraw–Hill, 1987.

M. Ohba. "Software Reliability Models." *IBM Journal of Research and Development* 28, pp. 428–443, July 1984.

Rome Laboratory. *Military Handbook on Hardware/Software Reliability Assurance and Control.* U.S. Air Force Systems Command, Griffiss AFB, NY, draft February 1992.

G. J. Schick and R. W. Wolverton. "Assessment of Software Reliability." Presented at the 11th Annual Meeting of the German Operational research Society, DGOR, Hamburg, Germany; also in *Proceedings on Operational Research.* Virzberg-Wien: Physica-Verlag, 1973, pp. 395–422.

N. F. Scheidewind, "Analysis of Error Processes in Computer Software," Proceedings of the 1975 International Conference on Reliable Software. Los Angeles, pp. 337–346, 1975.

M. L. Shooman. "Probabilistic Models for Software Reliability Prediction." In: W. Freiberger (Ed.), *Statistical Computer Peformance Evaluation.* New York: Academic Press, 1977, pp. 485–502.

S. Yamada, M. Ohba, and S. Osaki. "S-Shaped Software Reliability Growth Models and their Applications." *IEEE Transactions on Reliability* R-33, 289–292, October 1984.

M. Zhao and M. Xie. "Applications of the Log-Power NHPP Software Reliability Model." In: *Proceedings of the International Symposium on Software Reliability Engineering,* 1992.

CHAPTER 9

System Modeling

In Chapters 7 and 8 we discussed how the failure rate of an individual executing computer program is modeled. Often we are interested in the overall failure rate of several executing computer programs or in the failure rate of a system comprised of both hardware and software components. If you think about it, failure rates are additive: If one component has a failure rate of 4 failures per 10,000 hours and another component has a failure rate of 3 failures per 10,000 hours, then you can expect a failure rate of $3 + 4 = 7$ failures per 10,000 hours between them. This intuition is true, provided that certain conditions are met.

The failure rates of n hardware/software components can be added together to arrive at an overall system failure rate λ_w for the overall system, provided that the following conditions hold:

1. The components are logically in series, that is, the overall system is considered to have failed whenever any one or more of the components fails.
2. The components fail in an s-independent manner. When one component fails, it does not make it less likely or more likely that another component will fail.
3. The failure rates are expressed with respect to wall-clock time, system operating time, or some other common time frame. If all you know is the failure intensity expressed with respect to execution time, then you need to perform a conversion.
4. Care is taken not to double-count failures. This can occur if an erroneous external output of one of the components is pipelined as input to another component.

When these conditions are met, we have the formula

$$\lambda_w = \sum_{i=1}^{n} \lambda_{iw}$$

where λ_w is the combined failure rate (expressed with respect to system operating time or wall-clock time), n is the number of components being combined, and (λ_{iw} is the ith component's failure rate (expressed in the same time frame as λ_w).

As an example, suppose we have one component with a failure intensity of $\lambda_{1w} = 0.004$ per system operating hour, another with a failure intensity of $\lambda_{2w} = 0.002$ per system operating hour, and a third with a failure intensity of $\lambda_{3W} = 0.0063$ per system operating hour. Then the combined failure intensity is $\lambda_{SW} = \lambda_{1W} + \lambda_{2W} + \lambda_{3W} = 0.004 + 0.002 + 0.0063 = 0.0123$ failures per system operating hour.

How do you convert a component failure rate to system operating time or wall-clock time?

UTILIZATION

Hardware and software components do not necessarily operate continuously. Each component has a utilization, which is the fraction of system operating time (or wall-clock time) the component operates. This figure is sometimes called the component's *duty cycle*. For example, if a component operates for 15 seconds out of every minute of system operating (or wall clock) time, its utilization is 15 seconds/60 seconds = 0.25. This 15 seconds is cumulative and does not have to be in one continuous sweep. For example, the component may be active for 5 seconds, then pause 20 seconds, then be active 5 seconds, pause 20 seconds, be active 5 seconds and pause 5 seconds. In the case of several executing programs timesharing a CPU, the active periods could be measured in milliseconds. In the special case of a component operating continuously, its utilization is 100%. Often hardware components do operate continuously.

In the case of software, operating time is execution time. Utilization can exceed 100% when multiple copies of a computer program run simultaneously on different processors. For example, if a program uses up 60% of one CPU's time, and another copy of the program uses up 55% of another CPU's time, then the program's utilization is 115%. The copies have to be executing s-independent input streams. To convert a failure rate expressed with respect to component operating time to system operating time (or wall-clock time), you multiply the component-operating-time failure rate by the utilization. Let λ_i be a component's operating-time failure rate, and let u_i be its utilization. Then in terms of system operating time (or wall-clock time), we have $\lambda_{iW} = \lambda_i \cdot u_i$. One way the additivity of failure rates can be shown is to note that the combined failure rate can be expressed as expected failures over time:

$$\lambda_W = \frac{\text{expected failures}}{T}$$

where T is the time unit (e.g., one system operating hour). The expected number of failures contributed by the ith component is $\lambda_i \cdot T \cdot u_i$. Thus the expected failures contributed by all the components together is $\Sigma(\lambda_i \cdot T \cdot u_i)$, and

$$\lambda_W = \frac{\sum_{i=1}^{n} (\lambda_i \cdot T \cdot u_i)}{T} = \sum_{i=1}^{n} \lambda_{iW}$$

We may also wish to express the combined reliability of several components. It turns out that while the failure rates are additive, the reliabilities are multiplicative. The reliability function is $R(T) = \exp[-\lambda_W T]$, which is $R(T) = \exp[-\Sigma \lambda_{iW} T]$. Because the reliability of component i is $R_i(T) = \exp[-\lambda_{iW} T]$, we have $R(T) = \exp[-\Sigma \lambda_{iW} T] = \prod R_i(T)$.

Reliability Block Diagrams

Hardware components can be logically interconnected in ways other than series relationships. Systems in which there is hardware fault tolerance and no software fault tolerance are best modeled through a *reliability block diagram*. Whenever a group of components are in series, they appear in a horizontal sequence, as illustrated in Figure 9-1.

As we have seen, the combined failure rate λ_G is the sum of the component failure rates:

$$\lambda_G = \sum_{i=1}^{n} \lambda_i$$

The combined reliability is the product of the component reliabilities:

$$R_G(t) = \prod_{i=1}^{n} R_i(t)$$

The combined mean time-to-failure (MTTF) is the reciprocal of the combined failure rate: $1/\lambda_G$.

In hardware, the reliability of a design is often increased by using redundancy. The simplest form of redundancy is putting a group of components in parallel. If the components are in parallel, it means that they all have to fail before the group fails; if at least one component survives, then the group succeeds. Contrast that with a series group: If any member of the group fails, then the group is considered to have failed. A group of parallel components appear one atop the other, as shown in Figure 9-2. To save space, the group can be more compactly represented by stacking them like a slightly spread-out deck of cards (Figure 9-3). When components are in parallel, the reliability R_G of a group of n components is given by the formula

$$R_G = 1 - \prod_{i=1}^{n} (1 - R_i)$$

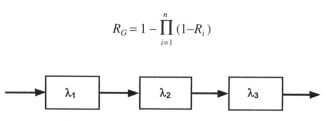

Figure 9-1. Three components in series.

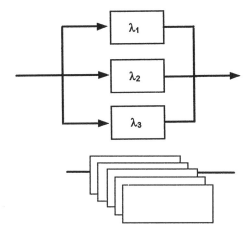

Figure 9-2. Three components in parallel.

Figure 9-3. Alternate representation for parallel components.

where R_i is the reliability of the ith component in the group. The MTTF is

$$\frac{1}{\lambda_1} + \frac{1}{\lambda_2} - \frac{1}{\lambda_1 + \lambda_2}$$

For the case of a group of two components with the same failure rate λ, the MTTF is $3/2$, λ and the failure rate turns out to be a function of time:

$$\lambda(t) = \frac{2\lambda \exp[-\lambda t] \, (1-\exp[-\lambda t])}{2 - \text{excp} \, [-\lambda \, t]}$$

We can have systems with mixed series and parallel elements, as exemplified in Figures 9-4 and 9-5. You would apply the formulas repeatedly, reducing each parallel or series group into a single box. The complex system of Figure 9-6 cannot be decomposed into series and parallel groups but can be solved by repeated application of Bayes' rule or by Monte Carlo simulation.

We can generalize the ideas of series and parallel groups to the idea of an M-out-of-N group. In this type of group there are N components in total, and the group succeeds whenever at least M of those components succeed (see Figure 9-7).

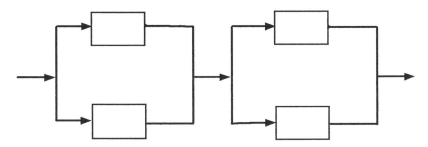

Figure 9-4. Parallel–series.

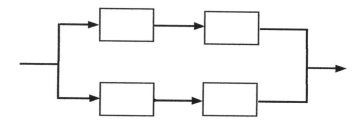

Figure 9-5. Series–parallel.

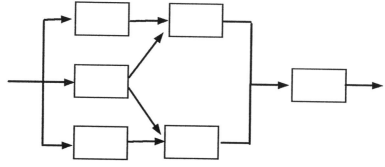

Figure 9-6. Complex system.

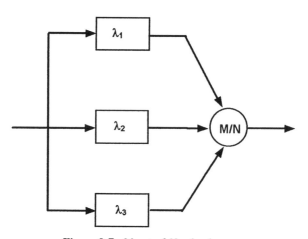

Figure 9-7. M-out-of-N redundancy.

The reliability R_G of the group is computed by summing the probabilities all the mutually exclusive ways M or more components can succeed. The formula for the case of all components having identical reliabilities is

$$R_G(t) = 1 - \sum_{i=0}^{M-1} \binom{N}{i} [R(t)]^i [1-R(t)]^{N-i}$$

where R is the reliability of an individual component. The failure rate is not con-stant, but an approximation based on time-to-first-failure is (Rome Laboratory, 1993).

$$\lambda_G \approx \frac{\lambda}{\displaystyle\sum_{i=M}^{N} \frac{1}{i}}$$

where λ is the failure rate of each component in the group.

Another form of redundancy is standby redundancy, as illustrated in Figure 9-8. When one component in the group fails, then another component in the group is switched-in to take over the job. If that component fails too, then the next component in the group is switched in, and so on, until there are no components left in the group, at which time the group is considered to have failed. If the n components in the group have equal failure rates λ, the formula is

$$R(t) = \sum_{i=0}^{n-1} \frac{(\lambda t)^i}{i!} \exp[-\lambda t]$$

The MTTF is $(n+1)/\lambda$.

AVAILABILITY

Availability is an index of a system's operational effectiveness. It is the fraction of time the system is up. If, on average, a system is down a cumulative total of one day a year, its unavailability is 1/365 (ignoring leap years) and its availability is $1 - 1/365 = 364/365$. The index combines reliability and maintainability. It is an important consideration in complex systems such as air traffic control, transportation

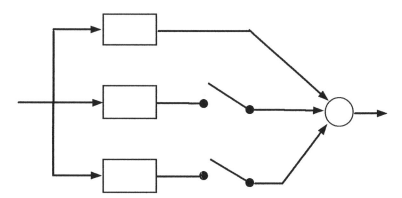

Figure 9-8. Standby redundancy.

systems, and power stations. A system alternates between periods when it is up and when it is down. Steady-state availability gives the long-term fraction of time the system is in an up state or, equivalently, what the probability is that the system will be up at a randomly chosen moment in time. The steady-state availability can expressed as

$$\frac{\text{MTTF}}{\text{MTTF} + \text{MTTR}}$$

As before, MTTF is the mean time-to-failure— that is, the average amount of time the system is up. MTTR is the mean time-to-repair— that is, the average amount of time the system is down after it fails. Hardware repair time is influenced by accessibility, ease of test and diagnosis, the presence of built-in test (BIT), and hardware testability. It is necessary to be clear about what is included in repair time. "Operational availability" includes the following in repair time:

- Storage time
- Preventive maintenance time
- Corrective maintenance time
- Administrative and logistics delay time (waiting for spares, etc.)

"Achieved availability" is more limited and includes only the following activities in repair time:

- Preventative maintenance time
- Corrective maintenance time

Preventive maintenance includes periodic chores such as cleaning, lubrication, calibration, and inspecting for incipient failures (by noticing cracks, etc.).

For hardware, according to MIL-HDBK-472, MTTR elements included in corrective maintenance are

- Preparation
- Fault Isolation
- Disassembly
- Interchange
- Reassembly
- Alignment
- Checkout
- Reassembly

For software, a computer program is not normally debugged after a software failure occurs; the software is not "repaired." Programmers do not come in and track down the bug. Rather, the software is "restored" by restarting the software from a known good state. If the computer system has crashed, a reboot will be required. The program will have to be reloaded. If a file or database on disk has been corrupted, then some type of recovery action will be required. The MTTR for software is computed as the average of the times of the different possible restoration scenarios, weighted by their respective probabilities of occurrence. (Meanwhile, some type of bug report is submitted, and the programmer will look at the problem later, off line, and include the fix in the next version. That time spent off line does not affect the MTTR.) There *is* a software quality factor called "maintainability." It refers to the ease with which software can be modified for the purposes of

- Correction (of faults)
- Adaptation (to new hardware and software environments)
- Perfective maintenance (adding features in response to user requests)

But note that maintainability has nothing to do with the uptime and downtime of operational software. Again, when operational software fails, it is restarted; no change is made to the code, so software maintainability is not relevant to availability.

MARKOV MODELING

Markov modeling is an approach that can be applied to the behavior of systems that vary with respect to time. As time goes on, the system transitions between a set of states. Some examples of states are:

- One processor down due to transient hardware fault
- Two processors down
- Application down
- Processor being repaired
- Application being restarted

In Markov modeling, the future states of the system are considered independent of all past states except for the immediately preceding state; the history of how the system got to the preceding state is unimportant. Also, the behavior of the system is assumed to be stationary: The probability of making a transition from one particular state to another particular state is independent of time.

In a Markov model, states are represented by ellipses (Figure 9-9). A number on the left-hand side uniquely identifies the state. An "S" on the right-hand side indicates that a state is a "success" state: one in which the system is considered to be up. An "F" indicates that the state is a "failure" state: one in which the system is considered to be down. In the middle of the ellipse is a compact description of the state. This description does not follow any particular convention and varies from model to model. Usually it is a list of the status of components or activities. For example, if

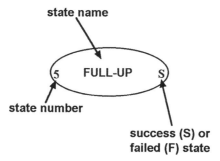

Figure 9-9. State depiction.

the system consists of four components, the state description may be a list of the up/down status of those four components.

A possible transition from one state to another is indicated by a directed arc (line or curve with an arrow at the end) appearing between the two states involved (Figure 9-10). The arrow indicates the direction of the transition, and the arc is labeled with the transition rate (Figure 9-11). The transition rate is the average number of transitions from the state the arc originates at to the state the arrow points to. The transition rate is usually understood to be in units of transitions per hour. The rate can be a number like 0.04 or can be a symbolic expression. The expression typically involves failure rates λ('s), repair rates μ('s), and coverages (C's). For example, λ_{SW} stands for software failure rate, and μ_{HW} stands for hardware repair rate. Depending on the subscript, a coverage is the probability that an error condition will be detected (C_d),

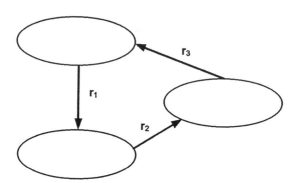

Figure 9-10. Transition arcs between states.

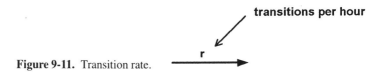

Figure 9-11. Transition rate.

isolated (C_i), or recovered from (C_r). Total coverage is $C = C_d + C_i + C_r$. A particular subscripted failure rate, repair rate, or coverage may appear in multiple transition rate expressions throughout a model. These quantities (λ's, μ's, C's) serve as the parameters of the model. When the model is evaluated to obtain the overall system availability or other figure of merit, each parameter has to be associated with a predicted value. Different values can be substituted for the rates, to see the effects of different values and the sensitivity of the model to the parameter values within the range of uncertainty.

"Solving" a Markov model is to determine the steady-state probabilities of being in each state. This amounts to solving a set of simultaneous differential equations, and a software tool is often employed to do the solving. Examples of such tools are SHARPE (Sahner and Trivedi, 1993), SURE (Butler, 1985), Hi-Rel (Bavuso and Dugan, 1992), ASSIST (Johnson, 1986), and MARKOV (at Hughes Information Systems).

The output of the tool is the long-term (steady-state) probability that the system is in each state. The availability is then simply the sum of the probabilities of the model's "success" states. States are numbered 0, 1, . . ., with state 0 being the start state.

The transition rate is a hazard rate—the number of transitions per unit time (generally, per hour). Because one of the Markov assumptions is stationarity, the transition rates are constant. A transition rate of 0.0001 means one transition per 10,000 hours. A rate of 4 means four transitions per hour.

Examples of Markov Models

Figure 9-12 illustrates a general hardware redundancy model. The system starts out with N identical units. This is an M-out-of-N system, meaning that the system can survive with as few as M units operational. Thus the system can lose up to $(N - M)$ units and still be up. The failure rate of each of the N elements is λ_{HW}. The transition rate from the initial state (#0) to the 1-unit-down state (#1) is $N \lambda_{HW}$ because N units are exposed to failure. Once in state #1, the system transitions to state 0 when the

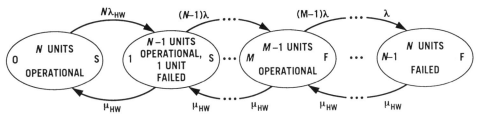

Figure 9-12. General hardware redundancy model. M required of N supplied identical elements.

repair of the failed unit is completed. While the system is in state #1, then until the repair is actually completed, a second unit can fail, with the result that the system transitions to state #2. The transition rate from state #1 to state #2 is $(N - 1)\lambda_{HW}$ because $(N - 1)$ units are exposed to failure (the Nth one is already out of commission). Note that the assumption is made that there is only one repair person, so only one unit can be repaired at a time.

Figure 9-13 shows three possible system configurations. System (a) is repairable. The hardware can be repaired and the software can be restarted. System (b) is a non-repairable system. The hardware cannot be repaired and the software cannot be restarted. System (c) has nonrepairable hardware, but the software can be restarted.

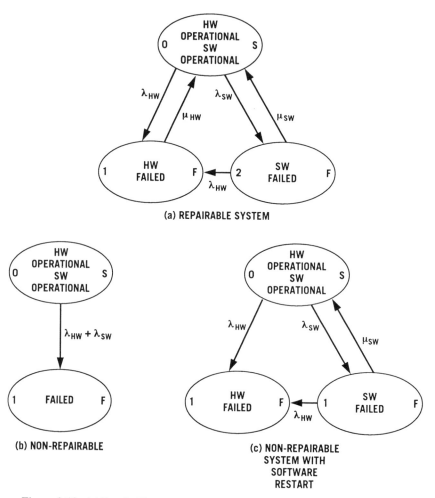

Figure 9-13. (a) Repairable system. (b) Non-repairable system. (c) Non-repairable system with software restart.

As we discussed under availability, the restart rate for software is usually an average of several different restoration possibilities, weighted by their relative frequencies. As a simple example of the averaging process, suppose that 90% of the time we can restore software by a restart that takes 20 minutes and that 10% of the time we can restore it by a reboot that takes 1.5 hours. The mean time-to-repair (MTTR) is $(0.9)(1/3)+(0.1)(1.5) = 0.45$ hours. The software restoration rate is $1/0.45 \approx 2.22$ per hour.

In Figure 9-14, a hot standby is available. If a hardware failure occurs, a switchover can take place to the backup element. Figure 9-15 is a simplified diagram of the hardware/software case. If a hardware or software failure occurs on the primary element, a switchover takes place to the backup element. The primary and the backup are loosely coupled. The primary merely periodically passes the backup enough information so that the backup stands ready to take over at any time. Because the logic being executed on the primary and backup is different (the primary does real work; the backup is just an "understudy"), in many cases the switchover

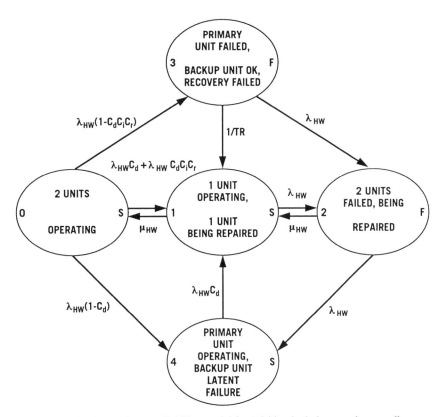

Figure 9-14. Hardware reliability model for 1:2 identical elements hot standby with automatic switchover.

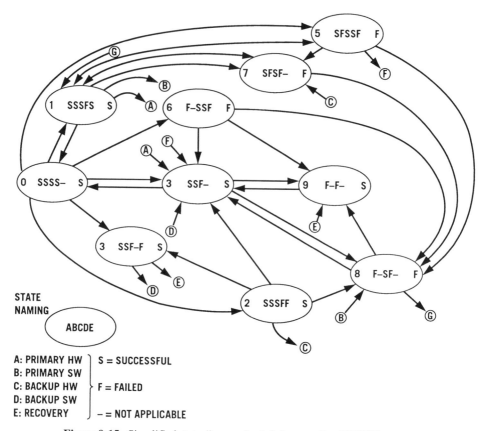

Figure 9-15. Simplified state diagram for 1:2, hot standby, HW/SW system.

can clear a software failure on the primary. In the event of the primary crashing, hanging, or being caught in an infinite loop, the backup has to take over. Typically, the primary would send out a "heartbeat" or "health message" on a continual basis. When the backup fails to receive an expected health message, the standby, preferably with consensus from other network devices, takes over and assumes the primary role (Rome Laboratory, 1992; Friedman et al., 1992).

In Figure 9-15, the state description is a comma-separated list in the following order: primary hardware, primary software, backup hardware, backup software, recovery. In that state-description list, "S" means success, "F" means failure, and "—" means don't care whether up or down.

We now describe each state in the diagram in detail and give the expressions for each transition rate. In the diagram, to avoid transition arcs crossing each other, the markers A–H each appear twice. The two places where the same letter appears are to be considered connected. For example, there is a transition arc from state 4 to state 3 because an arc is drawn from state 4 to a marker D and from another marker D to state 3.

State Descriptions

0 Fully operational state. This is the start state.

1 System is recovering from a detected failure in the standby.

2 System is operational, but the standby has a latent software failure.

3 System is operational, but the standby has a detected hardware failure.

4 System is operational, but the standby has a latent hardware failure.

5 Active's software has failed. Recovery to the standby has been unsuccessful. Manual intervention is required to restart the standby.

6 Active's hardware has failed. Recovery to the standby has been unsuccessful. Manual intervention is required to restart the standby.

7 Both active and standby have failed due to software. Manual intervention is required to restart either hardware platform.

8 The active's hardware has failed and the standby's software has failed. Manual intervention is required to restart the standby.

9 Both the active's and standby's hardware have failed.

Symbols Used in Transition Rate Expressions

λ_{HW}: hardware failure rate

λ_{SW}: software failure rate

μ_{HW}: hardware repair rate

μ_{HW}: software restoration rate

Cd_{HW}: hardware error detection coverage

Cd_{SW}: software error detection coverage

C_{HW}: total hardware error coverage

C_{SW}: total software error coverage

Transition Rate Expressions

From state 0 to state

1: $\lambda_{SW}Cd_{SW} + \lambda_{SW}C_{SW}$

2: $\lambda_{SW}(1 - C_{SW})$

3: $\lambda_{HW}Cd_{HW} + \lambda_{HW}C_{HW}$

4: $\lambda_{HW}(1 - Cd_{HW})$

5: $\lambda_{SW}(1 - C_{SW})$

6: $\lambda_{HW}(1 - C_{HW})$

From state 1 to state

0: μ_{SW}

3: λ_{SW}

7: λ_{SW}

8: λ_{HW}

From state 2 to state

3: $\lambda_{HW}Cd_{HW}$

4: $\lambda_{HW}(1 - Cd_{HW})$

7: λ_{SW}

8: λ_{HW}

From state 3 to state

0: μ_{SW}

8: λ_{SW}

9: λ_{HW}

From state 4 to state

3: $\lambda_{HW}Cd_{HW}$

8: λ_{SW}

9: λ_{HW}

From state 5 to state

1: $1/TR_{SW}$

3: λ_{HW}

7: λ_{SW}

8: λ_{HW}

From state 6 to state

3: $1/TR_{SW}$

8: λ_{SW}

9: λ_{HW}

From state 7 to state

1: μ_{SW}

8: $2\lambda_{SW}$

From state 8 to state

1: μ_{HW}

3: μ_{SW}

9: λ_{HW}

From state 9 to state

3: μ_{HW}

Markov Chains

Once we formulate a Markov model for a system, we can use that model to compute system availability and other system parameters. If we view time as advancing in discrete steps, we have what is called a *Markov chain*. The state the system is in at time n is the random variable X_n. If $X_n = i$, then at time n the system is in state i. We thus have a sequence of random variables, a stochastic process: $\{X_n\}$. The probability p_{ij} that the system will transition from state i to state j is

$$P_{ij} \equiv \Pr\{X_{n+1} = j \mid X_n = i\}$$

The system can be represented in matrix form by

$$\mathbf{P} = \begin{bmatrix} P_{11} & P_{12} & P_{13} & \cdots & P_{1n} \\ P_{21} & P_{22} & P_{23} & \cdots & P_{2n} \\ P_{31} & P_{32} & P_{33} & \cdots & P_{3n} \\ \vdots & \vdots & \vdots & \vdots & \vdots \\ P_{n1} & P_{n2} & P_{n3} & \cdots & P_{nn} \end{bmatrix}$$

The row indicates the *from* state and the column indicates the *to* state, so p_{ij} is found in row i, column j, and is the probability of transitioning from state i to state j, given that the system is presently in state i.

CONVERTING MARKOV TRANSITION RATES TO TRANSITION PROBABILITIES

The Markov models that we've seen so far have had their transition arcs labeled with rates. To convert that kind of Markov model to a Markov chain (where arcs are labeled with probabilities), we take the following approach:

Notation

r_{ij}: transition rate from state i to state j (per hour or other time period.)

$r_{ii} = 0$ (In the original Markov diagram, where arcs are labeled with transition rates, there is no arc from any state back to itself.)

p_{ij}: probability of transitioning from state i to state j during one time period

Rate of transitioning out of state i:

$$u_i = \sum_j r_{ij}$$

Because the transition rates are constant, the exponential distribution applies. The probability of staying in state i is

$$P_{ii} = \exp[-u_i]$$

Transition probabilities are proportionally allocated out of the probability $(1 - p_{ii})$ of leaving the state, so that $p_{ij} \propto r_{ij}$, $i \neq j$.

$$P_{ij} = (1-p_{ii})\frac{r_{ij}}{u_i}$$

Note that the probability of staying in a state plus the probability of leaving a state will always add up to unity:

$$P_{ii} + \sum_j P_{ij} = 1$$

Analysis of Markov Models

To determine the probability that the system is in each state after m time intervals, we compute $\mathbf{P}^m$, which is $\mathbf{P}$ to the mth power, the matrix $\mathbf{P}$ multiplied by itself m times. The top row of the matrix gives the probabilities: p_{11}^m is the probability of ending up in state 1 after m time intervals, p_{11}^m is the probability of ending up in state 1 after m time intervals, and so on.

The steady-state, long run average proportion of time spent in each state can be computed as follows: Denote the steady-state probability of being in state i as p_i. These probabilities form a matrix

$$\pi = [\, \pi_1\ \pi_2\ \cdots\ \pi_n\,]$$

The following matrix equation must hold true:

$$\pi\,\mathbf{P} = \pi$$

along with

$$\sum_1^n \pi_i = 1$$

Each state is either an up state or a down state. The steady-state availability is simply the sum of the steady-state probabilities of those states for which the system is considered "up." For example, consider a system that has six states. Suppose that states 1, 2, 4, and 6 are up states and that states 3 and 5 are down states. Then the steady-state availability A is given by

$$A = \pi_1 + \pi_2 + \pi_4 + \pi_6$$

Another classical analysis of a Markov chain is "first passage times." Cheung (1980) used the approach for microanalysis of software reliability: Cheung associates each of a program's modules with a state and adds two more states: S for success and F for failure. The states are divided into two classes: absorbing and transient. A state i is absorbing if $P_{ii} = 1$; the probability of leaving the state is 0. Thus, a state is called *absorbing* if it's impossible for the system to leave the state once it enters there; otherwise it's *transient*. Each of a program's modules are transient states, and the states S and F are absorbing states. State 1 is distinguished as the start state, and state n is distinguished as an end state.

The matrix is set up as a matrix composed of four submatrices:

$$P = \begin{bmatrix} P_1 & 0 \\ V_i & Q \end{bmatrix}$$

where the matrix P_1 contains the transition probabilities among the absorbing states, Q contains the transition probabilities among the transient states, and V_1 contains the transition probabilities from the transient states to the absorbing states. Cheung assumes that the transition probabilities among states is known (goes in submatrix Q) and that the reliability R_i of each module is known.

Note the following logical conclusions in constructing the matrices:

1. Successful module: The probability of transitioning from state i to state j is q_{ij} times the reliability of module i.
2. Module failure: The probability of state i transitioning to state F is $1 - R_i$.
3. The probability of transitioning from an absorbing state to any other state is zero.
4. The probability of transitioning from an absorbing state to itself is 1.
5. The probability of transitioning from any other state to the start state (state 1) is 0.
6. The probability of transitioning from the end state (state n) to another transient state (state 2 through n) is 0.
7. The probability of any of states 1 through $(n-1)$ transitioning to state C is 0.

The matrix

$$H = (I - Q)^{-1}$$

is called the *fundamental matrix*. The entry h_{ij} gives the expected number of times in the transient state j when the system was started in the transient state i. The reliability $R(k)$ of the program is the probability is the probability of reaching state C at or before the kth step, which is

$$R(k) = H_{1k}$$

Littlewood (1979) modeled sequential software systems via a *semi-Markov model.* In a semi-Markov model, there is a *sojourn time* the system spends in a state before transitioning to the next state. Littlewood assumes a system of n software components. Let the failure rate of the ith component be denoted λ_i. Control passes from component i to component j with probability P_{ij} and then stays in the state for a sojourn of mean duration m_{ij}. If the component failure rates are small, then the overall program failure rate is

$$\lambda = \frac{\text{total failures}}{\text{total time}}$$

$$= \frac{\displaystyle\sum_{k=1}^{n}\sum_{l=1}^{n} \pi_k P_{kl} \mu_{kl} \lambda_k}{\displaystyle\sum_{k=1}^{n}\sum_{l=1}^{n} \pi_k P_{kl} \mu_{kl}}$$

We can augment the formula by taking into account the probability q_{kl} of a failure occuring during transition from module k to module l:

$$\lambda = \frac{\displaystyle\sum_{k=1}^{n}\sum_{l=1}^{n} \pi_k P_{kl} (\mu_{kl} \lambda_k + q_{kl})}{\displaystyle\sum_{k=1}^{n}\sum_{l=1}^{n} \pi_k P_{kl} \mu_{kl}}$$

SUMMARY

This chapter showed how the failure rates of multiple software and hardware components can be combined to arrive at an overall system reliability figure of merit. When hardware redundancy is present, reliability block diagrams are useful models. When fault tolerance and repair are present, then Markov and semi-Markov models are appropriate.

REFERENCES

S. J. Bavuso and J. B. Dugan. "Hi-Rel: Reliability/Availability Integrated Workstation Tool." In: *Proceedings of the Reliability and Maintainability Symposium*, pp. 491–500, Jan. 21–23, 1992.

R. W. Butler. "The SURE2 Reliability Analysis Program," Technical Report 87593, NASA Langley Research Center, January 1985.

R. C. Cheung. "A User-Oriented Software Reliability Model." *IEEE Transactions on Software Engineering* SE-6(2), 118–125, 1980.

M. A. Friedman, P. Goddard, P. Y. Tran. "Reliability Techniques for Combined Hardware and Software Systems." Technical Report RL-TR-92-15, Rome Laboratory, U.S. Department of Defense, 1992.

S. C. Johnson. "Assist User's Manual." Technical Memorandum 87735, NASA Langley Research Center, August 1986.

B. Littlewood. "Software Reliability Model for Modular Program Structure." *IEEE Transactions on Reliability* R-28(3), pp. 241–246, 1979.

Rome Laboratory. *Military Handbook on Hardware/Software Reliability Assurance and Control.* U.S. Air Force Systems Command, Griffiss AFB, NY, draft February 1992.

Rome Laboratory. *Rome Laboratory Reliability Engineer's Toolkit: An Application-Oriented Guide for the Practicing Reliability Engineer,* April 1993, p. 90.

R. Sahner and K. S. Trivedi. "A Software Tool for Learning About Stochastic Models." *IEEE Transactions on Education*, February 1993.

CHAPTER 10

Software Reliability Prediction, Allocation, and Demonstration Testing

In Chapter 7 we discussed software reliability modeling, and in Chapter 8 we discussed software reliability growth modeling. In Chapter 9 we saw how multiple hardware and software reliability figures can be combined. In this chapter, we apply software reliability modeling to the tasks of software reliability prediction, allocation, and demonstration testing.

FAILURE INTENSITY AND FAULTS

A software fault is a susceptibility to failure—a missing, extra, defective, or out-of-sequence instruction or set of instructions that has caused, or has the potential to cause, a software failure. The presence of a software fault in the program code does not by itself guarantee the occurrence of a failure; a long time or even forever might go by before the fault triggers a failure. Whether and how often a fault is encountered depends on the fault's location in the program and the operational profile. A fault in an initialization part of a program may be hit every time. A fault in an exception handler for a rare condition may be encountered very seldom. Every time a fault is encountered during execution, a failure does not necessarily ensue; some faults will only cause a failure during certain machine states. For example, a particular fault might trigger a failure only when the machine state is such that the sum of the variables x and y exceeds 1000.

Even when a fault is encountered and the machine state is such that the fault is activated, a fault does not usually cause a failure immediately. The fault—the logical flaw—causes the system to enter an incorrect state in which one or more bits in some store or bus takes on an unintended value. In the PIE modeling of Chapters 2 and 3, this was called the *infection* step. If the software does not contain provision for fault tolerance, the error may propagate, resulting in erroneous output and hence a failure. The presence of incorrect data internal to the software does not constitute a failure; a failure occurs when erroneous output appears causing a user-observable effect on the system.

Considering now only software-caused software failures, a software fault is the totality of that which causes a particular software failure. Whatever you had to change in the software to get the failure not to recur is the fault. Whatever you did might not have been the only way. There might have been more than one way to change the software to accomplish this.

The set of input states that produces failure for a particular fault forms its *fail set.* In general, repair activity reduces the size of a fault's fail set and, ideally, makes the fail set null (empty). The ω faults existing in a program can be viewed as competing risks. The overall time-to-failure of the program, T, is the minimum of the ω individual faults' times-to-failure $T_1, T_2, \ldots, T_\omega$:

$$T = \min (T_1, T_2, \ldots, T_\omega)$$

The overall program failure intensity λ is the sum of the faults' hazard rates:

$$\lambda = \sum_{i=1}^{\omega} \mathrm{hr}\{t_i\}$$

As noted earlier, the contribution a fault makes to the overall failure rate is aptly described by a hazard rate because, ideally, the fault has a finite lifetime: Once the fault triggers a failure, the fault is removed from the program.

The ith fault's hazard rate can be dissected into three factors: the program's *linear execution frequency, f;* a structure factor, S_i; and a machine-state factor, M_i:

$$\phi_i = f \cdot S_i \cdot M_i$$

The linear execution frequency is found by dividing the processor speed by the number of object instructions in the program. It gives the number of "program passages" per unit time if the program's instructions were executed in linear sequence. The structure factor accounts for the fact that almost all programs contain loops and conditional and unconditional branches. The structure factor is the average number of times the fault is encountered per program passage. The machine-state factor is the probability that the fault, when encountered during execution, triggers a failure. The fault exposure ratio K we met in Musa's basic execution time model is simply the product of the average structure factor and the average machine-state factor, across all the faults in the program. His per-fault hazard rate is just $\phi = fK$. Note how K is similar to a testability measure. It is a function of execution, infection, and propagation.

OBJECTIONS

Adding together the fault hazard rates to produce the overall program failure intensity has been criticized because one fault could mask another (Ehrlich et al., 1991). Say fault A causes the system to crash every time it executed. It is on a line of code in front of another fault, fault B, that also crashes the system when encountered. Fault B will not trigger a failure until fault A has been detected and removed.

From the standpoint of a single version of the program, the resolution of this "problem" is simple: The hazard rate of fault A is what it is, and the hazard rate of fault B is zero.

In the case of reliability growth modeling, the fact that fault A masked fault B is only interesting until after fault A and fault B are removed. After that, the overall program failure intensity is simply the sum of the hazard rates of the remaining faults.

Let's say that there are 10 faults in the program all together, and the first two we encounter are fault A and fault B. Also, there is only one place where a fault masks another fault. Before we encounter fault A, our overall program failure intensity is 9ϕ. After we detect and remove fault A, the failure intensity is still 9ϕ. After we detect and remove fault B, the failure intensity is now 8ϕ. If fault A had not been masking fault B, we would have started off with 10ϕ. After detecting and removing fault A, it would be 9ϕ. After detecting and removing fault B, it would be 8ϕ. So in both cases we end up with 8ϕ. And in both cases, while faults A and B were being removed, the average failure intensity was the same: 9ϕ.

SOFTWARE FAILURE RATE PREDICTION

Software reliability prediction is the process of forecasting the reliability of a piece of software prior to the time the software can be actually tested as an integrated whole. Prediction can take place during the proposal/precontractual stage of a product and during development, up to the beginning of system test. Once the system test period begins, the history of failures during the system test allows the parameters of a software reliability growth model to be estimated (statistically inferred) and it's no longer necessary to use prediction techniques.

Hardware reliability is much easier to predict than software reliability because hardware is usually constructed from off-the-shelf parts of known reliability, whereas computer programs are generally newly written. Use of prediction handbooks such as MIL-HDBK-217 are routine in hardware reliability engineering.

The first step in software reliability prediction is to relate software failure intensity λ to software fault content ω. As introduced in Chapter 1, Musa et al. (1987) provided the following formula, based on a series of industry studies:

$$\lambda = \omega \cdot K \cdot r/I$$

where K is the fault exposure ratio, whose default value is 4.20×10^{-7}; r is processor speed (in, for example, instructions per second); and I is the number of object instructions in the program. If the processor speed is in instructions per second, the failure intensity will be in units of failures per CPU second. The presence of "number of instructions" in both the numerator and the denominator is not a mistake. The presence of the factor (ω/I) implies that software failure rate is ultimately dependent on fault *density,* not on the *number* of faults. If you felt that one program should have a higher failure rate than another on account of its length, you would have to capture that through predicting a higher fault density for the bigger program.

A higher fault density or a faster processor speed results in a higher rate of exposure of faults over time, and thus a higher failure rate. The higher failure rate due to faster processor speed is a phenomenon that arises because this failure rate is expressed in terms of execution time. When the failure rate is converted to a system-operating-time or wall-clock failure rate (by multiplying by the utilization), this speed dependency does not occur. Here is the formula for system-operating-time failure rate λ_s:

$$\lambda s = \omega_0 \cdot K \cdot u \cdot r/I$$

where u is utilization. If the processor speed r is doubled, the utilization u is halved, with no net change to λ_s.

In applying the formula it's necessary to predict the number of faults ω. Because the number of faults will change over time, we need to peg the prediction to a particular point in time. We will predict the fault content at the beginning of system test, a quantity we denote by ω_0.

One simple approach is to predict an average fault density for the program. A typical value is six faults per thousand lines of executable source code. If a program has 10,000 lines of executable source code, then the predicted number of faults is $\omega_0 = (6/1000) \times 10,000 = 60$. If the processor speed is 3 MIPS (million instructions per second) and each executable source statement expands to 6.5 object instructions, then the initial failure rate is

$$\lambda_0 = \omega \cdot K \cdot r/I = (6)(4.2 \times 10^{-7})(3,000,000)/(6.5 \cdot 10) = 0.1163$$

failures per CPU second. If this seems like a high failure rate to you, recall that this is the initial failure rate, before reliability growth takes place.

Other approaches include the use of software science principles (Halstead, 1977), which is based on information content. If you know or can predict the number of distinct operators η_1 and distinct operands η_2, then you obtain the program's "length" from the formula $N = \eta_1 \log_2 \eta_1 + \eta_2 \log_2 \eta_2$. The "volume" is then obtained as $V = N \log_2 (\eta_1 + \eta_2)$. Finally, the predicted number of inherent faults is $\omega_0 = V/3000$.

CASE STUDY: INITIAL FAULT CONTENT

Let us use the data from the case study on utilization to predict the initial number of faults in the flight data processor software. Table 10-1 reproduces several columns from our ongoing case study and adds a new column, "FAULTS ω_0". Using the default value of 6 faults per thousand lines of executable source code, we multiply the KSLOCs column by 6 to obtain the initial number of FAULTS ω_0.

TABLE 10-1. Predicted Fault Content

CSCI	MIPS	UTIL	MIPS USED	KSLOCs	FAULTS ω_0
ARP	95	0.00000411	0.00039045	26	156
SIM	95	0.0476761	4.5292295	50	300
FPA	95	0.00078948	0.0750006	50	300
FPP	95	0.0126658	1.203251	100	600
DBS	95	0.02707	2.57165	20	120
FLM	95	0.00238872	0.2269284	72	432
MAM	95	0.0394509	3.7478355	85	144
ENV	95	0.00142326	0.1352097	24	144
SMC	95	0.00152	0.1444	35	210
COM	95	0.150358	14.28401	5	30

CASE STUDY: PREDICTION OF INITIAL FAILURE RATE

Continuing our air traffic control flight data processor example from the previous chapter, we will use the basic execution time model prediction equation to predict the initial failure intensity of the software. The formula is

$$\lambda_0 = \omega_0 \cdot K \cdot r/I$$

where ω_0 is the initial fault content, K is the fault exposure ratio (default value 4.20×10^{-7}), r is processor speed, and I is number of object instructions. In terms of the table columns, and using CPU seconds as the time unit, the formula becomes

$$\frac{\text{FAULTS} \cdot K \cdot \text{MIPS} \cdot 1{,}000{,}000}{\text{KSLOCs} \cdot 1000 \cdot 6.1}$$

The way the number of object instructions is computed is by taking the number of lines of code (KSLOCs • 1000) and multiplying by the typical code expansion ratio for Ada (6.1 object instructions per source line of code.) Table 10-2 contains columns NUM (the numerator of the formula), DENOM (the denominator of the formula), and λ_0 (the initial execution-time failure intensity = NUM/DENOM). Note that all the initial failure intensities come out to be the same (0.039246 failures per CPU second). This is because failure rate is a function of fault density, not fault content. Also, we assumed that all the code was newly developed, as opposed to reused code.

PREDICTION OF GROWTH MODEL PARAMETERS

To forecast the failure rate of the software for points in time beyond the start of system test, you need two parameters. The basic execution time model can be parameterized in several ways, but for our purposes the best parameterization is to have ini-

TABLE 10-2. Initial Failure Rate

CSCI	MIPS	UTIL	KSLOCs	FAULTS	NUM	DENOM	λ_0
ARP	95	0.00000411	26	156	6,224.4	158,600	0.039246
SIM	95	0.0476761	50	300	11,970	305,000	0.039246
FPA	95	0.00078948	50	300	11,970	305,000	0.039246
FPP	95	0.0126658	100	600	23,940	610,000	0.039246
DBS	95	0.02707	20	120	4,788	122,000	0.039246
FLM	95	0.00238872	72	432	17,236.8	439,200	0.039246
MAM	95	0.0394509	85	510	20,349	518,500	0.039246
ENV	95	0.00142326	24	144	5,745.6	146,400	0.039246
SMC	95	0.00152	35	210	8,379	213,500	0.039246
COM	95	0.150358	5	30	1,197	30,500	0.039246

tial failure intensity λ_0 and the decrement-in-failure-intensity-per-failure β be the parameters. Why? Because in this chapter we have already shown how to obtain λ_0. To obtain the other parameter, β, you apply the formula

$$\beta = B\frac{\lambda_0}{\omega_0}$$

The quantity B is the fault reduction factor, whose default value is 0.955. This formula is easy to interpret: The fraction takes the initial failure rate and divides it by the initial fault content to yield the per-fault hazard rate (symbolized ϕ in this book). Every time a fault is removed, the failure intensity drops by ϕ. Because of imperfect debugging, the average net number of faults removed per failure experienced is not 1 but B. So the decrement in failure intensity per failure experienced is $\beta = B\phi$.

In the growth model parameter estimation equations, the parameterization is ν_0 and β. The parameter ν_0 is *total failures* and is obtained from the formula $\nu_0 = \omega_0/B$. This is the (*s*-expected) number of failures that have to be experienced to expose and remove all faults. Note also the relationship $\lambda_0 = \beta\nu_0$.

CASE STUDY: FORECASTING FAILURE RATE AFTER PERIOD OF GROWTH

In our continuing case study, we will now see what happens to the failure rate after 40 hours of system operation (144,000 seconds). In Table 10-3 column labeled UTIL is that CSCI's utilization. The column labeled λ_S is the initial failure rate expressed with respect to system operating seconds ($\lambda * $ UTIL). The sum of this column is 0.01112, the overall software failure rate. The column labeled SYS τ is the number of CPU seconds expended in system test. The column labeled CSCI TAU is the number of CPU seconds the individual CPU gets (CSCI TAU = SYS $\tau * $ UTIL). The column labeled β is the basic execution time model β parameter. The column labeled

Table 10-3. Predicted Failure Intensity

CSCI	UTIL	λ_s	SYSτ	CSCIτ	β	$\lambda(\tau)$	$\lambda_s(\tau)$	$\lambda_H(\tau)$
ARP	0.00000411	1.61×10^{-7}	144,000	0.59184	0.000240255	0.0392403	1.61×10^{-7}	0.0005
SIM	0.0476761	0.001871	144,000	6865.35	0.000124933	0.0166454	0.000794	2.8569
FPA	0.00078948	3.1×10^{-5}	144,000	113.685	0.000124933	0.0386924	3.05×10^{-5}	0.1099
FPP	0.0126658	0.000497	144,000	1823.87	6.24664E-05	0.0350198	0.000444	1.5967
DBS	0.02707	0.001062	144,000	3898.08	0.000312332	0.0116156	0.000314	1.1319
FLM	0.00238872	9.36×10^{-5}	144,000	343.975	8.67589E-05	0.0380919	9.1×10^{-5}	0.3275
MAM	0.0394509	0.001548	144,000	5680.92	7.34899E-05	0.0258511	0.00102	3.6714
ENV	0.00142326	5.59×10^{-5}	144,000	204.949	0.000260277	0.0372072	5.3×10^{-5}	0.1906
SMC	0.00152	5.97×10^{-5}	144,000	218.88	0.000178475	0.0377423	5.74×10^{-5}	0.2065
COM	0.150358	0.005901	144,000	21,651.5	0.001249328	$7.01742E^{-14}$	$1.06-10-14$	3.8×10^{-11}

$\lambda(\tau)$ is the CSCI's failure intensity after one hour of system test. The column labeled $\lambda_S(\tau)$ is the failure rate expressed with respect to system operating seconds. The column labeled $\lambda_H(\tau)$ is the failure rate expressed with respect to system operating seconds. This calculation, like the prediction for λ_0, can be easily performed on a spreadsheet.

SOFTWARE RELIABILITY ALLOCATION

Software reliability allocation involves taking an overall software reliability requirement and translating that requirement into reliability goals for lower-level software elements. For example, a software subsystem might consist of 10 executing programs. A contractual requirement (or an objective produced from a higher-level allocation) dictates an overall subsystem failure rate of one failure per 10,000 system operating hours. The system test period will last six months. What failure intensity should be allocated to each of the 10 programs?

Software reliability allocation must be based on what failure rates are achievable. In terms of software reliability modeling, a program's achievable failure rate is a function of its initial failure rate λ_0, its growth curve, and the amount of growth time it will have available to it during system test. The higher a program's utilization factor, the more growth time (execution time) it will experience.

First, a prediction is made of each program's initial failure rate λ_0. It is assumed that parts of the program that have a higher complexity have been paid more attention to, so that the overall fault density is fairly uniform. Also, any parts of the program that are critical to safety or reliability have been paid more attention to, so that the effects of all failures are fairly uniform. Next, a software reliability growth model is invoked to determine how much each program's reliability will have an opportunity to grow during system test, in light of that program's utilization rate. The programs need not be integrated together all at once; they can be integrated one by one by means of a series of "builds." The achievable failure rates are then computed, and they are employed to assign a relative weight to each program. The allocation of failure rates to the programs is then made in proportion to those weights.

Suppose that there are J programs to which we can allocate a failure rate requirement Λ_{REQD}, expressed with respect to system operating time. The programs comprising the subsystem are in series: The failure of one program results in failure of the subsystem. The utilization rate of the lth program is u_l, and its predicted initial failure rate is λ_{0l}. Let t_l be the amount of system operating time that the lth program will spend in system test. The earlier the program is integrated into the system configuration, the longer this amount of time will be. Then, according to the basic execution time model, the failure rate, with respect to system operating time, of the lth program at the end of system test is given by

$$\lambda_l(t_l, u_l) = \lambda_{0l}\exp[-B\phi_l t_l u_l]u_l, \quad l = 1, \ldots, J$$

where ϕ_l is the lth program's predicted per-fault hazard.

The next step is to compute the overall failure rate Λ of the subsystem. Because the programs in the subsystem are in series, the system-operating-time failure rates are added to obtain Λ:

$$\Lambda = \sum_{l=1}^{J} \lambda_l(t_l, u_l)$$

Next, the lth program is assigned a relative weight

$$w_l = \frac{\lambda_l(t_l, u_l)}{\Lambda}, \quad l = 1, \ldots, J$$

Note that

$$\sum_{l=1}^{J} w_l = 1$$

Finally, the system-operating-time failure rate to allocate to the lth program is

$$\lambda_{\text{ALLOC}\,l} = \Lambda_{\text{REQD}} \cdot w_l, \quad l = 1, \ldots, J$$

As a check, we'll show that the allocated failure rates add up to the required subsystem failure rate:

$$\sum_{l=1}^{j} \lambda_{\text{ALLOC}\,l} = \sum_{l=1}^{j} \Lambda_{\text{REQD}} \cdot w_l$$

$$= \Lambda_{\text{REQD}} \cdot \sum_{l=1}^{j} w_l = \Lambda_{\text{REQD}}$$

CASE STUDY: ALLOCATION

The λ_l column in Table 10-4 gives the CSCI's system-operating-time failure rate (taken from the preceding case study). The ω_l column gives the CSCI's relative weight; the formula is $\omega_l = \lambda_l / \Sigma \lambda_l$. The $\lambda_{\text{ALLOC}\,l}$ column gives the allocated failure rate, which is the product of the required system-operating-time failure rate Λ_{REQD} and the CSCI's relative weight ω_l.

In Table 10-4 the system-operating-time failure rate to be allocated is $\Lambda_{\text{REQD}} = 0.0004$. The allocated execution-time failure rates for each CSCI can be obtained by dividing the $\lambda_{\text{ALLOC}\,l}$ column by the utilization.

Table 10-4. Allocated Failure Rates

l	CSCI	λ_l	ω_l	λ_{ALLOC_l}
1	ARP	1.61×10^{-7}	5.75×10^{-5}	2.3×10^{-8}
2	SIM	0.000794	0.283076	0.000113
3	FPA	3.05×10^{-5}	0.010896	4.36×10^{-6}
4	FPP	0.000444	0.158217	6.33×10^{-5}
5	DBS	0.000314	0.11216	4.48×10^{-5}
6	FLM	9.1×10^{-5}	0.032457	1.3×10^{-5}
7	MAM	0.00102	0.363784	0.000146
8	ENV	5.3×10^{-5}	0.018889	7.56×10^{-6}
9	SMC	5.74×10^{-5}	0.020463	8.19×10^{-6}
10	COM	1.06×10^{-14}	3.76×10^{-12}	1.51×10^{-15}

DEMONSTRATION TESTING

Toward the end of the system test phase, a software reliability demonstration test can be performed to prove, to a stated degree of statistical confidence, that the software meets its reliability requirement. The test plan includes the criteria for accepting or rejecting the software. When the test has been completed, a decision is made on whether to accept or reject the software.

As we saw in Chapter 7, an executing program can be modeled as having a constant failure rate when its code is frozen and it is subjected to inputs randomly selected from a operational profile. Let λ be the true failure rate of the software. It is unknown. In designing a demonstration test, two failure rates, λ_0 and λ_1, must be specified ($\lambda_0 < \lambda_1$). A good test plan will reject, with high probability, software with a true failure rate that approaches λ_1. A good test plan will accept, with high probability, software with a true failure rate that approaches λ_0.

Relying on the results of the demonstration test for making an accept/reject decision entails two basic risks. First, if by chance good software happens to perform poorly (fails too many times during the test), then it will be rejected. Conversely, if, by chance, a bad piece of software performs well during the test, bad software will be accepted. These two decision risks must be specified in advance as parameters to the test. The "producer's risk" (risk to the developer) is the probability of rejecting software with a true failure rate equal to λ_0. The use of λ_0 in the remainder of this chapter has nothing to do with initial failure intensity. The "consumer's risk" (risk to the customer or end-user) is the probability of accepting software with a true failure rate equal to λ_1 (Friedman et al., 1994).

Three types of software demonstration tests are fixed-duration test, failure-free execution interval test, and sequential test.

A fixed-duration test is used when the amount of test time and cost must be known in advance. A fixed duration test provides demonstrated failure rate to a desired confidence level. A sequential test will accept software that has a failure rate much lower than λ_0 and reject software that has a failure rate much higher than λ_1

more quickly than a fixed-duration test having similar parameters. However, the total test time may vary significantly according to the true failure rate. A failure-free execution interval test will accept software that has a failure rate lower than λ_0 more quickly than a fixed-duration test.

Producer's and consumer's risks usually range from 10% (low risk) to 30% (high risk). The lower the risks, the longer the test. The ratio

$$d = \frac{\lambda_1}{\lambda_0}$$

is called the "discrimination ratio." The discrimination ratio establishes the power of the demonstration test in distinguishing between reliable and unreliable software. The lower the discrimination ratio, the more test time required. In Table 10-5, the time unit is chosen so that $\lambda_0 = 1$. Hence, $\lambda_1 = d$. As a typical example, if the original time unit was seconds, then the new time unit will be λ_0^{-1} seconds. The test time t is multiplied by λ_0^{-1} to convert to seconds.

ACCELERATING DEMONSTRATION TESTING

The higher a program's reliability, the longer a demonstration test is required. One way to speed up testing is to use a faster processor and adjust failure rates proportionally. For instance, if you test using a processor whose speed is twice that of the target processor, you would divide the execution time failure rate on the faster processor by two to obtain what it would be on the target. If you have more than one processor, another way to speed up testing is to run multiple copies simultaneously on s-independent input streams. When a failure occurs, it is considered to have taken place at a cumulative execution time that is the sum of the execution times accumulated on every copy. The total test time is also accumulated on all copies.

Table 10-5. Some Fixed-Duration Test Plans

Producer's Risk	Consumer's Risk	Discrimination Ratio d	Test Duration (Multiple of $1/\lambda_0$)	Reject If Number of Failures Is Greater Than or Equal to:
0.10	0.10	1.5	30.0	37
0.10	0.20	1.5	19.93	26
0.10	0.20	1.5	14.33	18
0.10	0.10	2.0	9.4	14
0.10	0.20	2.0	6.2	10
0.20	0.20	2.0	3.9	6
0.10	0.10	3.0	3.1	6
0.10	0.20	3.0	1.8	4
0.20	0.20	3.0	1.43	3

Yet another way to accelerate testing is to subject the software to an operational profile that is more "severe" than what the software would experience in field usage. Musa postulated the existence of a *testing compression factor* that would be multiplicative on the failure rate and indicate the severity of the operational profile compared to field usage. For example, if an operational profile's testing compression factor were 3, then the failure from testing under the operational profile would be divided by 3 to obtain what the failure rate would be under field usage. Musa has shown how to obtain the value of the testing compression factor in some cases. It is likely that the testing compression factor can be related to a testability measure. After all, testability is the degree to which a program reveals its faults with respect to a given operational profile.

For the case of when demonstration testing results in no failures, we saw in Chapter 3 how the squeeze play can be employed to relate testability to the statistical confidence that the software indeed has no faults: the higher the testability, the higher the confidence level that there are no faults.

SUMMARY

This chapter has covered the software reliability engineering front-end activities of software reliability prediction and allocation, as well as the back-end activity of software reliability demonstration testing. Prediction provides an early forecast of what the software failure rate will be. This forecast is made before the software has a failure history, because once the software enters system test, the failure times can be used to statistically infer the failure rate. Allocation goes hand-in-hand with prediction. Allocation apportions a failure rate requirement to multiple software components. Software reliability demonstration is performed according to a test plan that specifies a duration for the test and how many failures are allowed to occur. Statistical principles are used in constructing a test that quantifies and limits the decision risks to the producer and consumer.

REFERENCES

W. K. Ehrlich, A. Iannino, B. S. Prasanna, J. P. Stampfel, and J. R. Wu. "How Faults Cause Software Failures: Implications for Software Reliability Engineering." In: *Proceedings, International Symposium on Software Reliability Engineering*, Austin, TX, May 17–18, 1991. Los Alamitos, CA: IEEE Computer Society Press, 1991; pp. 233–241.

M. A. Friedman, P. Goddard, and P. Y. Tran. *Reliability of Software-Intensive Systems,* Series in Advanced Computing and Telecommunications. Park Ridge, NJ: Noyes Data Corp., 1994.

M. H. Halstead. *Elements of Software Science.* New York: Elsevier, 1977.

J. D. Musa, A. Iannino, and K. Okumoto. *Software Reliability Measurements, Prediction, Application.* New York: McGraw–Hill, 1987.

CHAPTER 11

Generating Test Cases

Both testability and reliability can only be assessed with respect to a specified environment. A computer program's environment certainly includes the hardware platform, the operating system version, and all the other hardware and software with which the program is integrated. An important aspect of the program's environment is its input environment, what we have been calling the program's operational profile (D). An operational profile associates each of the program's input states with a probability of occurrence. An input state is a distinct set of values for the software's input variables for a run.

As we have discussed, in software reliability engineering two kinds of testing are performed during the system test phase: software reliability growth testing and software reliability demonstration testing. In growth testing, the software is subjected to an input environment representative of field usage. When a software failure occurs, debugging activity ensues to isolate and remove the causative fault. Over the long run the reliability improves as software faults are removed. A software reliability growth model provides a family of reliability growth curves. The history of failure occurrence is used to determine point or interval estimates of the model's parameters. The growth curve describes the program's current reliability and can be employed to forecast information such as the amount of further testing needed before the software will be ready for release.

Toward the end of the system test stage, a software reliability demonstration test can be performed to prove, to a specified degree of statistical confidence, that the program has achieved its reliability requirement. For the duration of such a test, the program is stable; the code is not changed to remedy faults or for any other reason.

For meaningful results in both software reliability growth testing and software reliability demonstration testing, as well as testability assessment, an input environment representative of field usage must be maintained. Sometimes the customer will furnish a detailed written or recorded set of scenarios. For example, to test an air traffic control system, the customer might provide many hours of recorded output that the customer deems typical. When the input environment is specified via an operational profile, the input states need to be randomly selected in accordance with that operational profile. This type of testing, called *statistical testing*, is quite effective at improving reliability. Data from IBM (Adams, 1984) shows that statistical testing results in a significantly lower delivered failure rate than does coverage testing. The reason is that the faults that contribute the most to the overall program failure rate tend to be uncovered and removed early. It has also been shown to be cost-effective and to provide nearly total branch coverage anyway (Duran and Ntafos, 1984).

Performing statistical testing requires a source of randomness. The basic ingredient is a means for generating independent, uniformly distributed random numbers in the range (0, 1). A routine to generate such numbers is almost universally available in the math routine libraries that come with most compilers and interpreters. For example, in Basic the routine is RND( ), and the VAX/VMS Run-Time Library routine is MTH$RANDOM. Because library routines vary widely in quality, a better alternative is to consult a book on simulation or Monte Carlo methods for a proven pseudorandom number routine that exhibits desirable statistical properties.

This chapter describes techniques for generating input states in accordance with an operational profile.

For a random variable X, the cumulative distribution function (Cdf) $F(x)$ gives the probability that X is less than or equal to a real number x: $F(x) \equiv \Pr\{X \leq x\}$. The fundamental theorem upon which the input selection algorithms are based is the probability integral transform: If the random variable U is uniformly distributed over the interval (0, 1), then the random variable $X = F^{-1}(U)$ has cumulative distribution function $F(x)$. The notation F^{-1} denotes the inverse function of F.

OPERATIONAL PROFILE

Recall that a program's input space is the set of all possible input states. Quantization in the digital computer makes this set finite. Let a program's input states be numbered 1, 2, . . ., N. The operational profile is described by the probability mass function (pmf) function $p(i)$, which gives the likelihood that the ith input state is chosen for execution. Because the input space exhausts the possible input states, it follows that

$$\sum_{i=1}^{N} p(i) = 1$$

An alternative means of expressing the operational profile is via the Cdf $P(i)$. $P(i)$ gives the probability that the input state selected for a run is numbered less than or equal to i and is defined by

$$P(i) = \sum_{j=1}^{i} p(j), \qquad i = 1, 2, \ldots, N$$

It is assumed that each run represents a statistically independent trial; data corruption from one run is not allowed to contaminate the next run. Some degree of order dependency may exist; that is, some input states may tend to be followed by other input states. Musa et al. (1987) approached this problem by formulating a Markov model and solving for the steady-state probabilities.

GENERATING INPUT STATES FROM AN OPERATIONAL PROFILE

When the input space is big enough that you can't do an exhaustive search but is still of manageable size, a simple algorithm to select an input state is as follows:

1. Generate a uniformly distributed $(0, 1)$ random number U.
2. Set $i \leftarrow 1$.
3. While $P(i) < U$ do $i \leftarrow i + 1$.
4. Return i.

This amounts to a linear search. Any book on algorithms and data structures can suggest a number of ways to speed up the search—for example, by using a binary or interpolation search. A particularly fast method is to set up a table in advance and use an indexed search, as in Algorithm 11-1.

Algorithm 11-1. Fix m and let

$$g_i = \min_i \left[P(i) \ge \frac{j}{m} \right], \qquad j = 0, \ldots, m-1$$

1. Generate U.
2. $k \leftarrow \lfloor mU \rfloor$; $i \leftarrow g_k$
3. While $P(i) \le U$ do $i \leftarrow i + 1$.
4. Return i (Ripley, 1987).

IMPLICIT PROFILE

For many programs, as a practical matter, there may be too many input states to be individually enumerated. As an example, suppose that a program's input state consists of three unconstrained 16-bit integers. The number of possible input states is astronomical (10^{48}). An alternative method to the operational profile is to characterize the distribution of input states by means of an *implicit profile*.

A functional profile lists the relative frequencies of end-user functions. For example, the specification of a functional profile for a transaction-oriented system might look like

ADD   0.3
MODIFY   0.44
DELETE   0.26

If the distributions of input variables other than those determining the end-user function are known, then those distributions can be used to generate input values. When the distributions are not known, we make the assumption that all their permissible values are equally likely. For now, we will assume that the input variables' values are *s*-independent. Later, we will relax that assumption.

To select an input state for a test case, first the end-user function is randomly selected according to the functional profile. This can be done using the search method described above. A fast way to select the function in a program is through a table lookup in random-access memory. In the example, a program would declare a 100-element array (call it *X*) and fill its elements 1, 2, . . ., 100 with 30 letter *A*'s, followed by 44 *M*'s, followed by 26 *D*'s. The procedure to select the end-user function is as follows:

1. Generate a uniformly distributed random number *U*.
2. The selected function is found by evaluating *X*[*U*].

In our example, if *X*[*U*] is an '*A*', the selected function is ADD. If *X*[*U*] is an '*M*', the selected function is MODIFY. If *X*[*U*] is a '*D*', the selected function is DELETE.

A 100-element array was used because the relative frequencies were expressed to two decimal places (hundredths). If they were expressed to three decimal places (thousandths), a 1000-element array would have to be used.

The end-user function is only part of the input state. The next step is to generate a value for each of the remaining input variables. At the simplest level, all input quantities are single values (scalars). An array, for example, is just a collection of scalars identified by subscripts. In a record structure, the scalars are identified by field names. A scalar is characterized by having a *type*, a set of distinct, ordered values that the variable can assume.

A *discrete type* is a range of integers or a sequence of values that can be mapped to a range of integers. For example, characters can be mapped to integers by means of their ASCII codes. Booleans can be mapped to integers by taking FALSE = 0 and TRUE = 1. The values of user-defined enumerated type such as "(club, diamond, heart, spade)" can be assigned ordinal numbers 0, 1, 2, ... A discrete variable can be based on one of several types of scales:

Nominal Scale. The numbers are used merely to separate categories. For example,

EXEMPT → 1
NON-EXEMPT → 2
UNION → 3

Here, the numbers 1, 2, and 3 are arbitrary. Values can only be compared for equality, such as 2 = 2. Algorithm 11-1 is applicable, but Algorithm 11-2 is not.

Interval Scale. This is a measurement of something in constant units. The difference in units between 3 and 1 is the same as that between 2 and 4.

For an input variable that is an integer whose range is $[a, b]$, the procedure for selecting an input value is as follows:

1. Generate a uniformly distributed $(0, 1)$ random number U.
2. Return $a + (b - a)U$, rounded to the nearest integer.

The following listing shows an Ada generic function for randomly selecting a value from any discrete type:

```
with SYSTEM, MTH;
myseed: SYSTEM.UNSIGNED_LONGWORD := 31;
generic
   type DISCRETE_TYPE is (<>);
function SELECT_DISCRETE return DISCRETE_TYPE;
function SELECT_DISCRETE return DISCRETE_TYPE is
U: FLOAT;
begin
   MTH.RANDOM(RESULT => U, SEED => myseed);
   return DISCRETE_TYPE'val
      (
       DISCRETE_TYPE'pos(DISCRETE_TYPE'first)
       + integer(float(DISCRETE_TYPE'pos(DISCRETE_TYPE'last)
       - DISCRETE_TYPE'pos(DISCRETE_TYPE'first))
       * U)
      );
end SELECT_DISCRETE;
```

An example of the use of this listing is to declare "type suit is (club, diamond, heart, spade)" and then to perform the instantiation "function select_suit is new select_discrete (suit)". Invoking the function select_suit returns a random value of type *suit*. Real types such as floating point and fixed point types are handled similarly (Friedman 1993). If the range of the real input variable is $[a, b]$, the procedure for randomly selecting the input value is as follows:

1. Generate a uniformly distributed $(0, 1)$ random number U.
2. Return $a + (b - a)U$. The processor itself will choose the closest machine-representable floating or fixed-point value to the true mathematical result.

EMPIRICAL DISTRIBUTION

Recall that the cumulative distribution function (Cdf) is the function that gives the probability of the random variable X being less than or equal to any number x:

$$F(x) \equiv \Pr\{X \leq x\}$$

We can use the observed values of X to construct an "empirical Cdf" and then generate input values from that Cdf. The empirical Cdf, symbolized $\hat{F}(x)$, can be constructed as follows: Let the observed values be denoted

$$X_1, X_2, \ldots, X_n$$

Then the value of the empirical distribution function is defined by a step function that increases by $1/n$ at each of the order statistics:

$$X_{(1)} \le X_{(2)} \le \cdots \le X_{(n)}$$

This distribution function is

$$\hat{F}(x) = \frac{1}{n} \# (X_k \le x), \qquad -\infty < x < +\infty$$

where "#" means "number of." The empirical distribution function is a consistent estimator of the true distribution function $F(x)$: As the sample size increases, the variance tends to zero and its s-expectation tends to the true value.

The accuracy of the empirical Cdf $\hat{F}(x)$ as an estimator of $F(x)$ is provided by the maximum distance between $\hat{F}(x)$ and $F(x)$—the Kolmogorov statistic. A confidence band can be constructed. The confidence is $1 - \alpha$ that the true $F(x)$ value lies within a confidence band of width $200d_{1-\alpha}$, that is,

$$\hat{F}(x) - 100d_{1-\alpha} \le F(x) \le \hat{F}(x) + 100d_{1-\alpha}$$

(Any portion of the confidence band that lies below 0 or above 1 is truncated because $0 \le F(x) \le 1$.) The value of $d_{1-\alpha}$ can be obtained from a table of percentiles of the Kolmogorov statistic. For large samples ($n > 50$), the asymptotic values are given in Table 11-1. The required sample size can be determined according to the following example:

Suppose one wishes to be 90% confident of containing $F(x)$ within an interval of width 10%. Then it is required that

$$d_{.90} = \frac{.1}{2} = 0.05$$

Looking up the value of $d_{.90}$ from Table 11-1, we now have

Table 11-1. Percentiles of the Kolmogorov Statistic

$1 - \alpha$	90%	95%	99%
$d_{1-\alpha}$:	$1.22/\sqrt{n}$	$1.36/\sqrt{n}$	$1.63/\sqrt{n}$

$$\frac{1.22}{\sqrt{n}} = 0.05$$

or

$$n = \left(\frac{1.222}{.005}\right)^2 = 596$$

Because X is a continuous random variable, it can realize values between the observed values. To define $\hat{F}(x)$ for $x_{(i-1)} < x < x_{(i)}$, piecewise linear interpolation is employed. The data point pairs

$$\{((\hat{F}(x_{(1)}), \hat{F}(x_{(2)})), \ldots, (\hat{F}(X_{(n-1)}), \hat{F}(X_{(n)}))\}$$

are joined by a series of straight line segments (Figure 11-1). The formula (Bratley et al., 1987) is

$$\hat{F}(x) = \frac{i}{n} + \frac{x - x_{(ii)}}{n\,[x_{(I+1)} - x_{(i)}]}, \qquad x_{(i)} \le x \le x_{(i+1)}$$

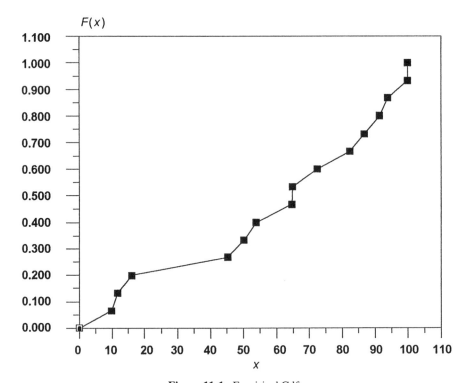

Figure 11-1. Empirical Cdf.

Algorithm 11-2 provides a means for generating random input values in accordance with such an empirical distribution.

Algorithm 11-2 (Continuous case)

1. Generate uniformly $(0, 1)$ distributed random number U.
2. Order the observations so that

$$X_{(1)} \le X_{(2)} \le \cdots \le X_{(n)}$$

3. Set

$$V \leftarrow nU$$
$$I \leftarrow \lfloor V \rfloor$$

4. Return

$$X = (V - I)* (X_{(I+1)} - X_{(I)}) + X_{(I)}$$

The procedure does not generate numbers below X_0 or above X_n. To remedy this, the lower and upper range limits can be included as pseudo-observations. For example, if the range of the input variable is (6, 300), then 6 and 300 are included, whether or not those values are actually observed.

DISCRETE: INTEGER, FIXED-POINT

The resolution r of an integer is 1. The resolution r of a fixed-point number is between 0 and 1. In this case the returned value must be rounded:

$$X' = \begin{cases} \left\lfloor X + \dfrac{r}{2} \right\rfloor, & X \ge 0 \\[2mm] -\left\lfloor \dfrac{r}{2} + X \right\rfloor, & X < 0 \end{cases}$$

DEPENDENT VARIABLES

When two or more input variables are statistically independent, random values can be generated using Algorithm 11-2 separately on each variable. When the variables are dependent, they are best modeled through their joint distribution. One way (Musa, 1992) is to partition the range of each input variable into a series of sub-ranges. For example, the range (-100.. + 100) can be partitioned into (-100.. -50), [-50..0),[0..50),[50..100). If the possible values of an input variable are purely nominal, then those values are divided into groups. The subranges or groups are selected in such a way that all input states within a single subrange or group are equally likely.

If we denote the input variables by $I_1, I_2, \ldots, I_n$, then we use the following notation for the ith input variable: Its range is partitioned into $N(i)$ subranges or groups $SR(i, 1), SR(i, 2), \ldots, SR(i, N(i))$. We define the set $partition(i)$ to be $\{SR(i, 1), SR(i, 2), \ldots, SR(i, N(i))\}$.

We form the Cartesian product $S = partition(1) \times partition\ (2) \times \cdots \times partition\ (n)$. Each n-tuple $(s_1, s_2, \ldots, s_n)$ is called an *input category*. An operational profile associates each input category with a probability of occurrence. All the probabilities, of course, have to add up to 1, since $\Pr\{S\} = 1$. Then Algorithm 11-1 can be used to generate a random input category. Then, using Algorithm 11-1 again, an input state is chosen randomly (uniformly) from within the input category.

Ideally, an input category represents an *equivalence class* (Myers, 1979): From knowledge of the computer program, the tester determines that all members of an input category exhibit the following property: If a run starting from one input state in the input category fails, then a run starting from any other input state in that category would also fail. If a run starting from one input state in the category succeeds, then they all succeed. Thus for all input states j in the input domain that is an equivalence class, either $e(j) = 0$ or $e(j) = 1$. We introduced the function $e(\ )$ in Chapter 7. Recall that the function $e(i)$ evaluates to 1 if the program fails when run from input state i, and evaluates to 0 if the program succeeds from input state i.

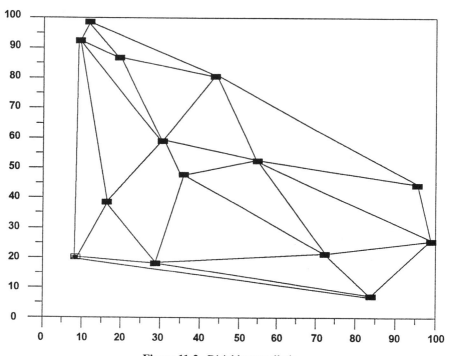

Figure 11-2. Dirichlet tessellation.

Another approach is to create a joint empirical distribution. In the univariate case the interpolation between pairs of consecutive points is linear. In the two-variable case a triangle spans trios of neighboring points. In the three-variable case the figure is a triangular pyramid. In the k-variable case the figure is a polytope of k vertices.

Let's look at the two-variable case in detail. Consider the data points

$$(x_1, y_1), (x_2, y_2), \ldots, (x_n, y_n)$$

We want to form the empirical Cdf

$$F(x,y) = \Pr\{X \le x, Y \le y\}$$

Neighboring data points are joined by means of line segments, forming triangular regions. This is a common task ("Dirichlet tessellation") in computational geometry, and several efficient algorithms are available (Figure 11-2).

The triangulation is performed by joining points for which the associated polygons have an edge in common. Figure 11-3 illustrates one of these triangular regions. Using trigonometry and the coordinates of the vertices, the triangle can be solved for its angles and the lengths of its sides. In the figure,

$$a = \sqrt{(x_2 - x_1)^2 + (y_2 - y_1)^2}$$

$$b = \sqrt{(x_1 - x_0)^2 + (y_1 - y_0)^2}$$

$$c = \sqrt{(x_2 - x_0)^2 + (y_2 - y_1)^2}$$

$$A = \cos^{-1} \frac{b^2 + c^2 - a^2}{2bc}$$

$$B = \cos^{-1} \frac{c^2 + a^2 - b^2}{2ca}$$

$$b' = \frac{c \sin B}{\sin(A + B)}$$

To select a uniformly random point from within the triangular region, a direction is first uniformly randomly selected. This direction determines a line segment from

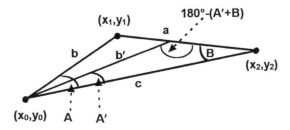

Figure 11-3. Triangular region spanning three data points.

(x0, y0) to a point on side a. Then a distance along that line segment is uniformly randomly selected. Together, the direction and distance specify a single point in the triangular region. The theoretical basis for concluding that the procedure generates points uniformly distributed over the triangular region is found in Smith (1984). Here is the algorithm:

First, the angle A' is selected as follows:

1. Generate U_1
2. Return $A' = U_1 A$.

To complete the selection:

1. Generate U_2.
2. Set $\beta = U_2 b'$.
3. Return

$$x = x_0 \beta \cos A'$$
$$y = y_0 \beta \sin A'$$

As an example, suppose that there are three xy data pairs: (18.133, 28.756), (47.741, 35.886), (52.505, 54.846). They are the vertices of a triangular region. Solving the triangle yields $A \approx 23.666°$ and $b' \approx 33.001$. Suppose $U_1 = 0.621$ and $U_2 = 0.884$. Then $A' \approx 14.697°$ and $\beta \approx 29.172$. The random (x, y) pair selected by the algorithm is then computed as $x = 18.133 + 32.321 \cos 14.697° \approx 50.494$, and $y = 28.756 + 32.361 \sin 14.697° \approx 36.966$.

Structure

The techniques we have described so far are applicable to scalar variables and to data structures that are reducible to a fixed number of scalars. A data structure that has an indefinite, varying number of elements cannot be reduced to a fixed number of scalars. The distribution of a data structure like this is often fruitfully described by means of a grammar. In particular, a context-free grammar (CFG) is denoted $G = (N, T, P, \Sigma)$, where N is a finite set of nonterminals. T is a finite set of terminals, disjoint from N. P is a finite set of productions, each of the form $A \rightarrow \beta$, where A (the "premise") is a nonterminal and β (the "consequence") is a string of symbols from $(N \cup T)^*$. S is a distinguished variable called the *start symbol*. In programming languages and data dictionaries, an alternative notation for context-free grammars is used that is called *Backus–Naur form* (BNF).

Specifying and Generating String Variables

A string is a finite sequence of symbols juxtaposed. If an input variable is a string type, each value the variable can take on is a finite-length sequence of characters. When the string values exhibit a recognizable structure, a syntactic approach can be taken. The syntax is defined by the programming language or in a data dictionary. In a stochastic CFG G_S, the productions are nondeterministic and a certain probability measure is assigned to each. Each production is of the form

$$\alpha_i \xrightarrow{\ p_{iij}\ } \beta_{ij}$$

where α_i is the ith distinct premise, and β_{ij} is the consequence of the jth production rule whose premise is α_i. The production probability p_{ij} is the probability of applying the rule whose consequence is β_{ij} among the n_i production rules whose premise is α_i, with $0 < p_{ij} \le 1$ and

$$\sum_{j=1}^{n_i} P_{ij} = 1$$

Given an unambiguous stochastic CFG, the production probabilities (see Table 11-2) can be inferred from sample information (Fu, 1982). Let the sample information be

$$S_t = \{(x_1, f_1), \ldots, (x_t, f_t)\}$$

where f_k is the relative frequency or subjective probability of string x_k. The strings are parsed, and the maximum-likelihood estimate for p_{ij} can be shown to be

$$\hat{P}_{ij} = \frac{\displaystyle\sum_{x_k \in S_t} f_k N_{ij}(x_k)}{\displaystyle\sum_{j} \sum_{x_k \in S_t} f_k N_{ij}(x_k)}$$

where $N_{ij}(x_k)$ is the number of times that the production $\alpha_i \to \beta_{ij}$ was used in parsing string x_k. As an example (Thomason, 1986), let $V_N = \{A_1, A_2\}$, $V_T = \{a, b, c, d\}$, $S = A_1$, and let P be

$$A \xrightarrow{0.2} bA_2A_1 \qquad A_2 \xrightarrow{0.9} a$$

$$A_1 \xrightarrow{0.8} dA_2 \qquad A_2 \xrightarrow{0.1} cA_2$$

Table 11-2. Production Probabilities

Production Probability	True	Estimated
p_{11}	0.2	0.20635
p_{12}	0.8	0.79365
p_{21}	0.9	0.90648
p_{22}	0.1	0.09352

A sample of 200 strings was generated from the grammar. The sample information appears in Table 11–3. The relative frequency f_k was computed by dividing the number of occurrences of string x_k by 200.

INPUT ARRIVAL TIMES

An input state generally consists of several input variables. All the variables can arrive at once, or subsets of the input variables can arrive together in groups. Just as the operational profile or functional profile describes the distribution of input states, each arriving group of variables must be described by a particular *arrival distribution* that characterizes the group's arrival pattern. Arrival distributions are not unique to statistical testing, and they have been extensively studied in the fields of queueing theory and simulation.

Queueing theory provides a system of three versatile arrival models that fit a great many real-world arrivals (see Table 11–4). The models in the system are (1) exponential, (2) Erlang, and (3) hyperexponential. These models are easy to use because the selection of which one of the three is applicable, as well as the estimation of parameters, depends solely on the mean and standard deviation of the interarrival times.

Based on sample input arrival times or prior theoretical information, the mean and standard deviation of the interarrival times are estimated. For example, a set of sample interarrival times for a particular group can be run through a statistical software package, such as SAS or SPSS, to obtain the required mean and standard deviation. The mean arrival rate Λ is a parameter of all three models and is found as the reciprocal of the mean interarrival time.

The key to determining which of the three models to use is to compute the *coefficient of variation, c,* of the interarrival times. The coefficient of variation is defined as the ratio of the standard deviation to the mean.

If c is zero, then the interarrival time distribution is constant; the inputs arrive according to a closely met schedule. The constant interarrival time is the mean.

Table 11-3. Sample Information

Sample String x_k	Number of Occurrences	f_k
bada	27	0.135
da	146	0.73
badca	4	0.02
dca	11	0.055
bccabadca	1	0.005
bcada	2	0.01
bcababada	1	0.005
babada	5	0.025
bcabcada	1	0.005
dcca	1	0.005
bcabada	1	0.005

Table 11-4. Summary of Arrival Models

Coefficient of Variation c	Arrival Distribution
$c = 0$	constant
$0 < c < 1$	Erlang
$c = 1$	exponential
$c > 1$	hyperexponential

If c is nonzero, then the interarrival time is random, and the mean provides only a measure of central tendency. The interarrival time distribution is suggested by whether c is close to one, less than one, or greater than one.

If c is close to one, then an exponential interarrival time distribution is a good model. The procedure for generating a random exponentially distributed interarrival time is as follows:

1. Generate a uniformly distributed [0,1] random variable U.
2. Return $(-\ln U)/\Lambda$.

Exponential interarrival times correspond to a homogeneous Poisson process. If the input arrival rate is nonstationary—that is, if it varies as a function of time—then a useful model is the nonhomogeneous Poisson process (NHPP). The arrival rate during a business's peak hours might be 50% higher than during the other hours, for example. The arrival rate at time t is denoted $\Lambda(t)$. NHPP interarrival times can be generated by a process called "thinning." Let Λ^* be high enough that $\Lambda(t) \le \Lambda^*$ for all t. (The quantity t is the running sum of the interarrival times generated so far. Initialize t to zero when generating the first interarrival time of the test.) The procedure to generate the next interarrival time from an NHPP is as follows:

1. Repeat

   Generate U_1 and U_2.
   Set $E := (-\ln U_1)/\Lambda$.
   Until $U_2 \le \Lambda(t + E)/\Lambda^*$.

2. $t := t + E$.
3. Return E.

If c is between zero and one, the interarrival times cluster more closely to the mean than the exponential; there are fewer small and large values. The model to use in this case is the Erlang distribution. The Erlang distribution has one parameter, k. The parameter k should be set to the largest integer less than or equal to $1/c^2$. The procedure to generate an interrival time from an Erlang distribution is as follows:

1. Generate uniformly distributed $(0, 1)$ random numbers $U_1, U_2, \ldots, U_k$.
2. Return

$$-\frac{1}{\Lambda} \ln \left(\prod_{i=1}^{k} U_i \right)$$

If c is greater than one, then the hyperexponential is a good model. The hyperexponential distribution has one parameter, p, in addition to the arrival rate Λ. Set p equal to

$$\frac{1}{2} - \frac{1}{2} \left[1 - \frac{2}{c^2 + 1} \right]^{1/2}$$

The procedure to generate a random interarrival time from a hyperexponential distribution is as follows:

1. Generate independent uniformly distributed $(0, 1)$ random numbers U_1 and U_2.
2. Let $Q = -\ln U_1$.
3. If $U_2 < p$, return $Q/2 \Lambda p$; else return $Q/2 \Lambda (1 - p)$.

SUMMARY

In software testability measurement, software reliability growth testing, and software reliability demonstration testing, it's necessary to subject the software to an operational profile representative of field usage. In this chapter we looked at methods for automatically generating input states in accordance with a given operational profile. We also looked at ways of automatically generating the arrival times of inputs, needed for testability measurement and reliability testing of real-time software.

EXERCISES

1. For one input variable, tessellation used line segments for the empirical distribution. For two dependent variables, the tessellation used triangles. Describe the corresponding geometric shape that would be used for three dependent input variables.

2. Can you think of a way to extend the stochastic grammar idea to a two-dimensional array of black/white pixels?

3. Write a program that implements automated generation of test cases for a set of three independent, integer input variables.

4. How would you extend the test generation concepts to graphical user interfaces (GUIs) that employ a pointing device (mouse, trackball, etc.).

REFERENCES

E. N. Adams. "Optimizing Preventive Service of Software Products." *IBM Journal of Research and Development,* June 1984.

P. Bratley, B. L. Fox, G. E. Schrage. *A Guide to Simulation,* 2nd edition. New York: Springer-Verlag, 1987.

J. W. Duran and S. Ntafos. "A Report on Random Testing." In: *Proceedings of the 5th International Conference on Software Engineering,* San Diego, March 1984, pp. 179–183.

M. A. Friedman. "Inference of and Generation from Operational Profiles for Software Reliability Testing." In: *Proceedings 2nd Annual AIAA Aerospace Design Quality Conference,* Irvine, CA, Feb. 1993.

K. S. Fu. *Syntactic Pattern Recognition and Applications.* Englewood Cliffs, NJ: Prentice–Hall, 1982.

J. D. Musa. "The Operational Profile in Software Reliability Engineering: An Overview." Presentation and handout, International Symposium on Software Reliability Engineering, Raleigh, NC, 1992.

J. D. Musa, A. Iannino, and K. Okumoto. *Software Reliability Measurement, Prediction, Application,* New York: McGraw-Hill, 1987.

G. J. Myers. *The Art of Software Testing.* New York: John Wiley & Sons, 1979.

B. D. Ripley. *Stochastic Simulation.* New York: John Wiley & Sons, 1987.

R. L. Smith. "Efficient Monte Carlo Procedures for Generating Points Uniformly Distributed Over Bounded Regions." *Operations Research,* 32 (6), 1296–1308, November–December 1984.

T. Thomason. "Syntactic Pattern Recognition: Stochastic Languages." In: T. Y. Young and K. S. Fu, (eds). *Handbook of Pattern Recognition and Image Processing.* Orlando, FL: Academic Press, 1986.